Historic Japanese Swords and Fittings

A Collection of Restored and Translated
Nineteenth Century Manuscripts

◆◆◆◆✿◆◆◆◆

THOMAS BUCK

Lloyd & Tutle Publishing, Limited

ISBN: 0-9843779-4-8
ISBN-13: 978-0-9843779-4-7

DEDICATION

Because the study of ancient manuscripts expands the appreciation of the importance of studying these functional sculptures in their cultural context, this book is dedicated to students of the Japanese art sword everywhere.

CONTENTS

ACKNOWLEDGMENTS

I would like to thank all those without whom this work would not have been finished. In particular, my appreciation goes to Donald J. Pierce, Librarian at the University of Minnesota in Duluth, for introducing me to the art of ancient manuscripts; and, to Robert Kosuth for introducing me to the study of translating classical Chinese and Japanese text.. My thanks especially goes out to my friend, editor, and love of my life, Andrea Novel Buck, who reviews all my works with a professionalism and care rarely seen in the publishing industry.

ACKNOWLEDGMENTS

1 A Brief Chronology

1.1 Koto: Early Sword Era

Ancient Period (before 794)

In Ancient Japan, all aspects of Japanese life, from politics to science, were strongly influenced by the continental cultures and technologies. The manufacture of swords was no exception and the domestic product was considered low-grade to the swords made in China and Korea, which led to a large import of arms from the continent. At its peak, the Empress Suiko (554-628) imported the bulk of the imperial house swords from the ancient Chinese province of Go. The earliest swords in Japan were of the Straight Sword (*Chokuto*) variety.

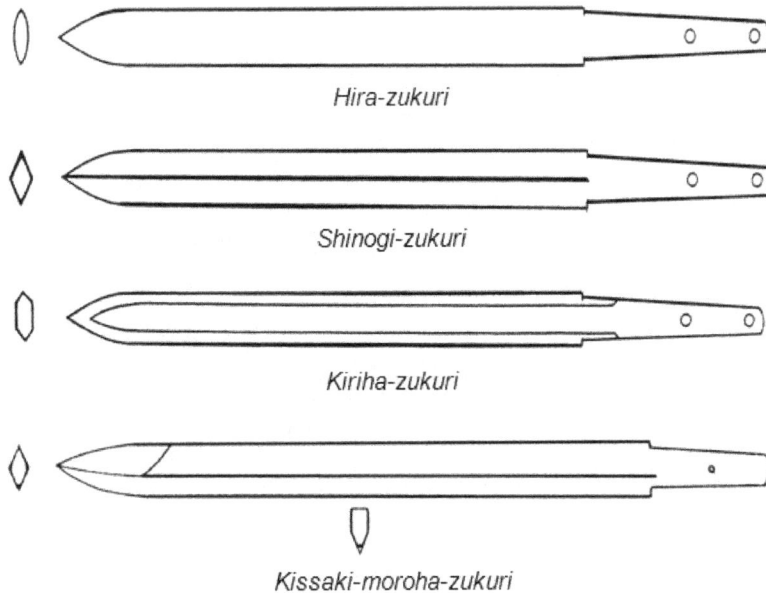

Hira-zukuri

Shinogi-zukuri

Kiriha-zukuri

Kissaki-moroha-zukuri

Figure 1.1 Varieties of Chokuto

Chokuto can be divided into four classifications: (1) *Hira-zukuri*, flat blades without a ridge line, or *Shinogi*, (2) *Shinogi-zukuri*, double-edged blades with a ridge line down the center, (3) *Kiriha-zukuri*, double-edged blades with a ridge line near the cutting edge, and

(4) *Kissaki-moroha-zukuri,* blades with a double edge only at the tip. *Hira-zukuri* and *Kiriha-zukuri* blades are the oldest, followed by *Kissaki-moroha-zukuri* blades, with the double-edged *Shinogi-zukuri* being the newest of the ancient styles.

These Ancient period swords were primarily thrusting weapons, and were hung from the waist edge-down.

Along with the import of these swords, came many Chinese and Korean craftsmen who began teaching their art of sword making to the indigenous smiths. This was a significant milestone in the evolution of the Japanese sword.

Toward the end of the Ancient Sword Period a transition from straight double-edged swords to single-edged curved blades began to occur. In fact, by the beginning of the Heian Period, although straight swords where still in wide use, the Japanese warrior class showed a marked preference for this new style of sword.

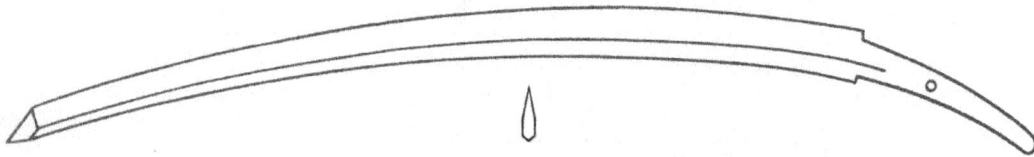

Figure 1.2 Single-edged curved blade of the *Shinogi-zukuri* style.

Heian Period (794 – 1184)

During the Heian Period, the warrior class in Japan began to gain power. The aristocrats, led by the Fujiwara family, had come into power by destroying the old clan system and flourished in conjunction with the development of the manor system of government in which land estates (or manors) were leased to lords and the peasants were made dependent on the land and on their lords. Along with the powerful families in the provinces, they found it necessary to form and maintain large military forces within their own families. In addition, separate warrior families grew up among the military groups attached to these manors. Among these the Genji and Heike clans made the most rapid rise to power.

In 1156, the Heike clan, under the leadership of Taira Kiyomori, succeeded in putting down a rebellion and took over the reins of the government in Kyoto. This is the first time in Japanese history that the government had been in the hands of a warrior family.

As a result, a significant shift occurred in the fighting methods: the old group warfare foot soldier method was being replaced in importance by the mounted warrior, and increased focus was placed more on individual hand-to-hand combat with swords, bows and arrows.

Around the mid-Heian Period, the curved single-edged Japanese Sword (*Nippon-to*) was perfected and came into general use. The adoption of the curved sword was not only due to the shift to horseback fighting techniques in which a striking sword rather than a stabbing sword became necessary, but was also due to the quality of the steel available and the great advance in forging techniques.

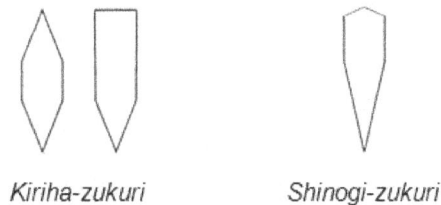

Kiriha-zukuri   *Shinogi-zukuri*

Figure 1.3 Blade cross sections.

As illustrated in Figure 1.3, the change from *Kiriha-zukuri* to *Shinogi-zukuri* was merely a moving of the ridge line (*Shinogi*) closer to the top ridge of the blade. This produced a much broader cutting surface and a more acute angle to the cutting edge, and added a dynamic keenness to the cutting edge.

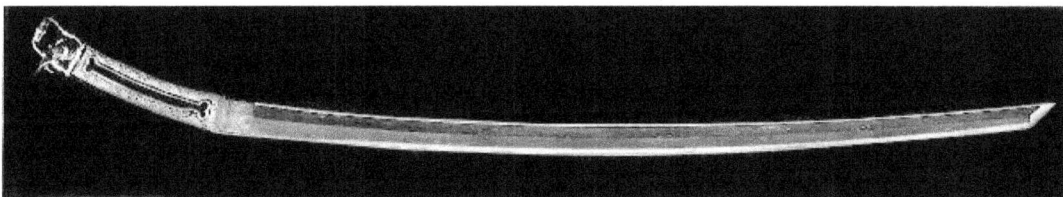

Figure 1.4 Kenuki-gata style tachi.

The evolution of the straight to the curved blade and from *Kiriha-zukuri* to *Shinogi-zukuri* was not a direct process. Intermediate stages in this process can be seen in the *Kenuki-gata* style *tachi* (Fig. 1.4) that is said to have been owned by Fujiwara Hidesato in the 10th century, and the famous *Kogarasu Maru tachi* (Fig. 1.5), a prized possession of the Heike family.

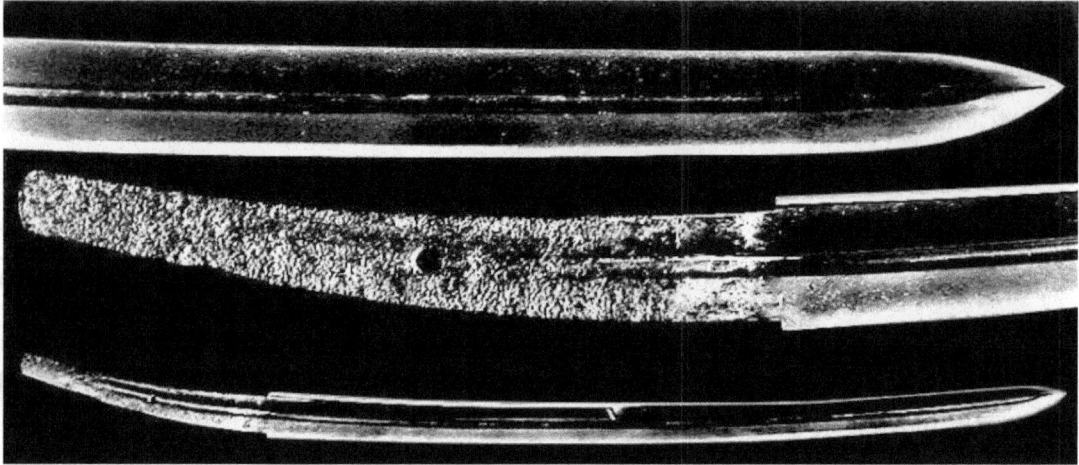

Figure 1.5 The Kogarasu Maru tachi, Circa 800

Because of swords like these, the classic curved Japanese Sword (*Nihonto*) came to replace the older straight sword because of both its greater practical applications, as well as progress in sword-making techniques and improvements in materials. Initially, the sword-making process of curving a blade would seem relatively easy, but the actual procedure involved in bending the folded steel back in the direction of the thick *mune* (back edge) from the thinner *ha* (cutting edge) are exceptionally complex and difficult. The birth of the curved sword was not only an improvement for battle tactics, but a significant accomplishment in engineering and metallurgy. And, by the end of the Heian Period, the evolution was complete, and the traditional curved single-edge of the *Shinogi-zukuri* style *Nihonto* was perfected.

Early Kamakura Period (1184 – 1231)

The 150 years of the Kamakura Period were divided into roughly three parts: under the leadership of Minamoto Yoritomo's new warrior government in Kamakura, the first 50 years redefined the warrior class; the next 50 years redefined the economy; and, the last 50 were redefined by stagnation. Although in many ways, the evolution of the Japanese sword mirrored these changes in society, Early Kamakura Period swords paralleled those of the previous period in design and function, such as the *Kitsune-ga-saki* blade (Fig. 1.6) made by Tametsugu from Bitchu. This was also exemplified by the large number of Bizen swordsmiths that still flourished under the imperial court as it had been during the last part of the Heian Period. The greatest change during this period occurred to the sword mountings and fittings, or *koshirae*.

Figure 1.6 The Kitsune-ga-saki blade by Tametsugu

During the Early to Middle Kamakura Period, three general types of *tachi koshirae* (sword mounts worn edge down) were used (Fig. 1.7): the *hiru-maki-no-tachi koshirae* is comprised broad metal bands wrapped in a spiral fashion around both the *tsuka* (handle) and *saya* (scabbard); the *hyogo-gusari koshirae* is covered with a combination of metal plates and bands; and the *ito-maki-no-tachi koshirae* has the saya wrapped, at least in part, in silk braid.

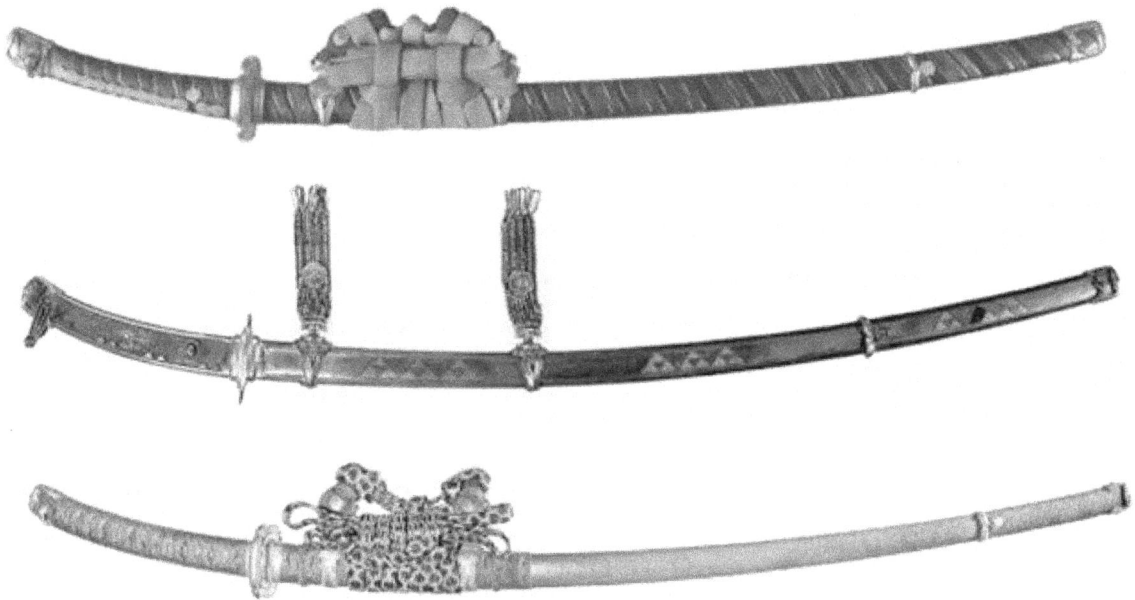

Figure 1.7 Three types of Early to Middle Kamakura Period sword mountings: from top to bottom, Hiru-maki-no-tachi Koshirae, Hyogo-gusari Koshirae, and Ito-maki-no-tachi Koshirae.

Middle Kamakura Period (1232 – 1287)

During the Kamakura Period, the samurai felt it necessary to be as austere and warrior-like as possible. To further this mindset, in 1232 an official code of ethics was established which focused on thrift and strength of character, as well as extensive martial training in archery, horsemanship and swords.

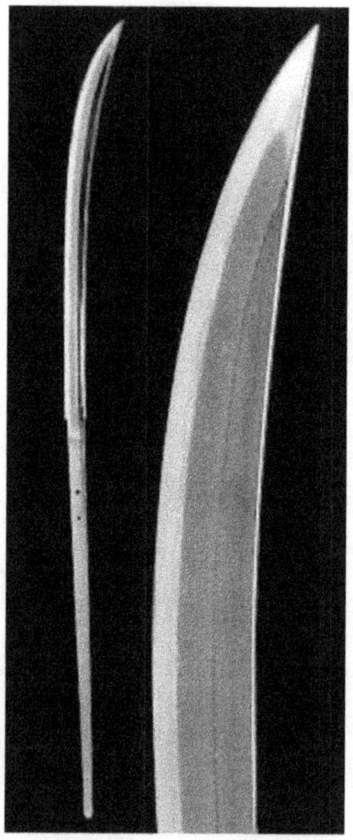

The Middle Kamakura Period was also a time of great advancement in the art of sword making. In general, the blades became stronger, broader and thicker. In particular, the Yamashiro school of Bizen became preeminent with its distinct curve and its variations of the *choji midare* temperline.

This part of the Kamakura Period was a time of refinement for the sword, and set the standards for all future Japanese swords. In addition to the long swords, *tanto* (daggers) *wakizashi* (short swords) and *naginata* (halberds) were all in large supply, and their production did not decline during this middle period. It was also during this time that five separate and distinct schools of sword making became formally established. Famous swordsmiths of this period include Kunitsuna of the Awataguchi school, Saburo Kunimune from Bizen, and Sukezane of the Ichimonji.

Figure 1.8 (Above) Late Kamakura *naginata* blade.

Late Kamakura Period (1288 - 1335)

The two Mongol invasions in 1274 and 1281 gave birth to drastic changes in Japanese war tactics and weapons. The Japanese discovered through this experience that group warfare was much more effective than the mounted individual combat style that they had been using up to that time.

The blades became longer and more even in width throughout their entire length and the sword mountings of this period became more refined, focusing on detail and quality. *Tanto* became straighter, thicker and slightly longer than those of the previous period, and *naginata* blades became curved (see Fig. 1.8).

The most significant effect the Mongol invasions brought was the awareness of the need for a strong national defense. This resulted in swordsmiths springing up in all parts of the country. The most famous swordsmith to appear during this period was a student of Shintogo Kunimitsu named Masamune. He inherited the traditions of his teacher's style and developed that style to produce stronger, more resilient, more beautiful swords.

Masamune's influence spread throughout the country and everyone began to imitate his style, even to the extent that during the Edo Period there were ten famous swordsmiths known as the Masamune Jittetsu, who made blades in his style but none of who seem to have had any direct relationship to the master himself.

The actual student of Masamune who is said to have succeeded the best in learning the master's style was Sadamune. He was active throughout the Late Kamakura and well into the Nanbokucho Period.

Nanbokucho Period (1336 – 1393)

During the Nanbokucho Period, also known as the Northern and Southern Courts period, the Japanese government was divided into two groups, with the Emperor Godaigo at Yoshino in the south (*Nan*), and the shogun Ashikaga Takauji and Emperor Komyo in the north (*Hoku*). Warring between these two factions didn't end until nearly sixty years later, when Emperor Gokomatsu took the throne in 1392.

Figure 1.9 The Kashiwa Tachi.

During this time, swords and pole arms became greatly exaggerated. Examples of this can be seen in the Nambokucho swords named Kashiwa Tachi, or the Oak Sword (Fig. 1.9), and the Tomomitsu Odachi (Fig. 1.10).

Figure 1.10 The Tomomitsu Odachi.

The blade of the Oak Sword has a *nagasa* (cutting edge) of 136.6 cm, with a *nakago* (tang) of 54.4 cm, and is *mumei* (unsigned); its *tsuka* and *saya* are black lacquered and wrapped in opposite directions with a thin strip of leather.

The Tomomitsu Odachi has a *nagasa* of 126.0 cm and a *sori* (curve) of 5.8 cm, and a *kissaki* of 6.7 cm in length; and it is signed by Tomomitsu and dated 1366.

Ironically, the primary significance of these oversized arms came during the following period when it became common practice to cut down the blades to make them a more useful length, as seen in Figures 1.11 and 1.12.

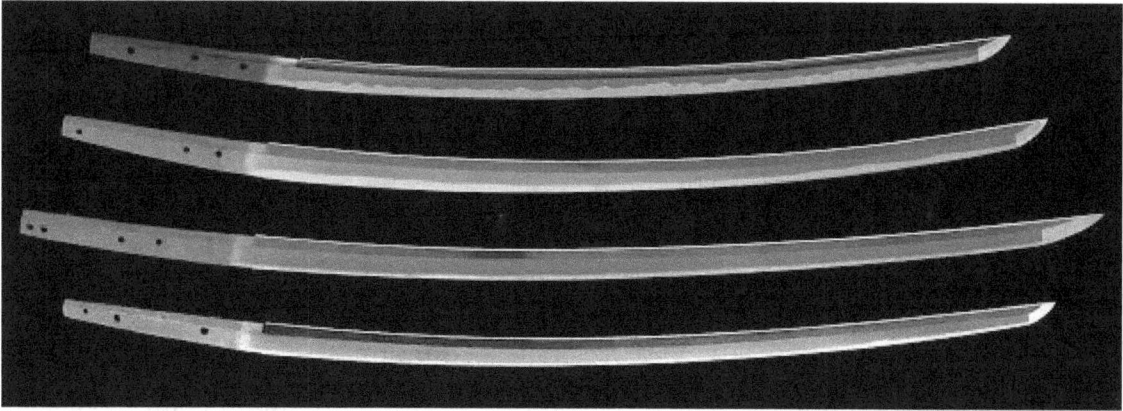

Figure 1.11 Shortened Nanbokucho Period swords.

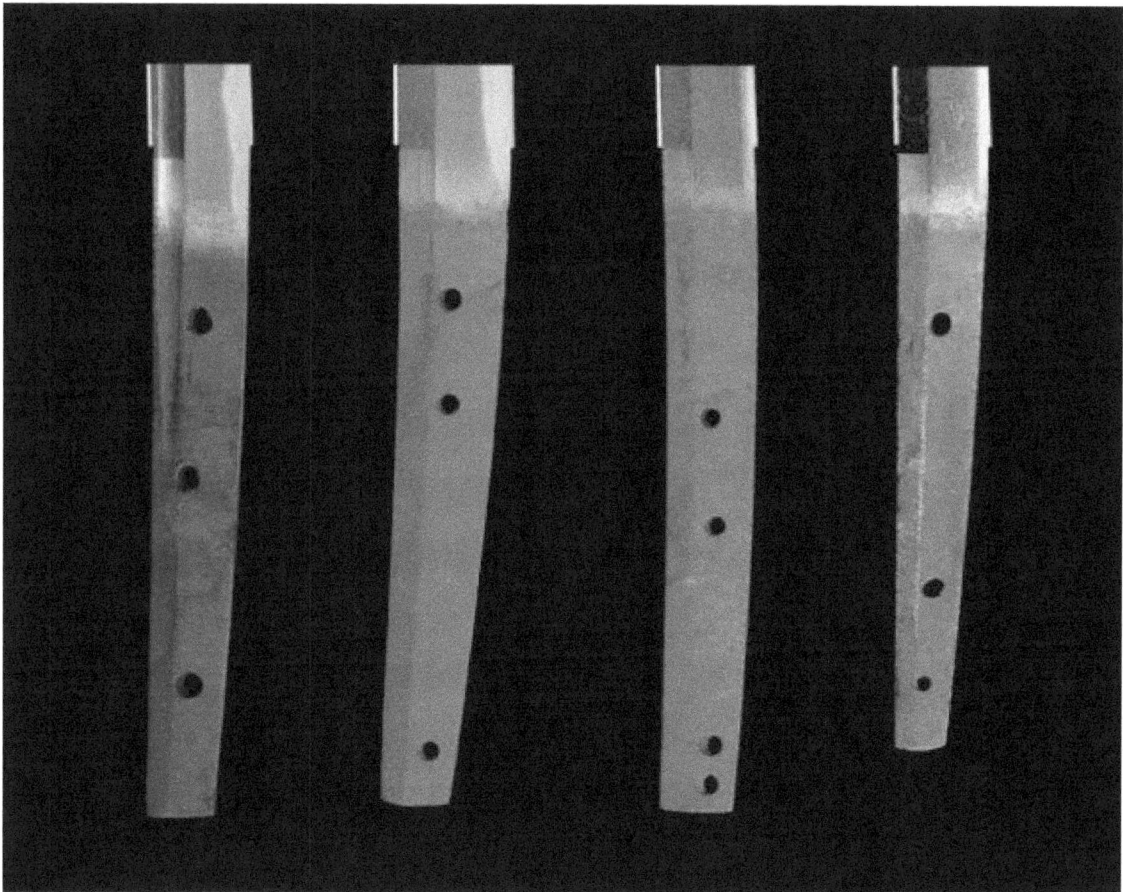

Figure 1.12 Nakago of shortened Nanbokucho Period swords.

From top to bottom (Fig. 1.11), and left to right (Fig. 1.12), mumei (unsigned) Omiya school sword with a blade length of 63.6 cm; mumei sword with a blade length of 69.7

cm; mumei Hoju school sword with a blade length of 82.0 cm; and, mumei Chikushi Ryokai sword with a blade length of 71.0 cm.

As a sign of things to come, there were also blades of only about 70 cm made that were worn unlike the *tachi*, thrust through the belt (*obi*) with the edge pointing up. This style became known as the *uchigatana*.

Muromachi Period (1392 – 1573)

In 1393 the north and south warring factions were united by emperor Ouchi Yoshihiro, allowing Ashikaga Yoshimitsu to become shogun, creating a general state of peace and ushering in the new age known as the Muromachi Period.

It was during this period that the *tachi* began to disappear and the *uchigatana* took its place. Similar to the *koshirae* in Figure 1.13, common features of *uchigatana koshirae* of this period include a *tsuka* wrapped with leather over black lacquered *same'*, and a black horn *kashira* (pommel) with the wrap crossing over its top. This shift in *koshirae* occurred primarily because of the change in battle tactics from mounted individual fighting back to the group combat on foot, and can be traced back to the two Mongol invasions (1274 and 1281).

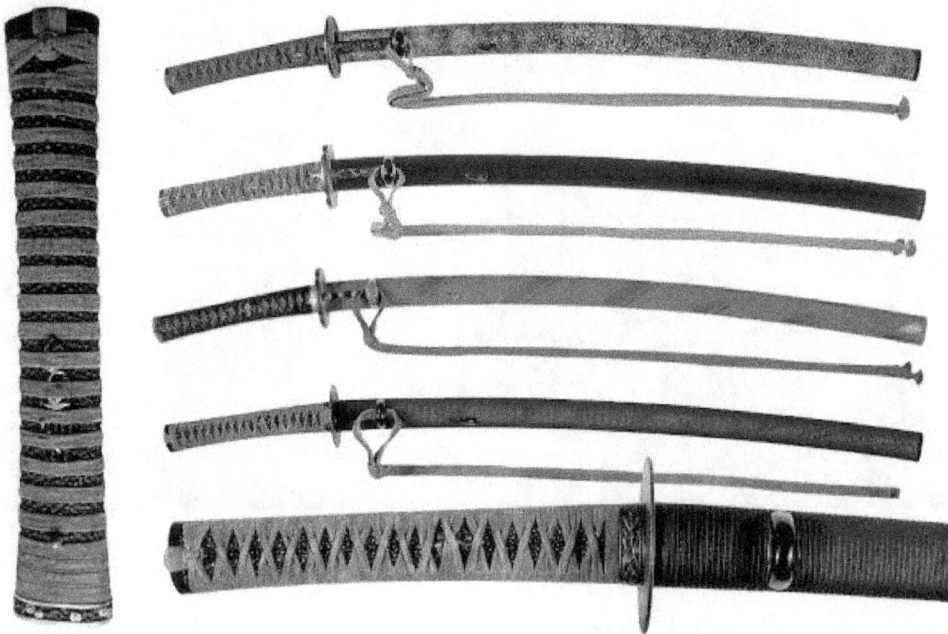

Figure 1.13 Modern reproductions of Muromachi Period akechi tsuka
& uchigatana koshirae by Kazuki Takayama and Yasuo Toyama

The Muromachi period was marked by repeated rebellions and civil war, including the Eikyo Rebellion in 1439 and the Onin Rebellion in 1467. After Yoshimitsu, the successor shoguns were relatively short-lived and changed rapidly, until the 15th Shogun was driven out of the capital by Oda Nobunaga in 1568.

In general, government was broken up among various regional feudal lords who established their own castle towns, which in turn became commercial centers where merchants and craftsmen could gather and supply the ever-increasing demand for weapons. Because of the constant stream of battles in all parts of the country, weapon production was at an all-time high, and, consequently, the quality of workmanship fell to an all-time low.

Sword mountings of this period covered the spectrum from inexpensive functional *akechi koshirae* (see Fig. 1.13), to elaborate high quality works for the nobility that in ways mirrored pieces from the Kamakura period.

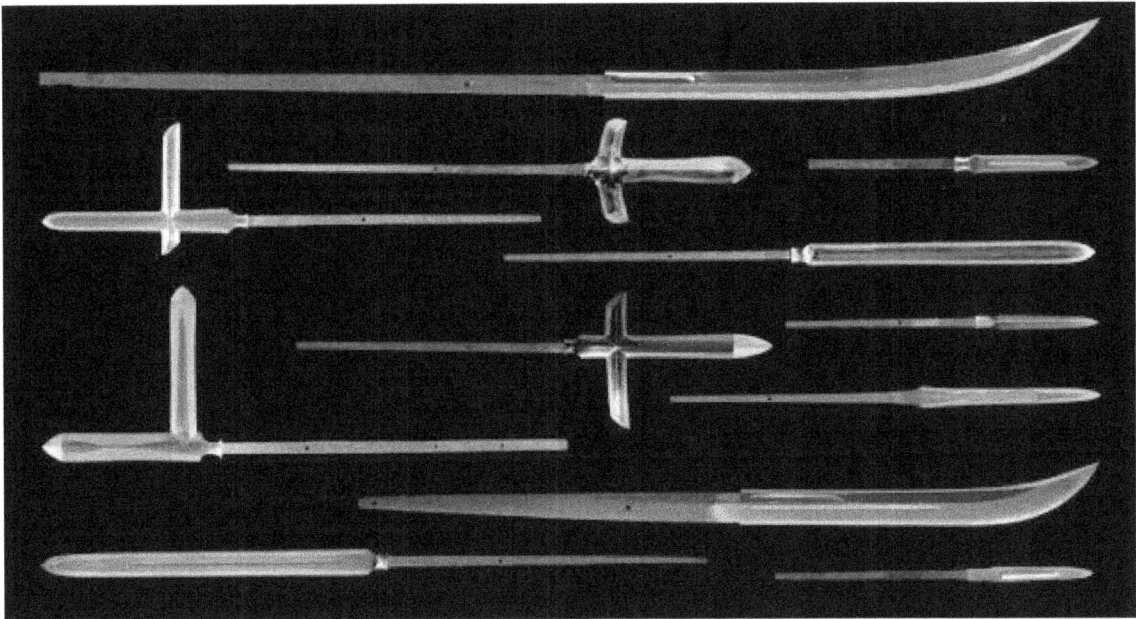

Figure 1.14 Examples of period naginata and yari blades.

Because of their usefulness in the new foot soldier battle tactics, a great variety of styles, shapes and sizes of pole arms were developed and produced (Fig. 1.14). In addition to *naginata*, the most common pole arms of the Muromachi period were *yari*, or lances, of which there are two major types, the *su yari* (those with straight blades) and *kama yari* (those with crossbars on the blade). Oversized *su yari* are referred to as *omi no yari*. *Jumonji yari* are *kama*

Figure 1.15 Muromachi
Period tanto

yari with crossbars of equal length, and *katakama yari* have either a single sided crossbar or crossbars of unequal length.

In addition to long swords and lances, a wide variety of *koshirae* for *tanto* (daggers) and *wakizashi* (short swords) were also introduced during this period, as shown in Figure 1.15 and 1.16.

During the 181 years of the Muromachi period, arguably the most dramatic change occurred in its last 30 years was the introduction of the gun to Japan in 1543. Its impact was felt across the Japanese social strata, and directly influenced sword production and battle tactics. The gun gave Oda Nobunaga the political and military edge he needed to end the period of civil wars and unify Japan.

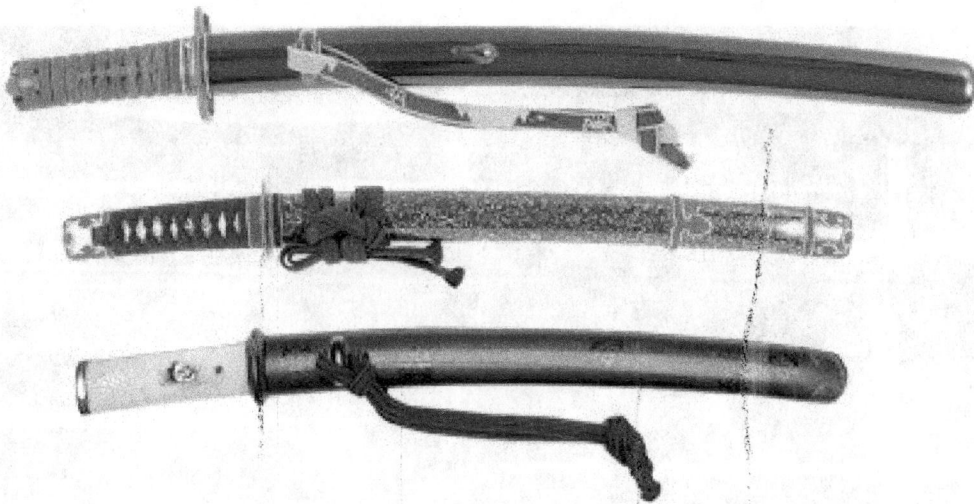

Figure 1.16 Muromachi Period wakizashi

1.2 SHINTO & SHIN-SHINTO: NEW SWORD ERAS

In the context of sword production, the Shinto Period is traditionally broken up into three distinct eras: the *Keicho Shinto* era (1596 – 1660); the *Kanbun Shinto* era (1661 – 1780); and the *Shin-shinto* (New New Sword) era, which began in 1781 and lasted until the end of the Tokugawa Period. In a historical context, the Shinto period arguably spans the Momoyama period, beginning in 1573, all the way through the end of the Meiji Restoration in 1868.

The period name *Shinto* (New Sword) wasn't derived simply from the production of new blades, but came about because of a change in styles and methods of production, as well as a societal shift in government and culture, characterized by a new prosperity and a revitalization of traditional social values and ideals.

Momoyama Period (1573 – 1615)

Although the Momoyama Period began in 1573, its foundations were laid in 1568 with the end of Ashikaga Shogunate. From that point on until his death in 1582, Oda Nobunaga's string of conquests and alliances brought the country under a more unified rule with a strong central government. By 1590, Hideyoshi, one of Nobunaga's former allies, had completed the unification of Japan, formalized his rule and issued an order banning the ownership of swords by farmers and peasants. It was during Hideyoshi's reign of peace that castle towns became less the fortresses of war and more the peaceful centers of politics, economies, transportation and culture, filled with craftsmen and merchants. The most direct influence this had on sword production was a shift from a focus on quantity to a greater interest in quality.

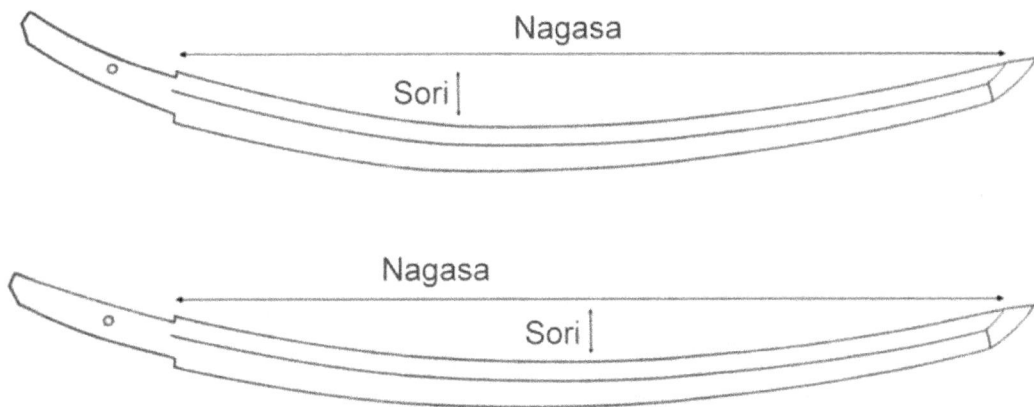

Figure 1.17 Shift from "Bizen-sori" (top) to "Saki-sori" (bottom).

One of the more noticeable differences in sword design directly attributed to the peaceful urbanization of the Momoyama Period was the shifting of the *sori* (curve) from being off centered and closer to the *nakago* (often referred to as a *"Bizen-sori"*) as seen on *tachi*, to a more central point (*saki-sori*) that made the sword easier to draw when worn edge up, as with a *katana*.

Early Edo Period

During the Edo Period the Tokugawa Shogunate government remained strong until the first half of the 18th century, and was still in control of the economies as well as the government. Thus the whole society was built upon warrior-like ideals and the demand for swords was great. Sword makers moved from the old capital Kyoto and gathered in the new capital Edo and in the thriving commercial center in Osaka. In 1629 an edict was passed defining the duties of a samurai, and required the wearing of a *daisho,* or a matched set of katana and wakizashi, when on official duty. These matching long and short swords were characterized by a great deal of artistry and refinement.

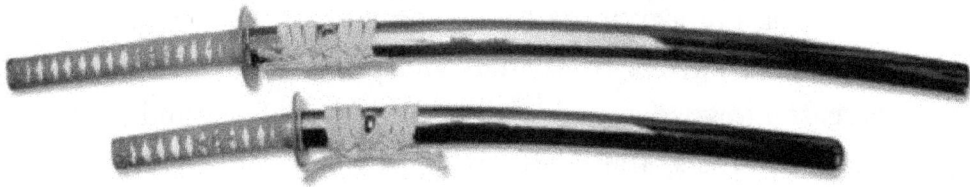

Figure 1.18 A Daisho, or matching set of a long and a short sword.

Late Edo Period

During the same 130 years after the Genroku Period until the end of the Shogunate, the creation of mountings and fittings was the most significant development in the evolution of the Japanese sword. All kinds and colors of metals, lacquers, woods and fabrics were used to produce extremely refined swords, incorporating works of artist from all aspects of Japanese society. These mounts in general are considered works of fine art by the international art community.

The coming of Commodore Perry to Japan with his 'black ships' in 1853 marked a period of unrest and internal strife that lasted until the Meiji Restoration in 1868. In the fourth year after the Meiji Restoration, 1871, the Emperor issued the Dampatsurei Edict, forcing the samurai to cut their top knots. This was followed in 1876 by the Heitorei Edict, a strict order for all citizens to stop the carrying of swords. Consequently, the sword lost its last use, causing the swordsmiths to literally go out of business. Swordsmiths went into such jobs as producing cookware and cutlery, and the fittings artists turned their hands to such things as jewelry, vases and sculpture.

2 HISTORIC JAPANESE SWORDS AND FITTINGS

2.1 RESTORATION OF THE MANUSCRIPT ILLUSTRATIONS

This chapter contains a collection of 81 digitally restored black-and-white hand-drawn illustrations, dating from 1810 to 1849, of famous ancient Japanese swords and fittings. These originals were heavily damaged through a combination of age, neglect, regular wear and tear, and bookworms. Below is an example of a manuscript in its original condition (left), and the same manuscript after its digital restoration (right).

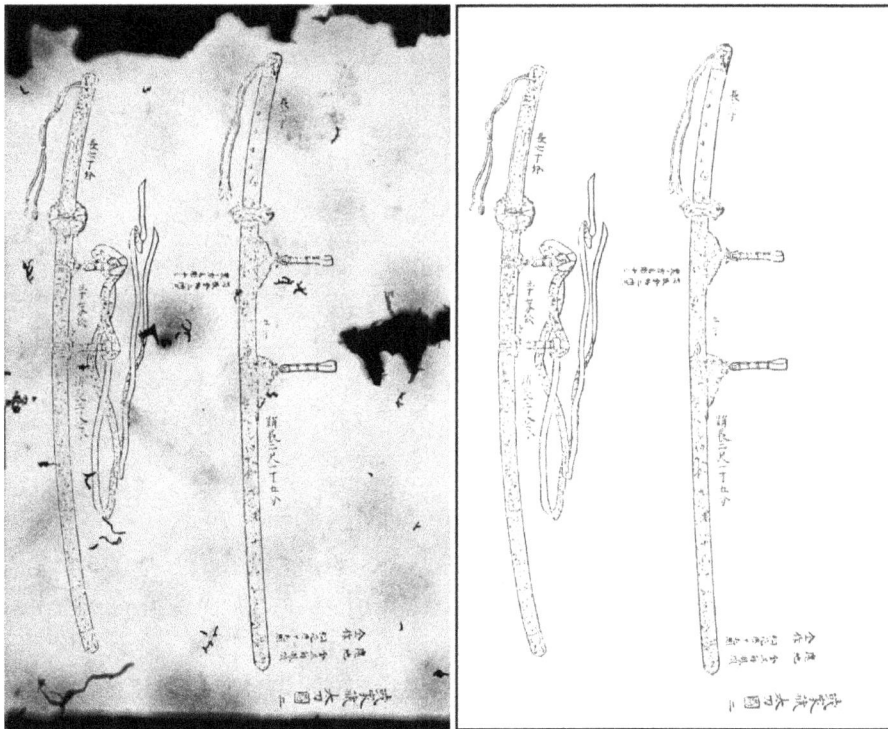

The preservation and restoration of these manuscripts was done in a two step process, first the original was stabilized to avoid any further wear, then it was digitized, cleaned, and restored. During this procedure, when possible, titles and text were taken from the manuscripts and translated into English by the author, Thomas Buck. The sections of text on the manuscripts include descriptions of the illustrations, measurements, and listing of their then current owners or locations. Of these, the vast majority of texts are dedicated to the measurements of various swords and parts, with only one or two larger captions per manuscript describing either the owner, the name of the sword, or the collection/shrine the sword is located in. The translations in this book focus on descriptions, not measurements. To read the measurements and other text not translated, included is a guide for quick reference to the sword components displayed in the manuscript illustrations, measurement translation instructions, a listing of the most commonly used characters for measurement, and a conversion table with both Japanese Shaku, Metric and English measurement systems.

2.2 MEASUREMENTS: INSTRUCTIONS FOR READING AND CONVERTING

Following is a general list of kanji for the sword parts, measurement units, and basic Japanese numeral system. As mentioned, the vast majority of the writings on these manuscripts are dedicated to measurements and sizes of particular sword parts. The basis of the Japanese length measurements is the shaku, the other units are all fixed fractions or multiples of this basic unit. The shaku was originally the length from the thumb to the middle finger (about 18 cm or 7.1 in), but its length is now standardized to 11.93 inches, or 303.0 millimeters.

Japanese Length Measurement Units					
Romanized	Kanji	Shaku	Centimeters	Inches	Feet
bu	分	$\frac{1}{100}$	0.303	0.1193	9.942×10^{-3}
sun	寸	$\frac{1}{10}$	3.030	1.193	0.09942
shaku	尺	1	30.30	11.93	0.9942

鞘 Saya
(naga -or- "length of")

長 Ni

二 Shaku

尺 San

三 Sun

寸 San

三 Bu

分

When reading a measurement, it is important to remember that it begins with the name of the object being measured, followed by the numbers and measurement units, from largest to smallest. For example, in the measurement to the left, it reads, "Saya naga ni shaku san sun san bu" —or— "Scabbard length is 2 shaku, 3 sun, 3 bu" [approximately 70 centimeters]. The word "naga" simply means "length of". Following are tables listing the Japanese numerals used in measurement, examples of kanji common in object measurement, and sword diagrams with labeled components.

Japanese Numerals 1 thru 10					
一	Ichi	1	六	Roku	6
二	Ni	2	七	Shichi	7
三	San	3	八	Hachi	8
四	Shi	4	九	Kyu	9
五	Go	5	十	Jyu	10

Common Japanese Kanji used in Measurements					
刀	Katana	Long Sword	刀	Katana	Long Sword
力	Ken	Straight Sword	刃	Jin	Sword
刀	Tachi	Long Sword	虵	Tsuka	Sword Handle
太	Ken	Sword /Saber	鍔	Tsuba	Sword Hand-guard
剣	Tanto	Short Sword /Dagger	脇差	Wakizashi	Short Sword
刀剣					
錕	Kon	Ancient Treasured Sword	分	Bu	Unit of Measurement 0.303 cm
長	Naga	Long; Length; Measure of	寸	Sun	Unit of Measurement 3.030 cm
鞘	Saya	Scabbard	尺	Shaku	Unit of Measurement 30.30 cm

2.3 COMPONENTS: SWORD MOUNTINGS

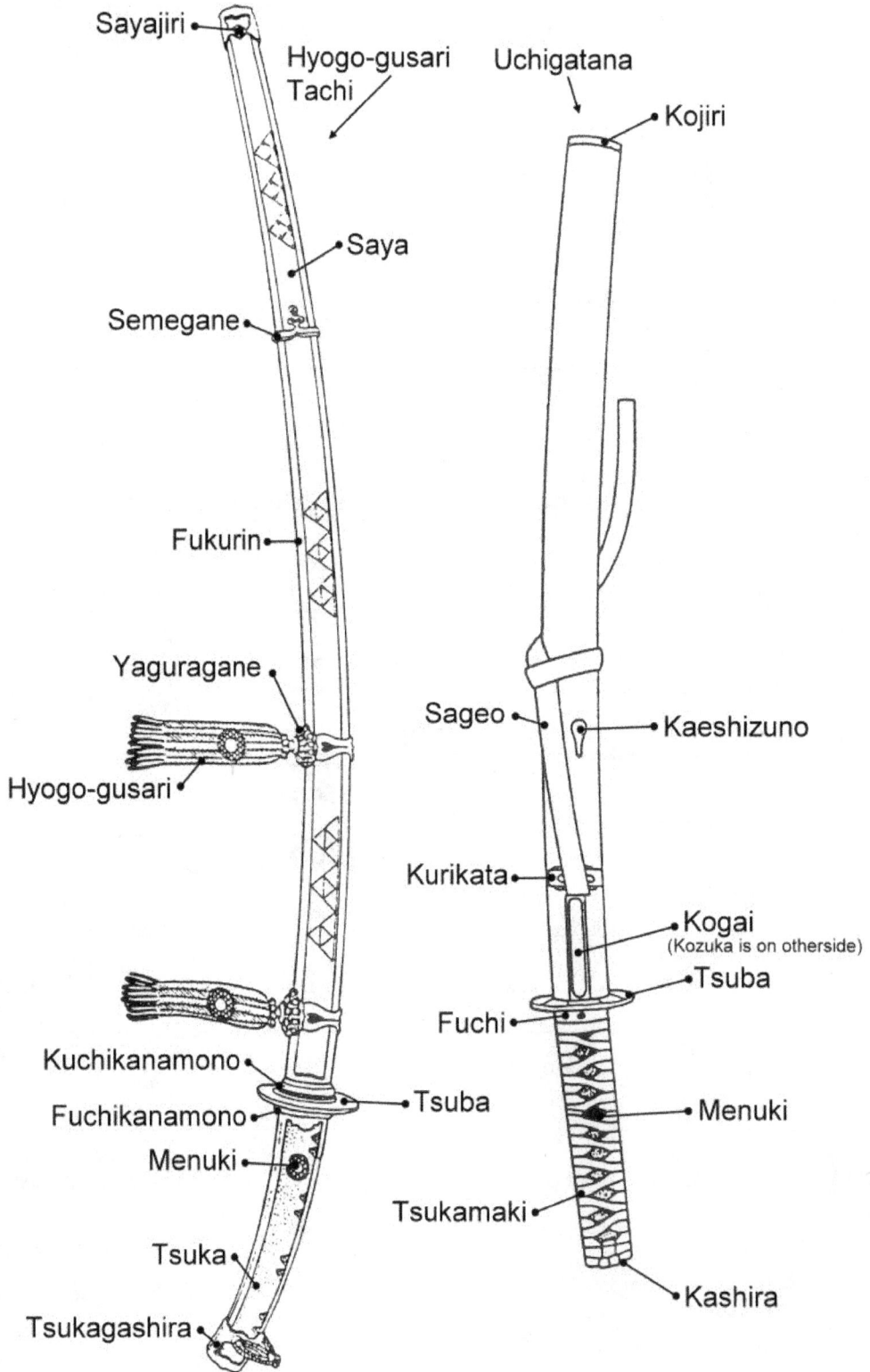

Sayajiri

Hyogo-gusari
Tachi

Uchigatana

Kojiri

Saya

Semegane

Fukurin

Yaguragane

Sageo

Kaeshizuno

Hyogo-gusari

Kurikata

Kogai
(Kozuka is on otherside)

Tsuba

Kuchikanamono

Fuchikanamono

Tsuba

Fuchi

Menuki

Menuki

Tsukamaki

Tsuka

Kashira

Tsukagashira

2.4 COMPONENTS: SWORD BLADE

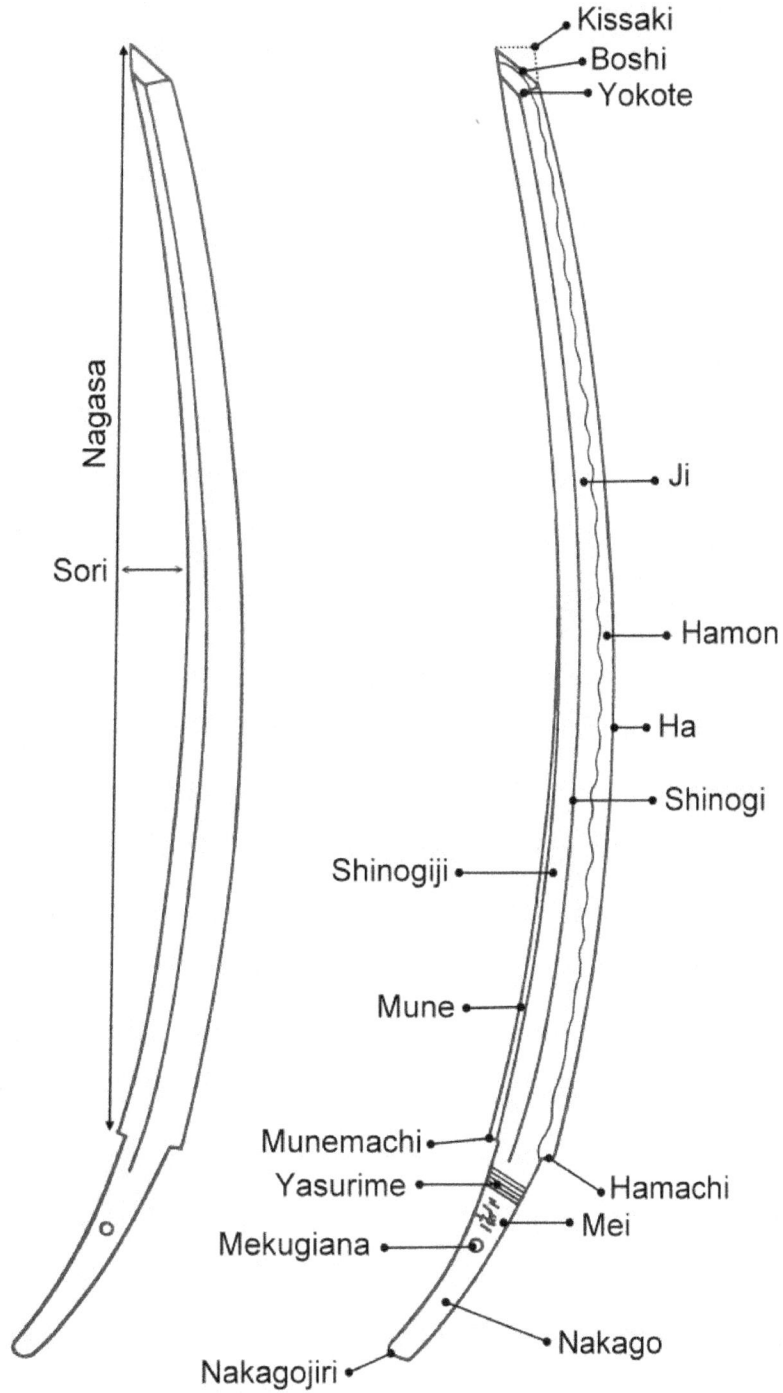

Kissaki
Boshi
Yokote

Nagasa

Sori

Ji

Hamon

Ha

Shinogi

Shinogiji

Mune

Munemachi

Yasurime

Hamachi

Mekugiana

Mei

Nakago

Nakagojiri

2.5 A COLLECTION OF RESTORED NINETEENTH CENTURY HAND-DRAWN ILLUSTRATIONS
(Figure 2.1 thru Figure 2.81)

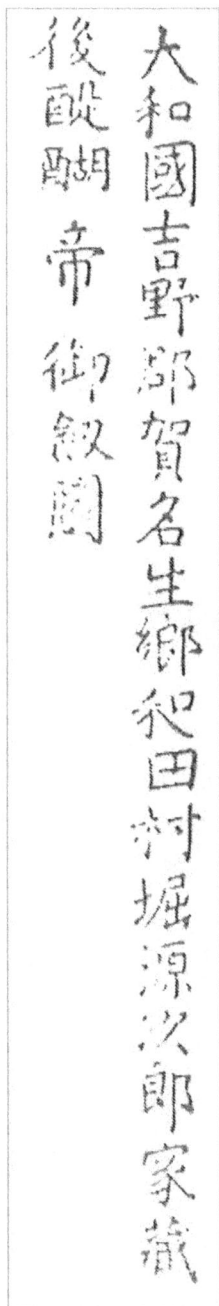

大和國吉野郡賀名生郷和田村堀源次郎家藏

後醍醐帝御叙閥

Figure 2.1 Tanto - Emperor Godaigo.

The description reads, "Drawing of a straight two-edged short sword (tanto) belonging to Emperor Godaigo, Collection of Genjiro Hori Family, Wada Village, Anou-go, Yoshino District, Yamato Province."

Emperor Go-Daigo (後醍醐天皇 Go-Daigo-tennō) (November 26, 1288 – September 19, 1339) was the 96th emperor of Japan, according to the traditional order of succession.

大和國吉野郡賀名生郷和田村堀源次郎家藏

後醍醐 帝 御劔箇

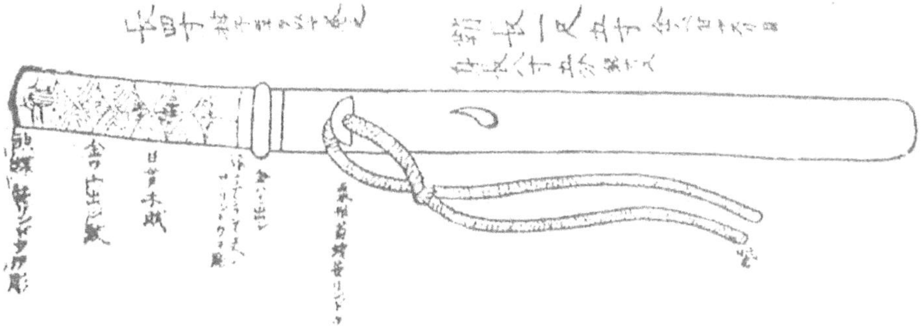

伊勢國太神宮藏太刀圖

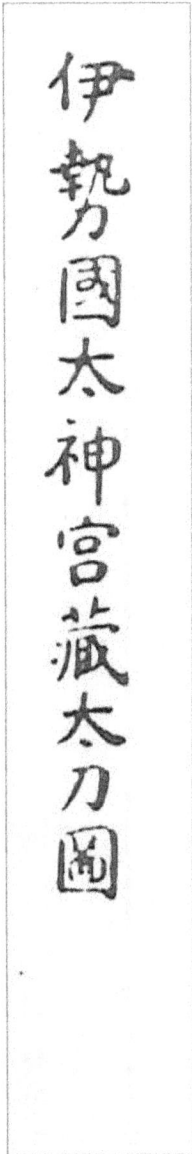

Figure 2.2 Tachi - Daijingu Shrine.

The description reads, "Drawing of long sword (tachi), Collection of Daijingu Shrine, Ise Province."

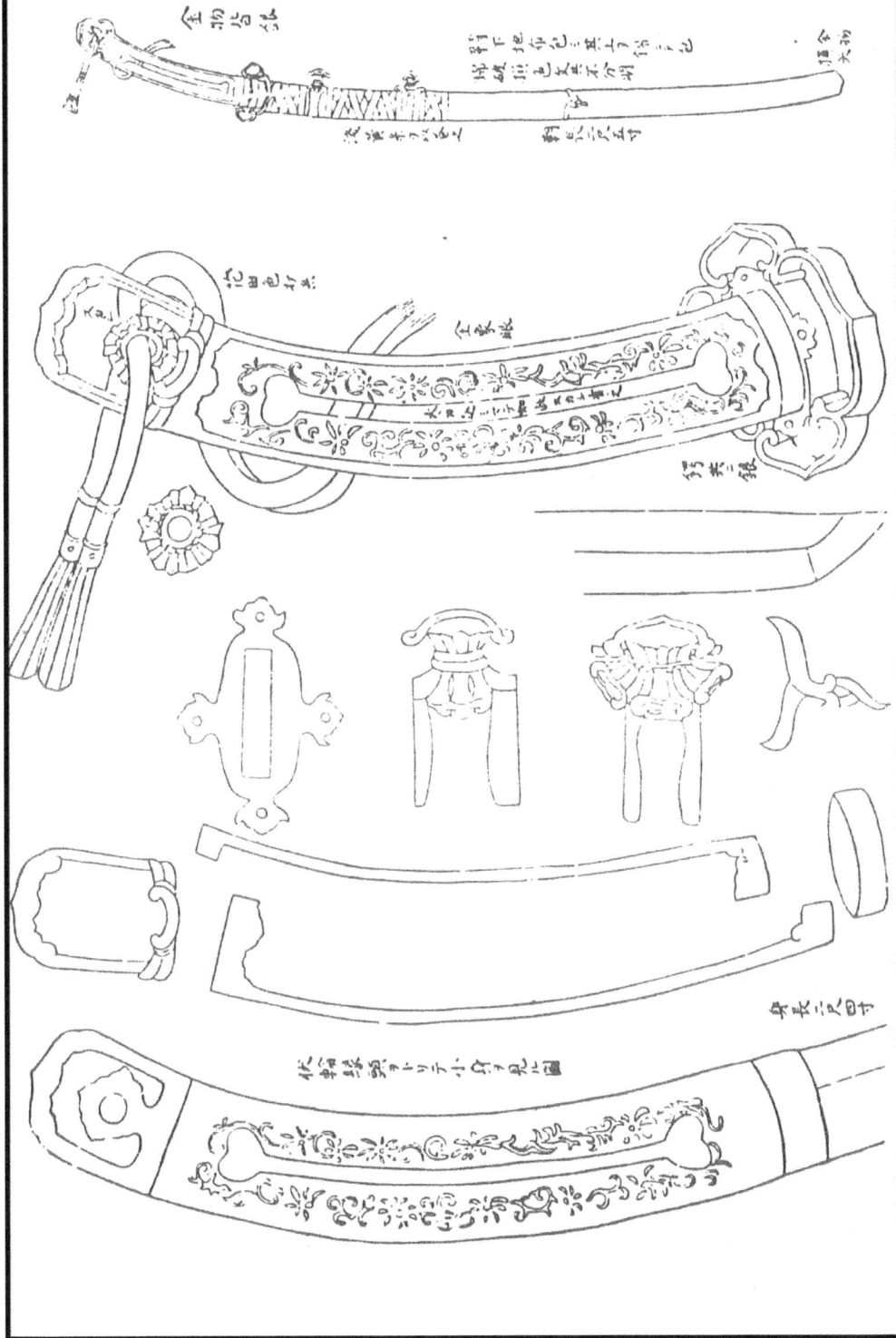

伊勢国大神宮御蔵太刀図

後白河帝御太刀圖 詳代夫

山城國鞍馬寺藏源義經朔臣太刀圖

Figure 2.3 Two Tachi - Emperor Goshirakawa
and Yoshitsune Minamoto.

The description reads, "Drawing of long sword (tachi) belonging to Emperor Goshirakawa, Collection unknown."

Emperor Go-Shirakawa (後白河天皇 Go-Shirakawa-tennō) (October 18, 1127 – April 26, 1192) was the 77th emperor of Japan, according to the traditional order of succession. His reign spanned the years from 1155 through 1158.

Description reads, "Drawing of long sword (tachi) belonging to Court Noble Yoshitsune Minamoto, Collection of Kurama Temple, Yamashiro Province."

Minamoto no Yoshitsune (源 義経, 1159 – June 15, 1189) was a general of the Minamoto clan in the late Heian and early Kamakura period. Yoshitsune was the ninth son of Minamoto no Yoshitomo, and the third and final son and child that Yoshitomo would father with Tokiwa Gozen. Yoshitsune's older brother Minamoto no Yoritomo (the third son of Yoshitomo) founded the Kamakura Shogunate. Yoshitsune's name in childhood was Ushiwakamaru (牛若丸). He is considered one of the greatest and the most popular warriors of his era, and one of the most famous samurai fighters in the history of Japan.

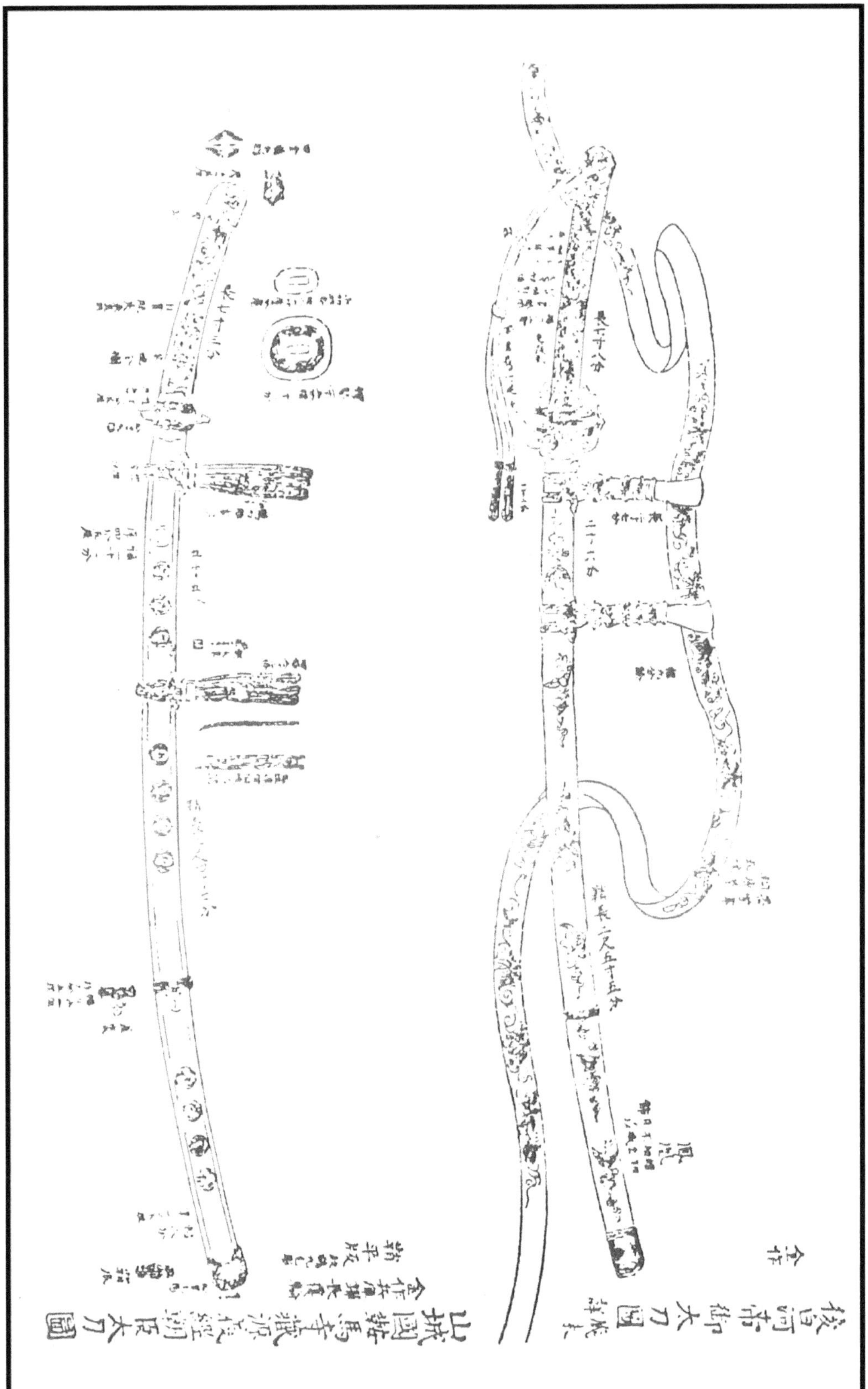
後白河帝御太刀図
金作
山城國鞍馬寺藏源義經朝臣太刀圖

伊勢國太神宮蔵俵藤太分鄉
蜈蚣切太刀圖

安藝國嚴嶋社蔵足利尊氏公佩刀圖

Figure 2.4 Tachi (The Centipede Slicer) - Toda Hidesato Tawara
and Wakizashi - Takauji Ashikaga.

The description reads, "Drawing of sword (tachi) 'The Centipede Slicer' belonging to Toda Hidesato Tawara, Collection of Daijingu Shrine, Ise Province."

In Japanese, Tawara Tōda [俵藤太 "Rice-bag Tōda"]), considered one of Japan's greatest warrior's, got his nickname "Rice-bag Tōda" from a fairy tale about a hero who kills the giant centipede Seta to help a Japanese dragon princess, and is rewarded in her underwater Ryūgū-jō 龍宮城 "dragon palace castle".

Description reads, "Drawing of short sword (wakizashi) belonging to Lord Takauji Ashikaga, Collection of Itsukushima Shrine, Aki Province."

Ashikaga Takauji (足利 尊氏, 1305 – June 7, 1358)[1] was the founder and first shogun of the Ashikaga shogunate. His rule began in 1338, beginning the Muromachi period. He ruled until his death in 1358.

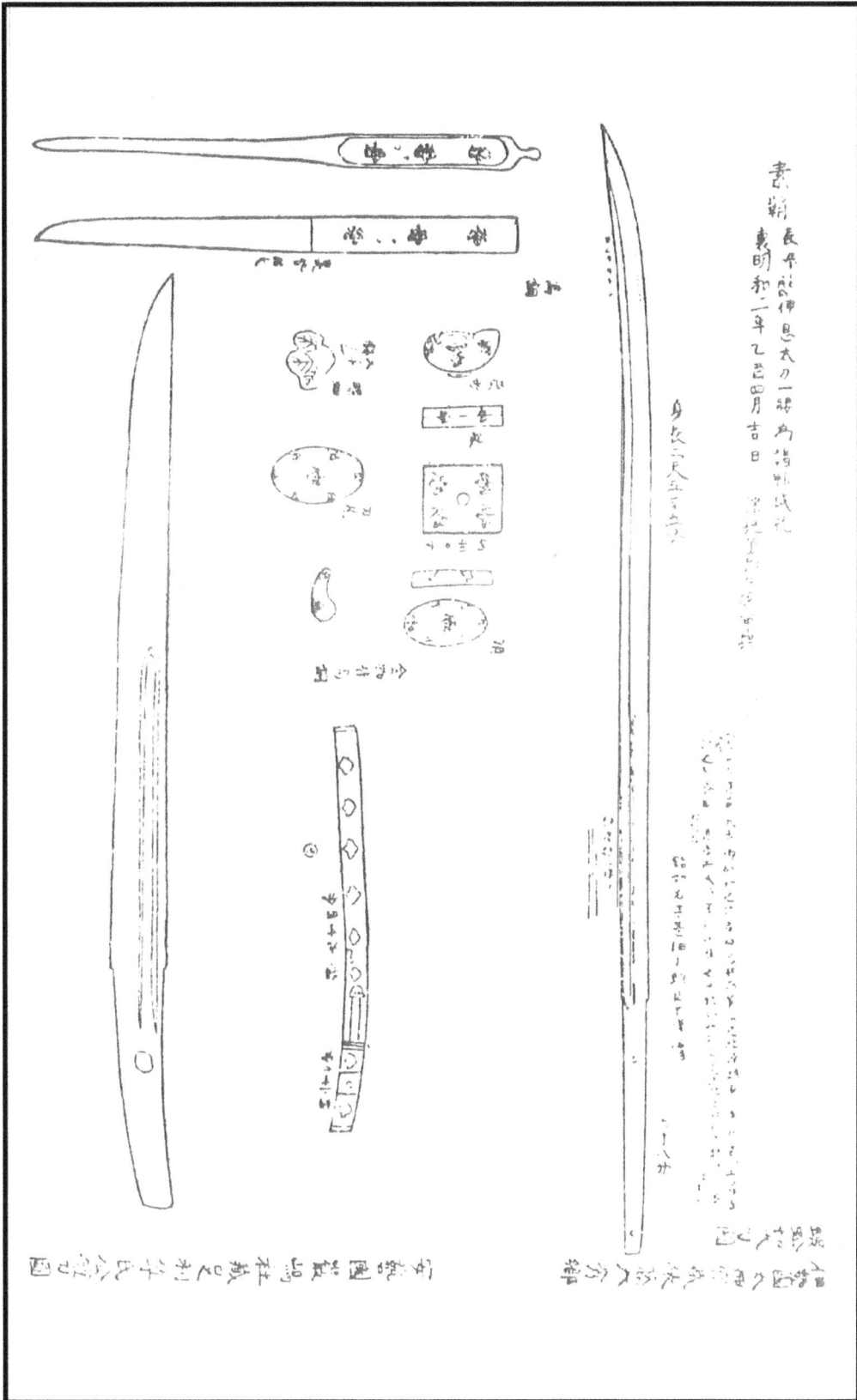

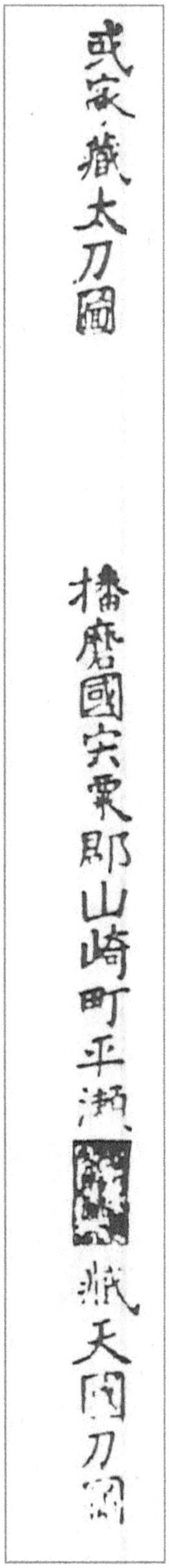

武家藏太刀圖

播磨國宍粟郡山崎町平瀬、瓶天國刀圖

Figure 2.5 Two Tachi

The descriptions read, "Drawing of long sword (tachi), Private collection;"

"Drawing of sword 'Amakuni' (full tang sword), Collection of Hirase [illegible], Yamazaki-cho, Shiso District, Harima Province."

Amakuni Yasutsuna (天國 安綱) is the swordsmith attributed with creating the first single-edged longsword (tachi) with curvature along the edge in the Yamato Province around 700 AD. His son, Amakura, was the successor to his work. There are almost no modern examples of signed works by Amakuni.

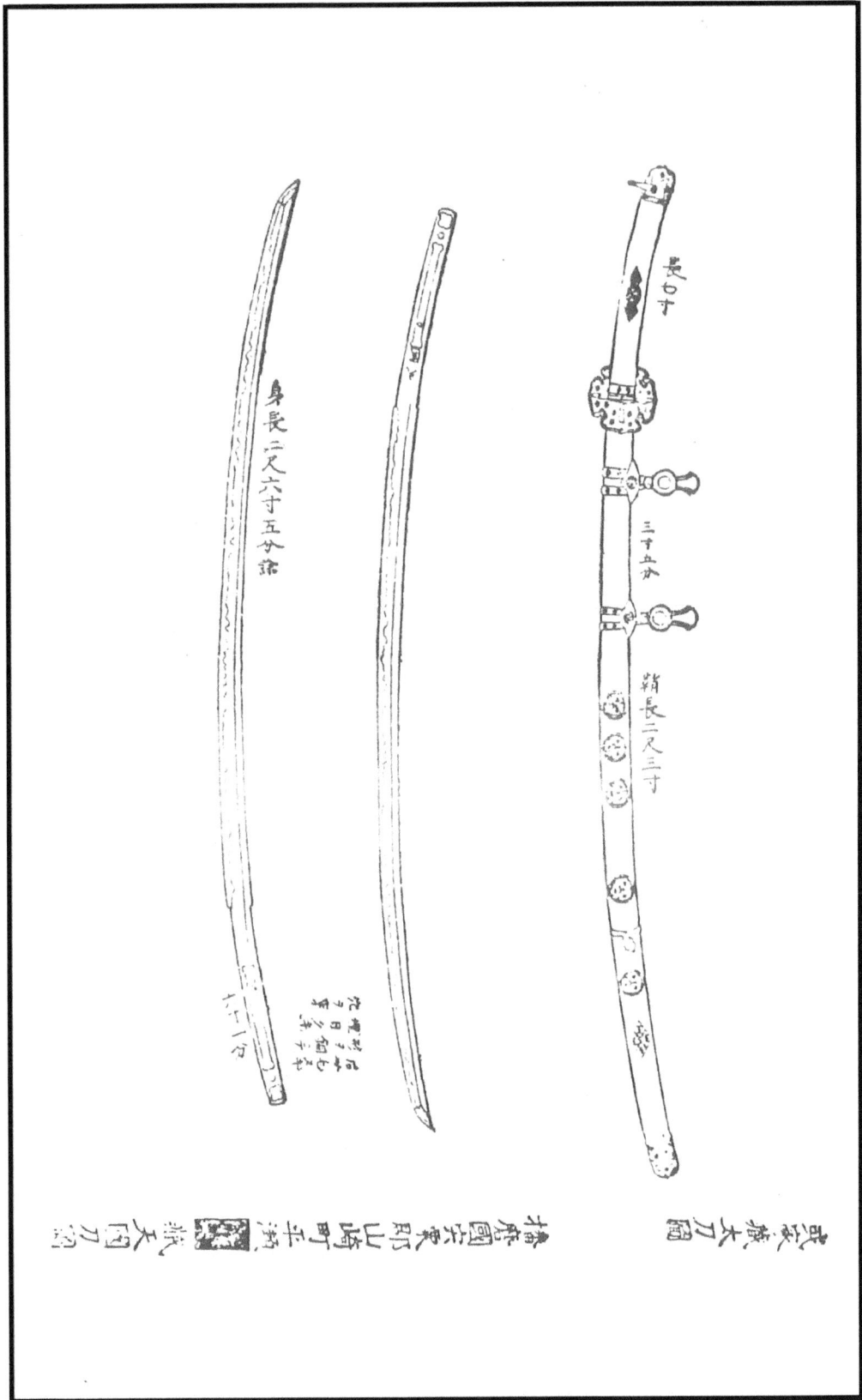

紀伊國熊野新宮藏太刀圖

若狹國遠敦郡靈應山神宮寺紙太刀柄鞘圖

Figure 2.6 Tachi and Koshirae.

The descriptions read, "Drawing of long sword (tachi) in collection of Kumano Shingu Shrine, Kii Province;"

"Drawing of long sword, hilt and scabbard (tachi koshirae), Collection of Reio-zan Jinguji Temple, Onyu District, Wakasa Province."

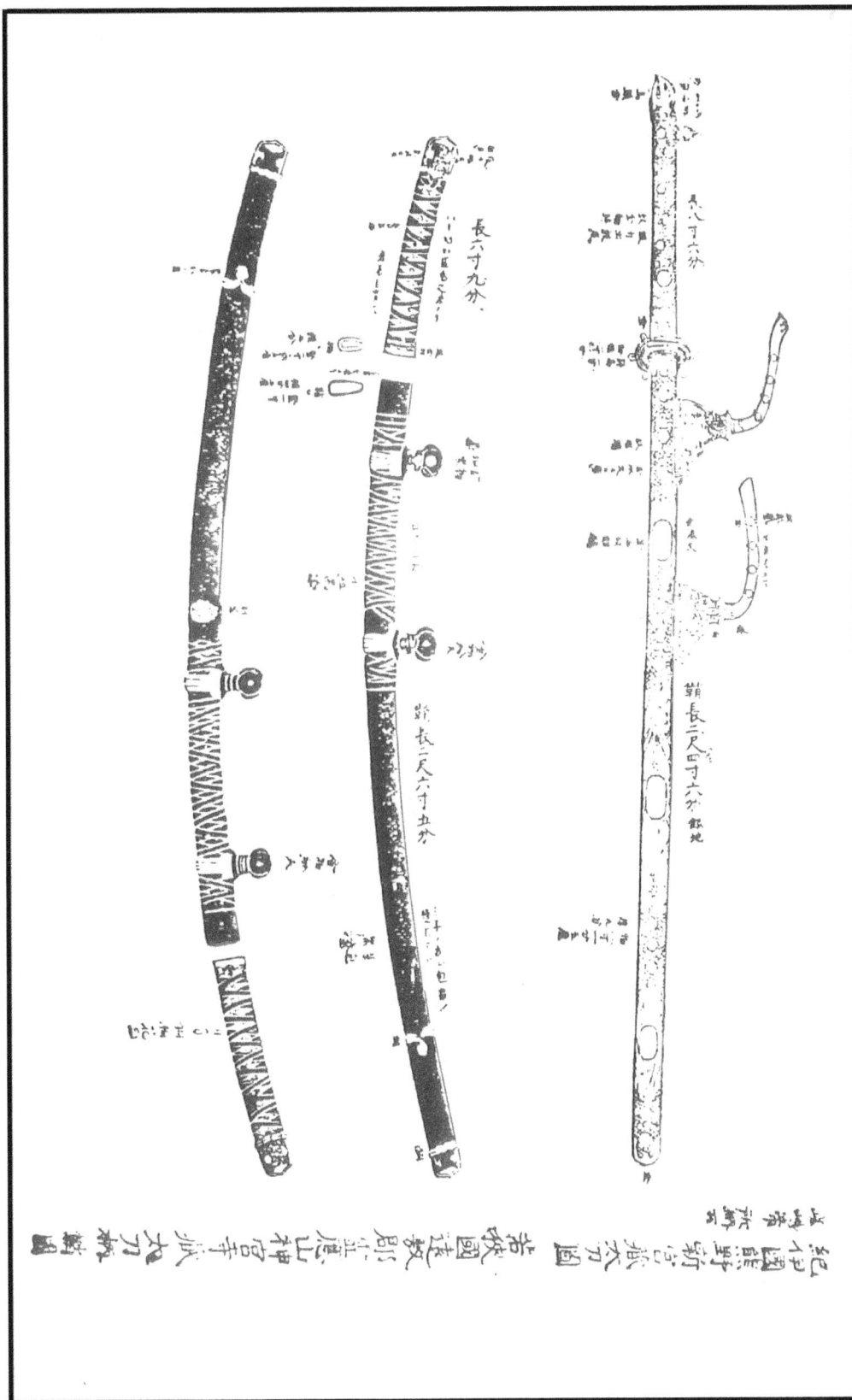

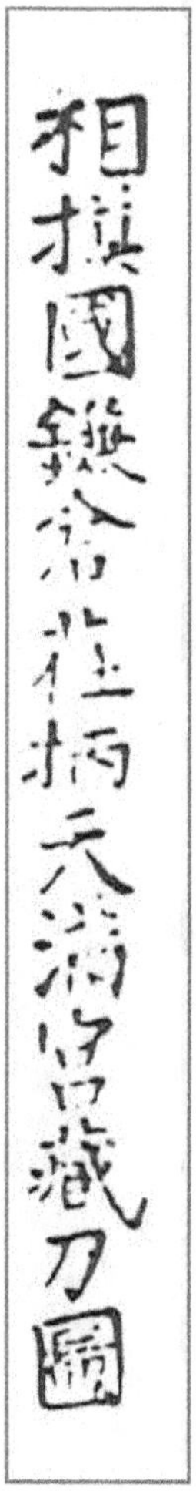

相模國鎌倉荏柄天満宮所蔵刀圖

Figure 2.7 Tanto - Egara Tenmangu Shrine.

Description reads, "Drawing of sword (tanto), Collection of Egara Tenmangu Shrine, Kamakura, Sagami Province."

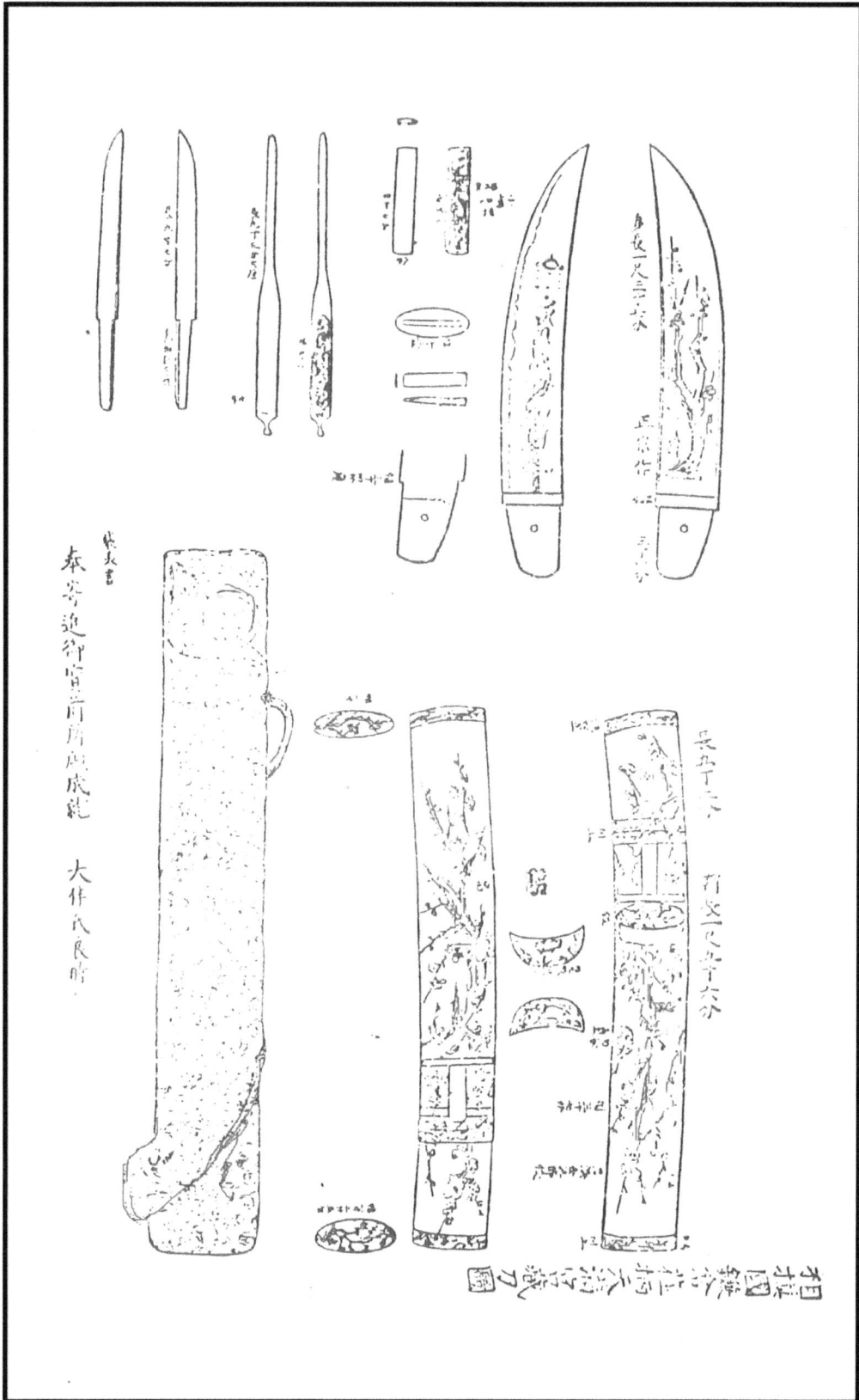

肥前國七郎宮藏刀飲圖

Figure 2.8 Ken - Shichirogu Shrine.

Description reads, "Drawing of sword (ken), Collection of Shichirogu Shrine, Hizen Province."

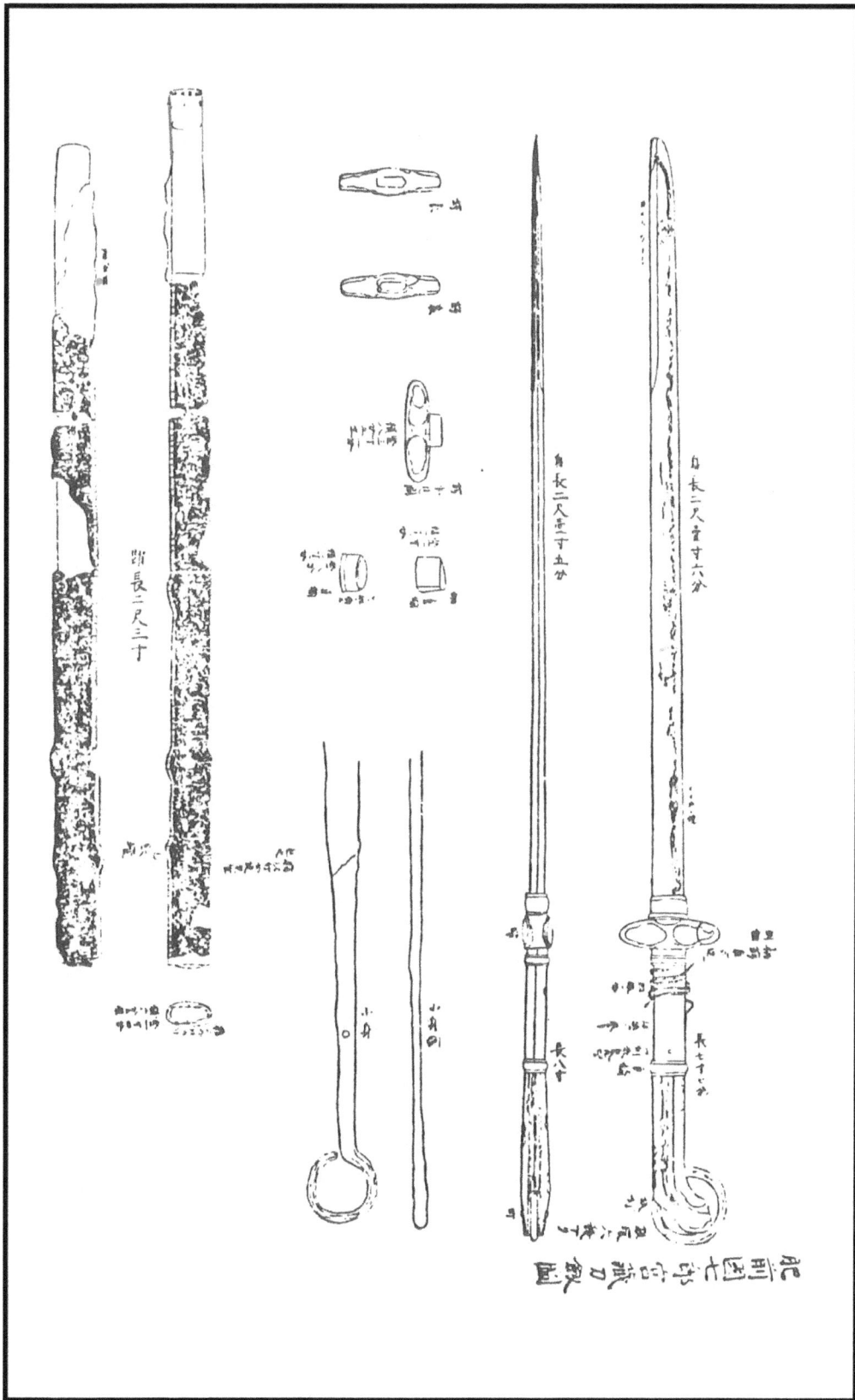

或家旅太刀圖二

Figure 2.9 Two Tachi.

Description reads, "Drawing of long swords (tachi), Private collection (2)."

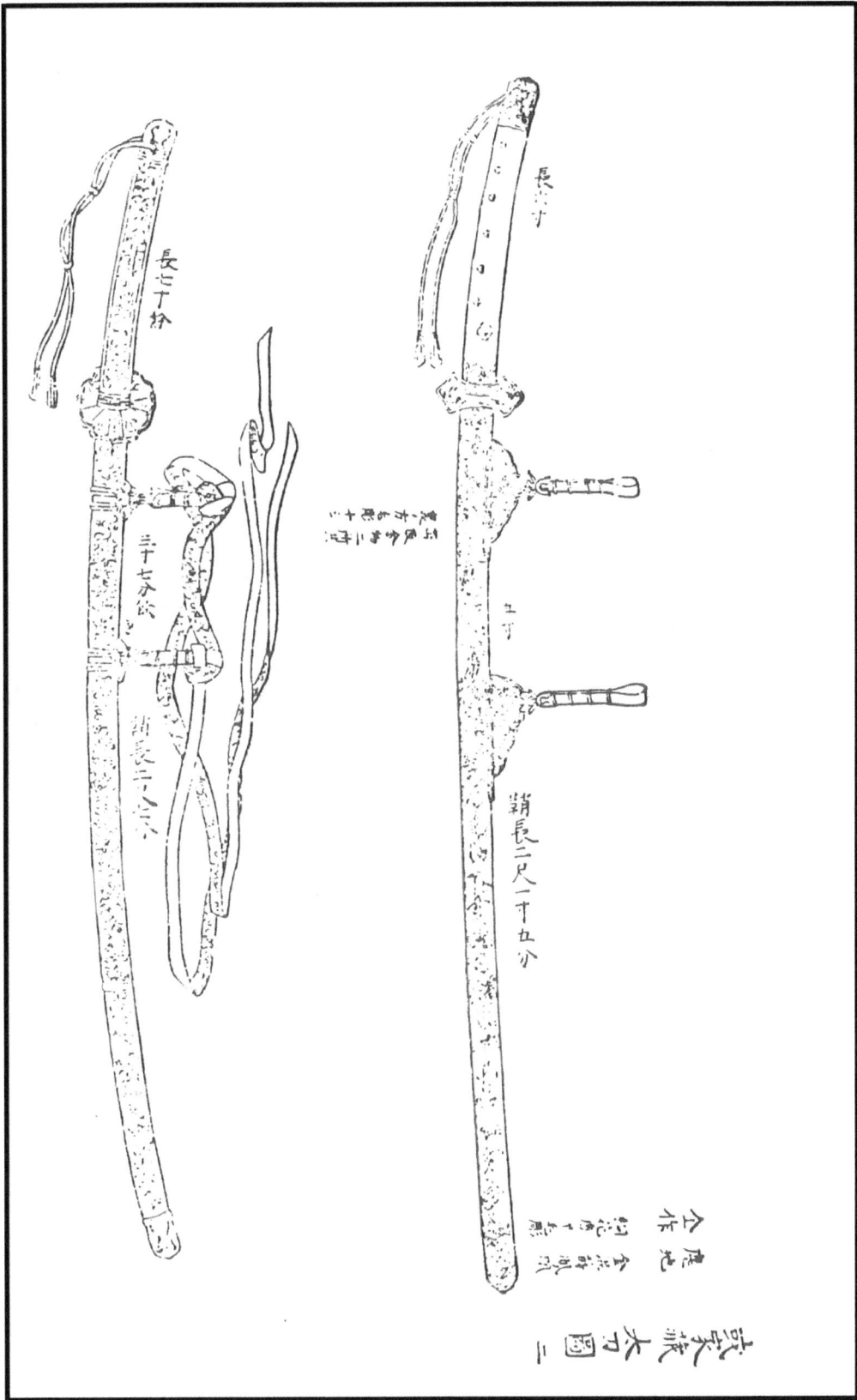

Figure 2.10 Tachi - Onimaru.

鬼
丸
太
刀
図

Description reads, "Drawing of long sword 'Onimaru'."

"Onimaru" (Ogre Boy) is a famous historical sword and is one of the famous "Tenka Goken" (Five Famous Japanese Swords). It was originally owned by the Hojyo family during the days of the Kamakura Shogunate. After the fall of the Kamakura Shogunate, the sword was taken over by the Ashikaga family of the Muromachi Shogunate and handed down through generations as a family treasure. Later the Tokugawa Shogunate placed Onimaru under the care of the Hon-ami family (famous sword polisher and appraiser). From the Meiji period, Onimaru has been in the possession of the imperial family.

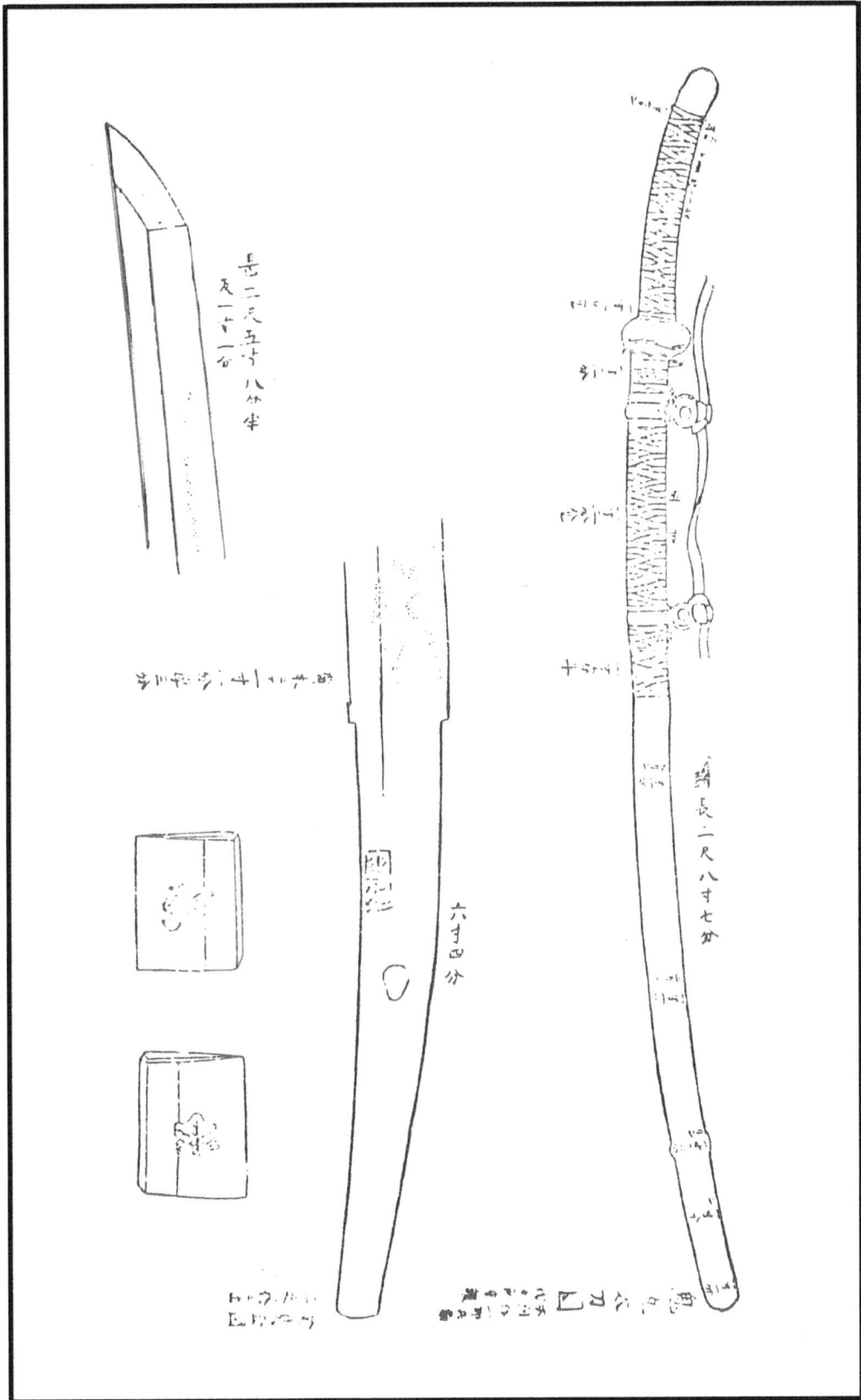

相模國鎌倉鶴岡八幡宮藏 杏葉太刀圖 二 金具全図之巻

Figure 2.11 Two Tachi - Tsurugaoka Hachimangu Shrine.

Descriptions read, "Drawing of long swords (tachi) 'Gyoyo' (The Guardian), Collection of Tsurugaoka Hachimangu Shrine, Kamakura, Sagami Province (2);"

"Appears in 'Complete Drawings of Metal Fittings'."

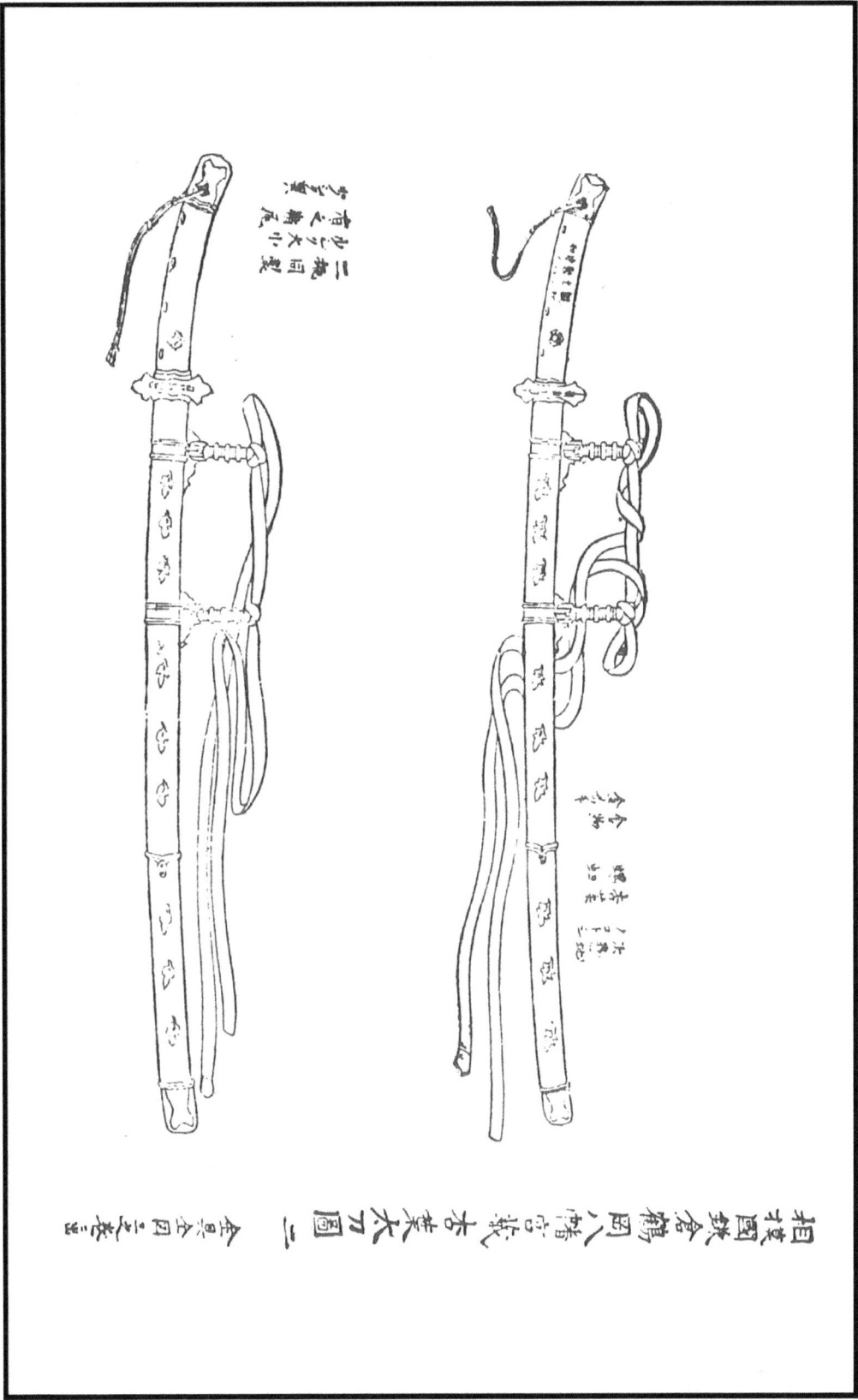

Thomas Buck

豊前國宇佐八幡宮藏短刀圖

Figure 2.12 Wakizashi and Tanto - Usa Hachimangu Shrine.

The description reads, "Drawing of short sword (wakizashi and tanto), Collection of Usa Hachimangu Shrine, Buzen Province."

42

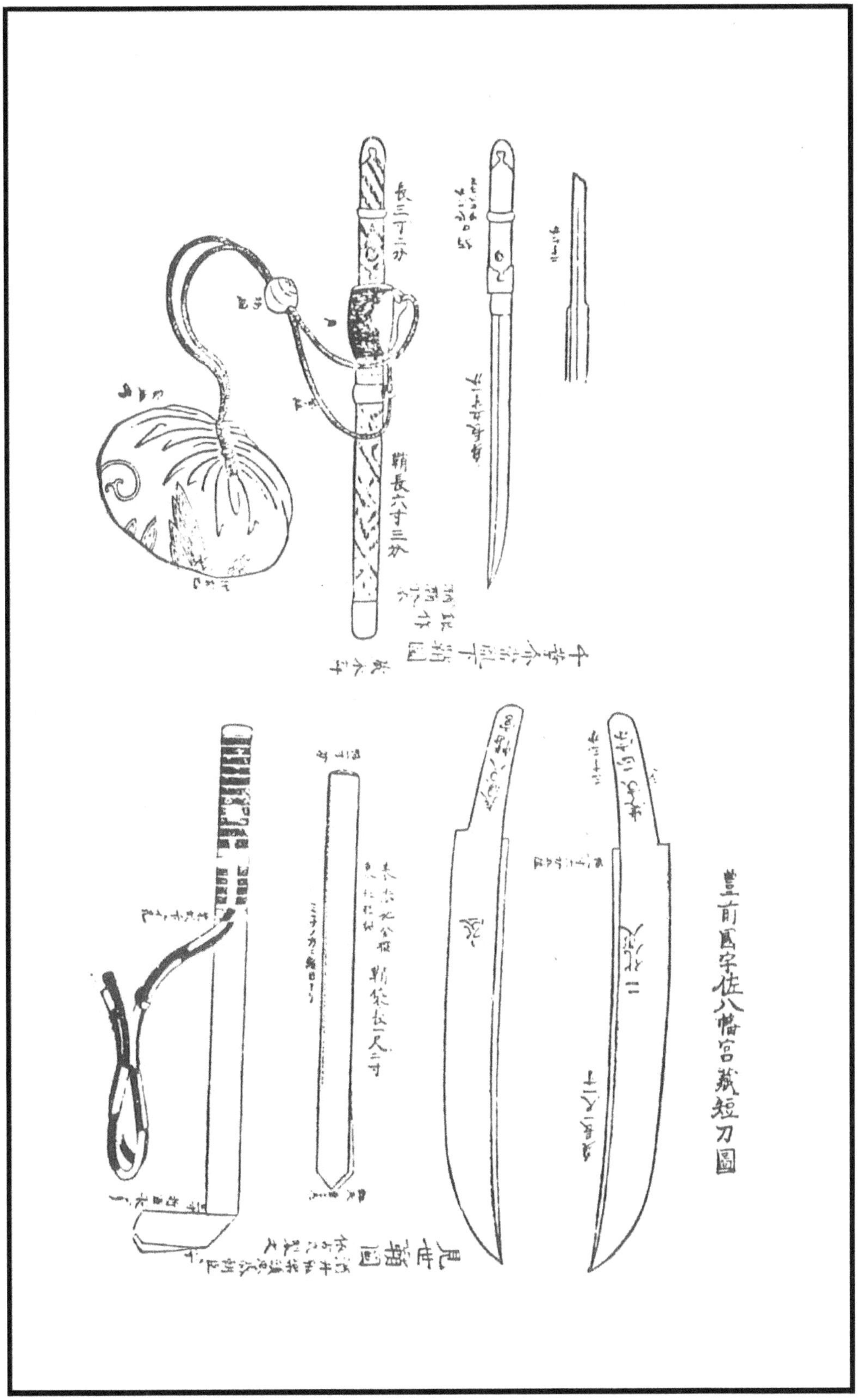
豊前國宇佐八幡宮藏短刀圖
長三寸二分
鞘長六寸三分

筑前國彦山無地所藏刀圖

恣云計

於丹波國大江山山中所獲の圖　同同

Figure 2.13 Two Ancient Swords.

The description reads, "Drawing of sword unearthed in Hikosan, Chikuzen Province, Collection unknown;"

Description reads, "Drawing of sword found in Mt. Oe, Tamba Province [illegible]".

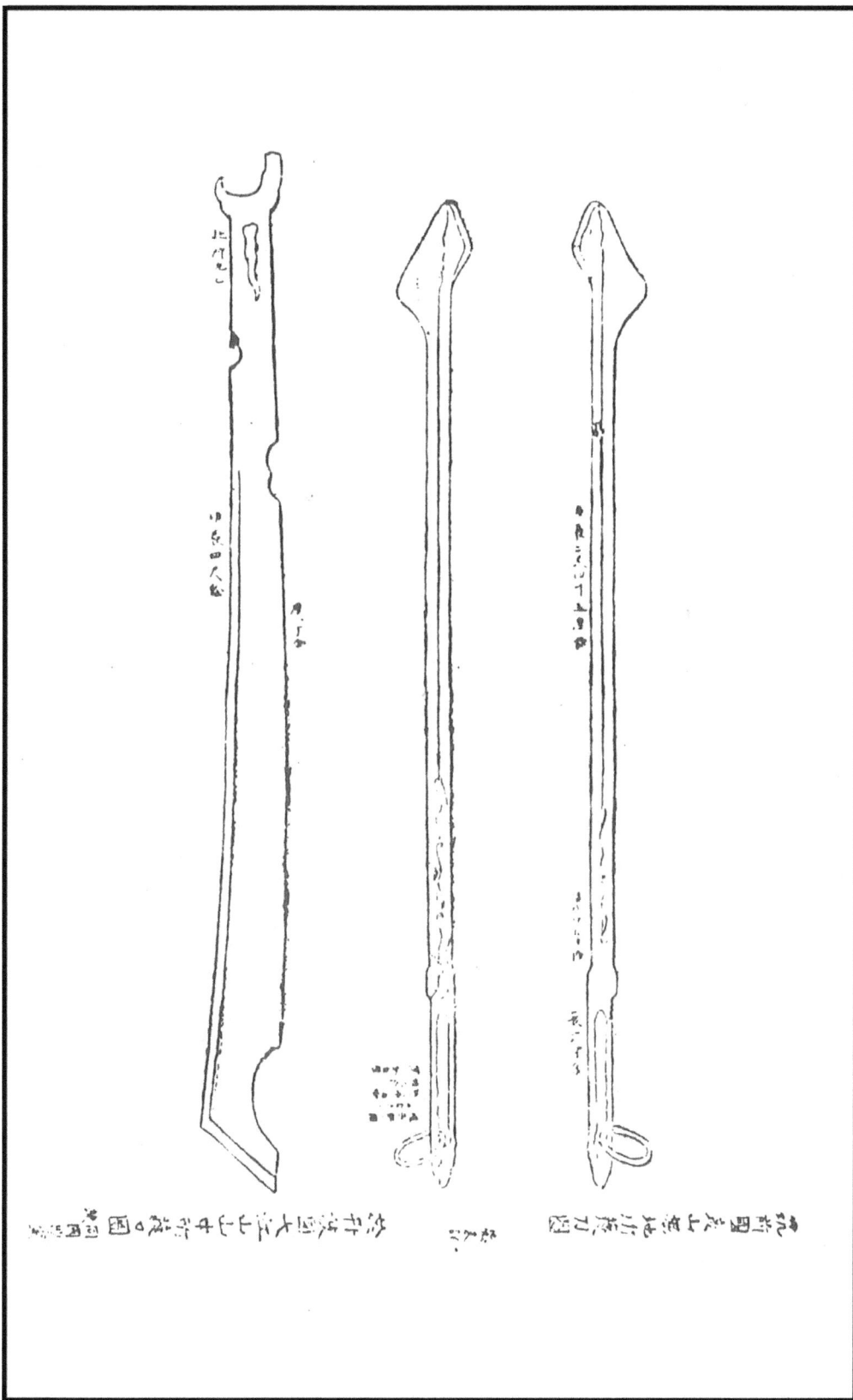

上野國高崎郡豊岡村堀地所發刀圖

Figure 2.14 Ancient Sword.

The description reads, "Drawing of sword unearthed in Toyooka Village, Takazaki District, Kozuke Province, Collection unknown."

身長一尺七八寸

上野國髙崎郡豐岡村堀地所發刀圖

五寸餘

長三寸七分

新長一尺三分

阪坂正宗延刀圖 蔵未詳

Figure 2.15 Tanto and Hachiwara - Masamune.

The description reads, "Drawing of short swords (tanto and hachiwara) by swordsmith Masamune (Iizuka?), Collection unknown."

Masamune (正宗, c.1264–1343 AD), is widely recognized as Japan's greatest swordsmith. The swords of Masamune have a reputation for superior beauty and quality, remarkable in a period where the steel necessary for swords was often impure.

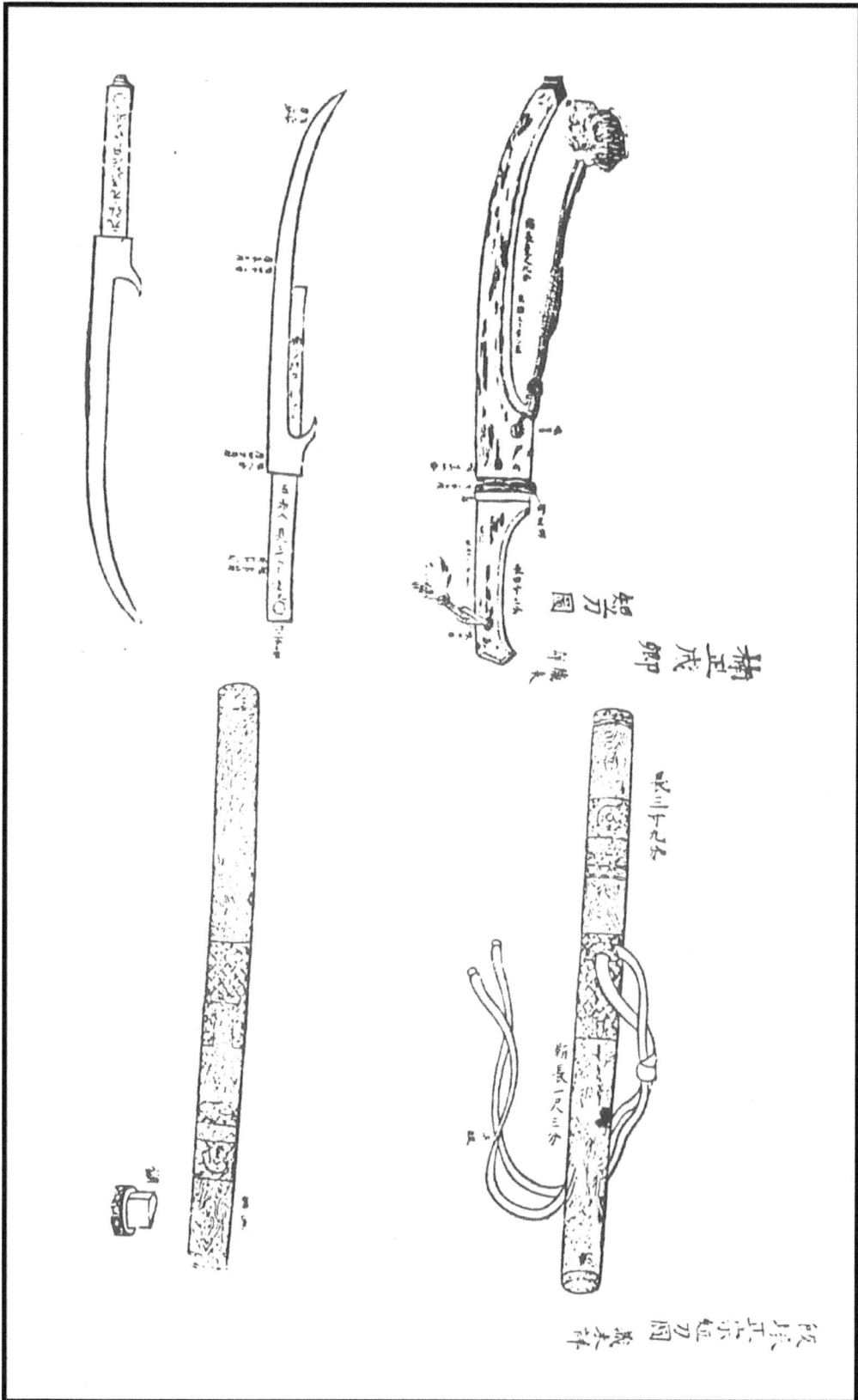

陸奥國南部本誓寺藏太刀

Figure 2.16 Two Tachi.

The description reads, "Long swords (tachi), Collection of Nambu Honsei-ji Temple, Mutsu Province."

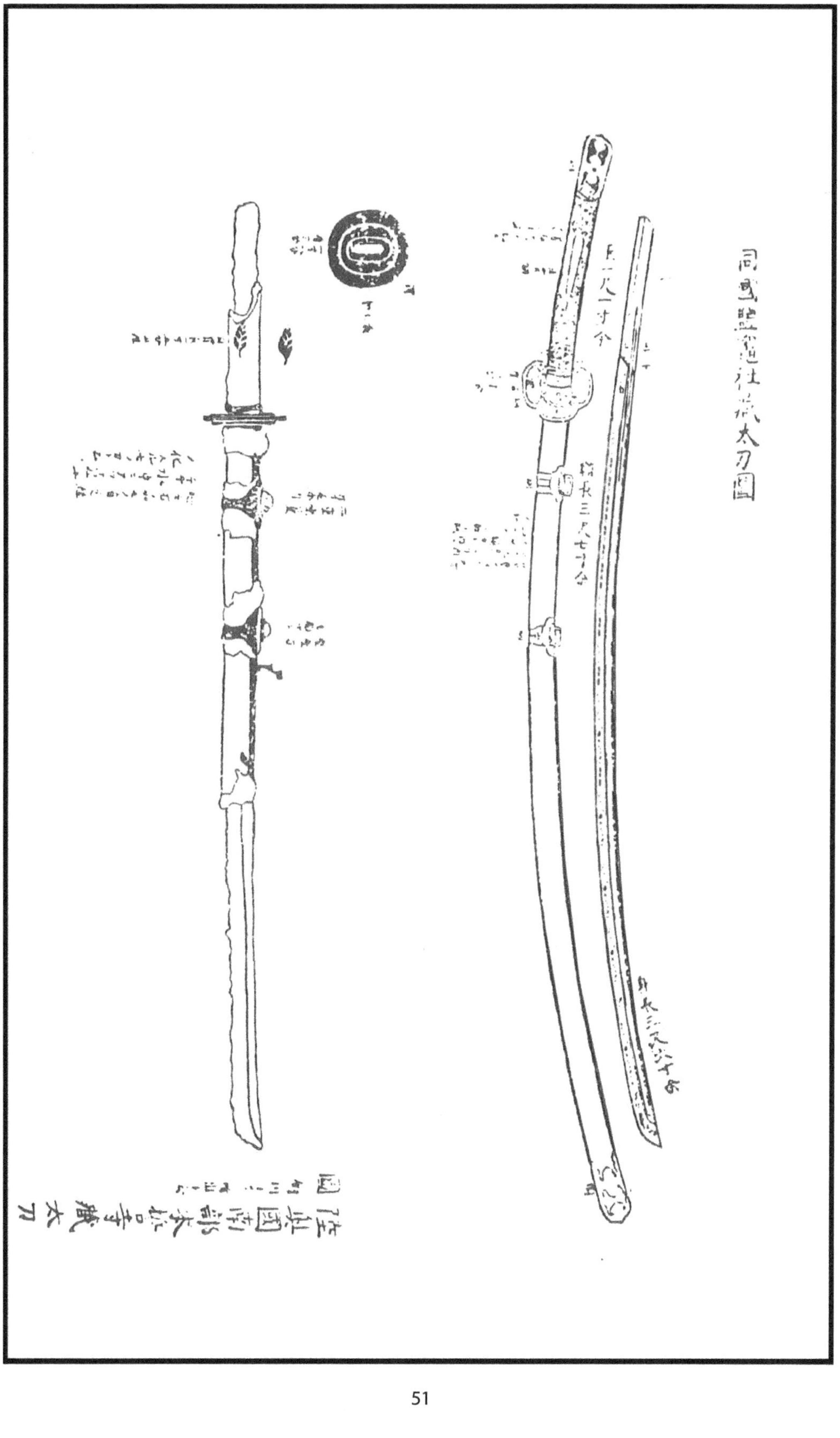
同國鹽竈社藏太刀圖

伊
豫
国
三
島
社
蔵
平
重
盛
太
刀
図

Figure 2.17 Two Tachi - Shigemori Taira.

The description reads, "Drawing of long sword (tachi) belonging to Lord Shigemori Taira, Collection of Mishima Shrine, Iyo Province."

Taira no Shigemori (平 重盛, 1138 – September 2, 1179) was the eldest son of the Taira clan patriarch, Taira no Kiyomori. He took part in the Hōgen and Heiji rebellions. He died of illness in 1179.

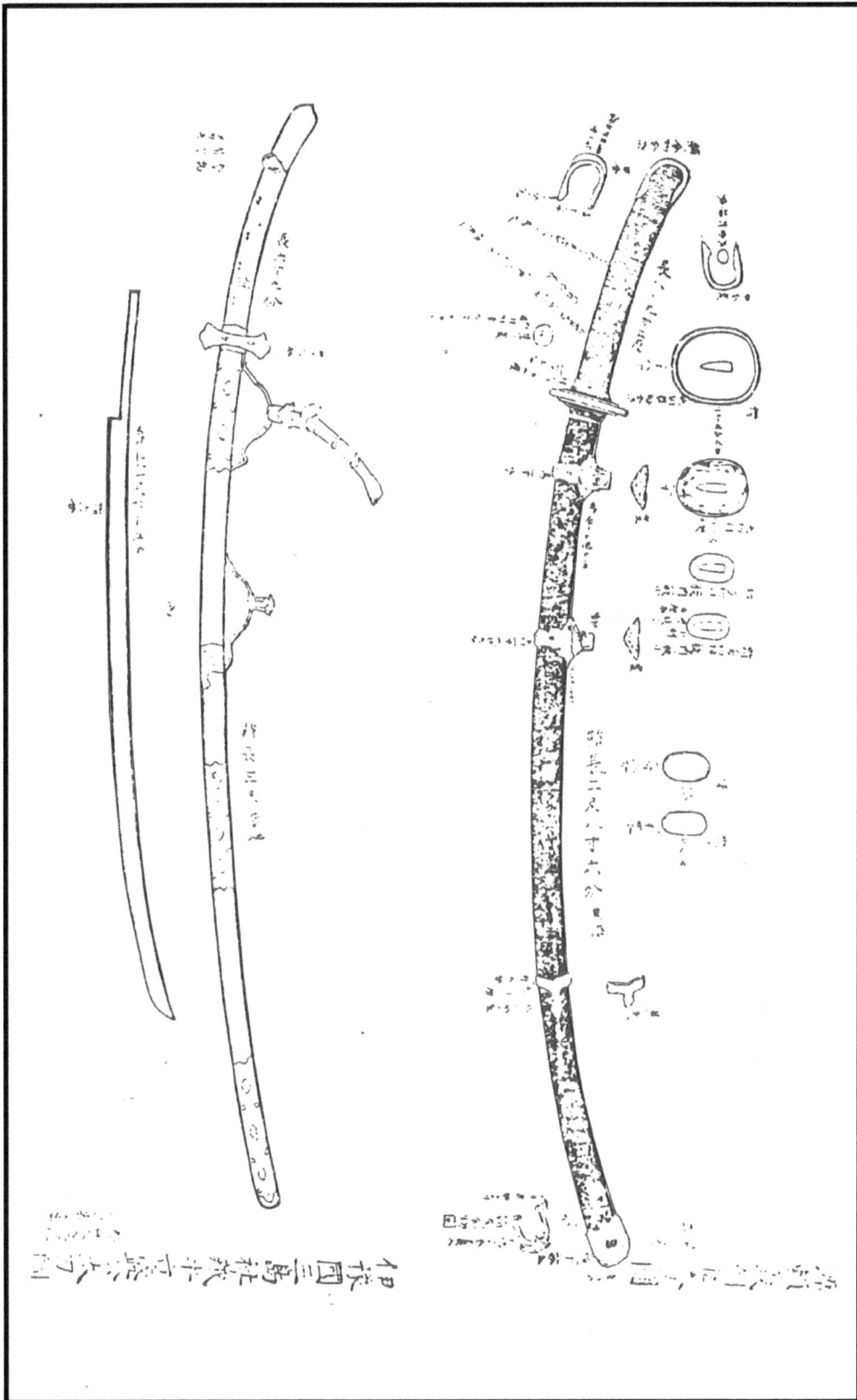

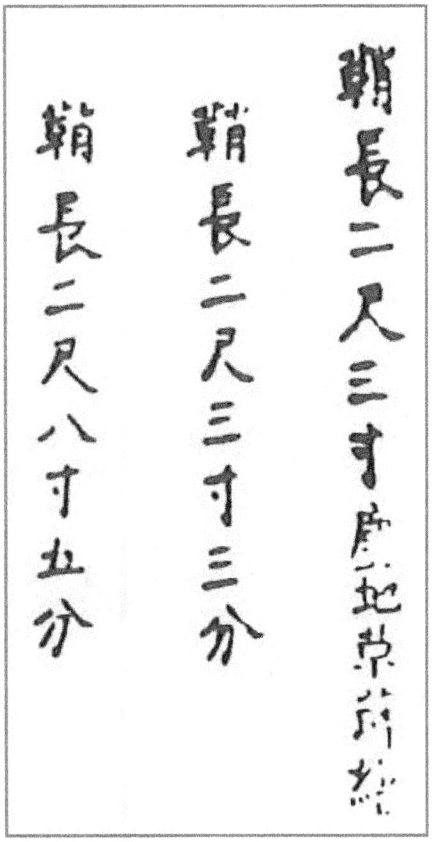

鞘長二尺三寸□□□□□□

鞘長二尺三寸三分

鞘長二尺八寸五分

Figure 2.18 Lengths of Three Tachi.

The description reads, "First sword length: Scabbard; 2 shaku, 3 sun [approximately 69 cm]; Second sword length: Scabbard; 2 shaku, 3 sun, 3 bu [approximately 70 cm]; Third sword length: Scabbard; 2 shaku, 8 sun, 5 bu [approximately 85.5 cm]."

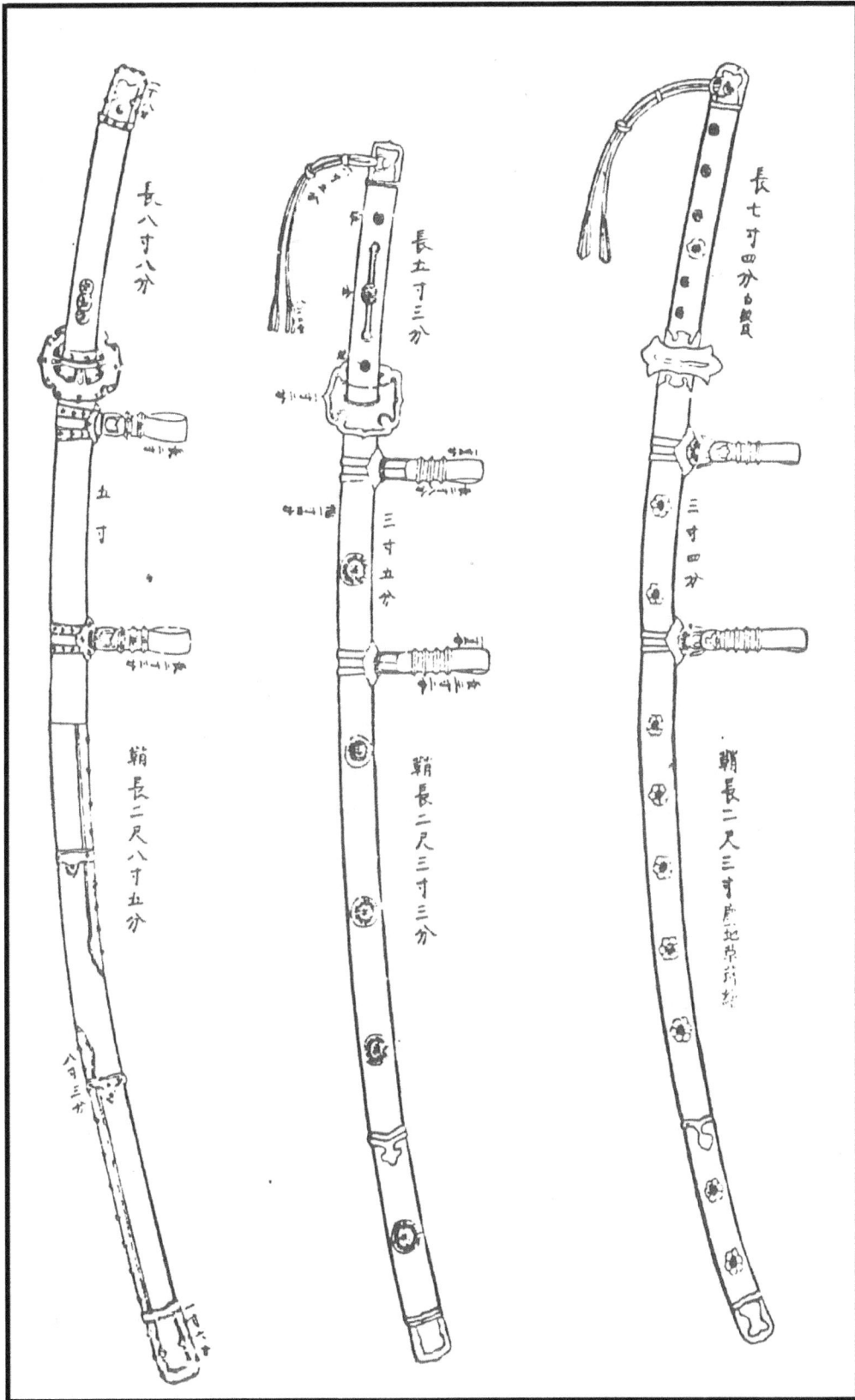

長八寸八分

五寸

鞘長二尺八寸五分

八寸三分

長五寸三分

三寸五分

鞘長二尺三寸三分

長七寸四分白鮫貝

三寸四分

鞘長二尺三寸廣地螺鈿塗

伊豆國三島社藏北条末耶納太刀圖二

Figure 2.19 Tachi blade with Two Koshirae.

The description reads, "Drawing of long sword (tachi) donated by Hojo Family (clan), Mishima Shrine, Izu Province (2)."

The Hōjō Family (clan) (北条氏) the hereditary title of shikken (regent) of the Kamakura shogunate between 1206 and 1333. The Hōjō are known for fostering Zen Buddhism, the development of Bushidō, and for leading the successful opposition to the Mongol invasions of Japan.

Left is the family crest (mon) of Hōjō Family; know as the "Tri-Force."

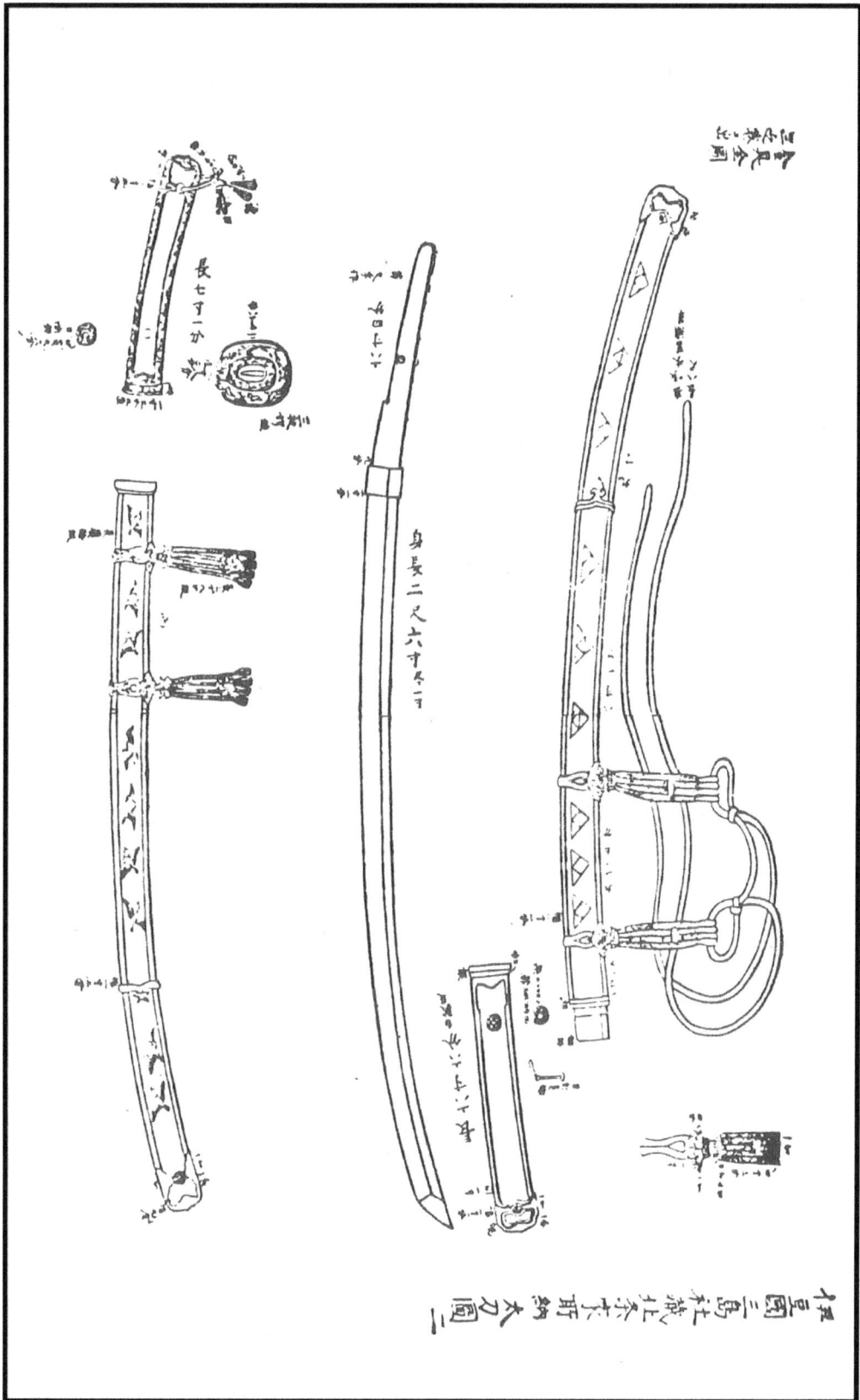

茎
二
寸
九
分

惚
芯
分
五
厘

Figure 2.20 Two Ken Nakago.

Descriptions read, "Tang (nakago): 2 sun, 9 bu [approximately 8.8 cm];"

"Width : 7 "bu", 5 "ri" [approximately 21.5 mm]."

茎
四
寸
九
分

惚
八
分
五
厘

"Tang (nakago): 4 sun, 9 bu [approximately 14.7 cm];"

"Width : 8 bu, 5 ri [approximately 24.5 mm]."

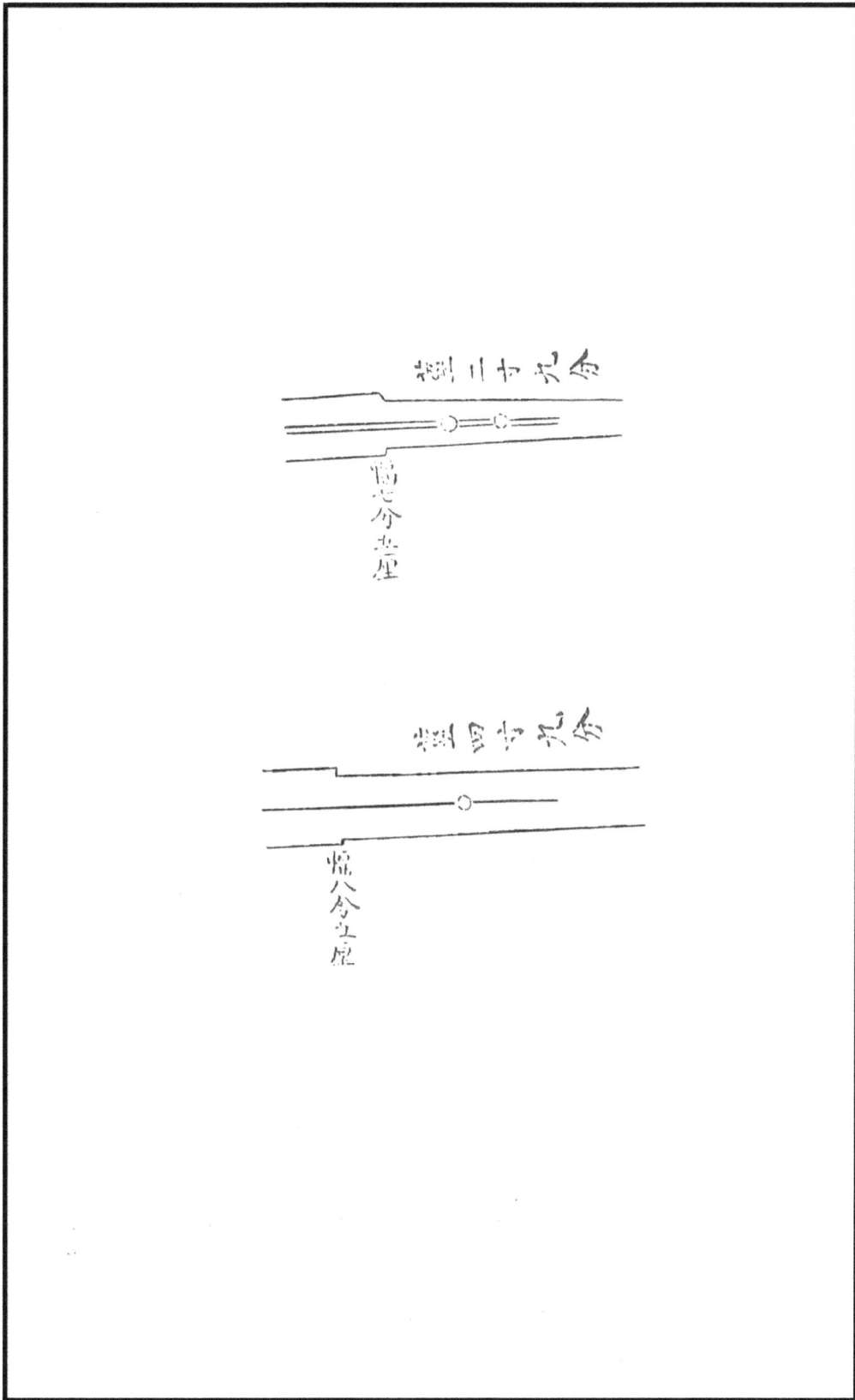

出雲國大社藏劒圖

Figure 2.21 Three Ken - Taisha Shrine.

The description reads, "Drawing of straight two-edge swords (ken) in collection of the Taisha Shrine, Izumo Province."

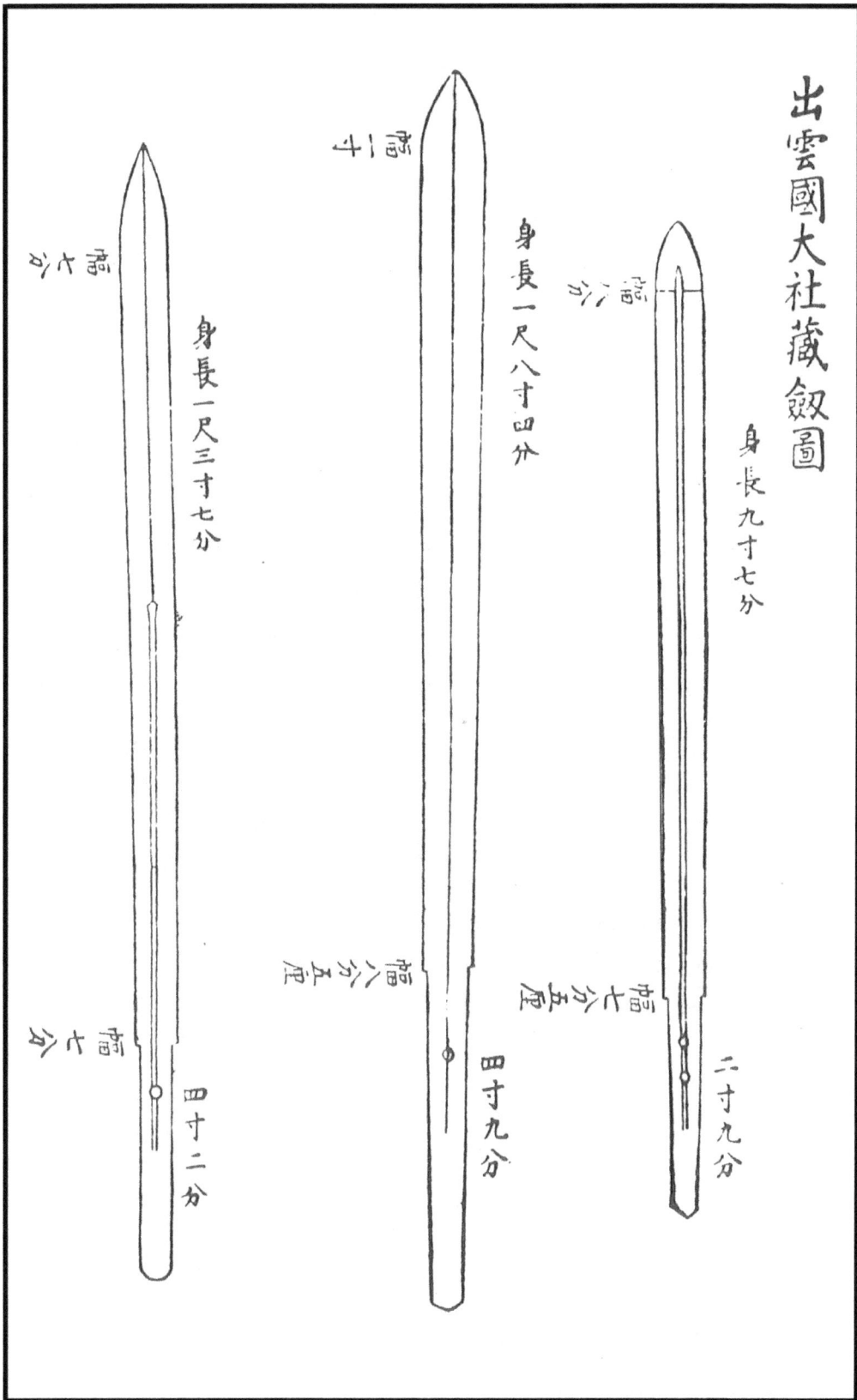

出雲國大社藏劔圖

身長九寸七分

身長一尺八寸四分

身長一尺三寸七分

二寸九分

四寸九分

四寸二分

河内國壷井八幡宮藏源義家朝臣太刀圖

源義家朝臣海老鞘卷短刀圖

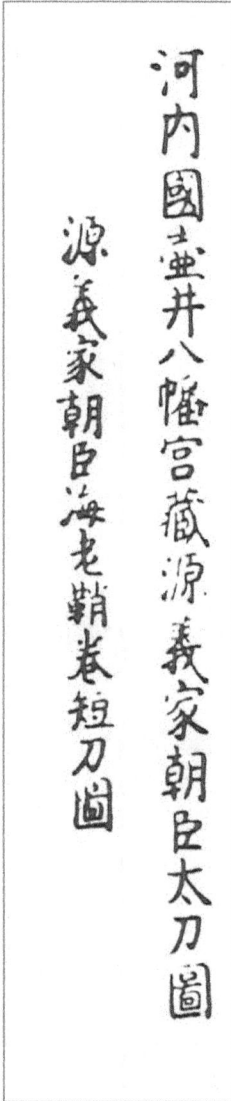

Figure 2.22 Tachi and Wakizashi - Yoshiie Minamoto.

First part of description reads, "Drawing of long sword (tachi) belonging to Court Noble Yoshiie Minamoto, Collection of Tsuboi Hachimangu Shrine, Kawachi Province;"

Second part reads, "Drawing of short sword (wakizashi) in sheath with shrimp pattern belonging to Court Noble Yoshiie Minamoto."

Minamoto no Yoshiie (源 義家; 1039 – 4 August 1106), was a Minamoto clan samurai of the late Heian period, and Chinjufu Shogun (Commander-in-chief of the defense of the North).

As the first son of Minamoto no Yoriyoshi, he proved himself in battle in the Zenkunen War (Early Nine Years' War) and in the Gosannen War (Later Three Years' War). Subsequently, he is considered an ideal of samurai skill and bravery.

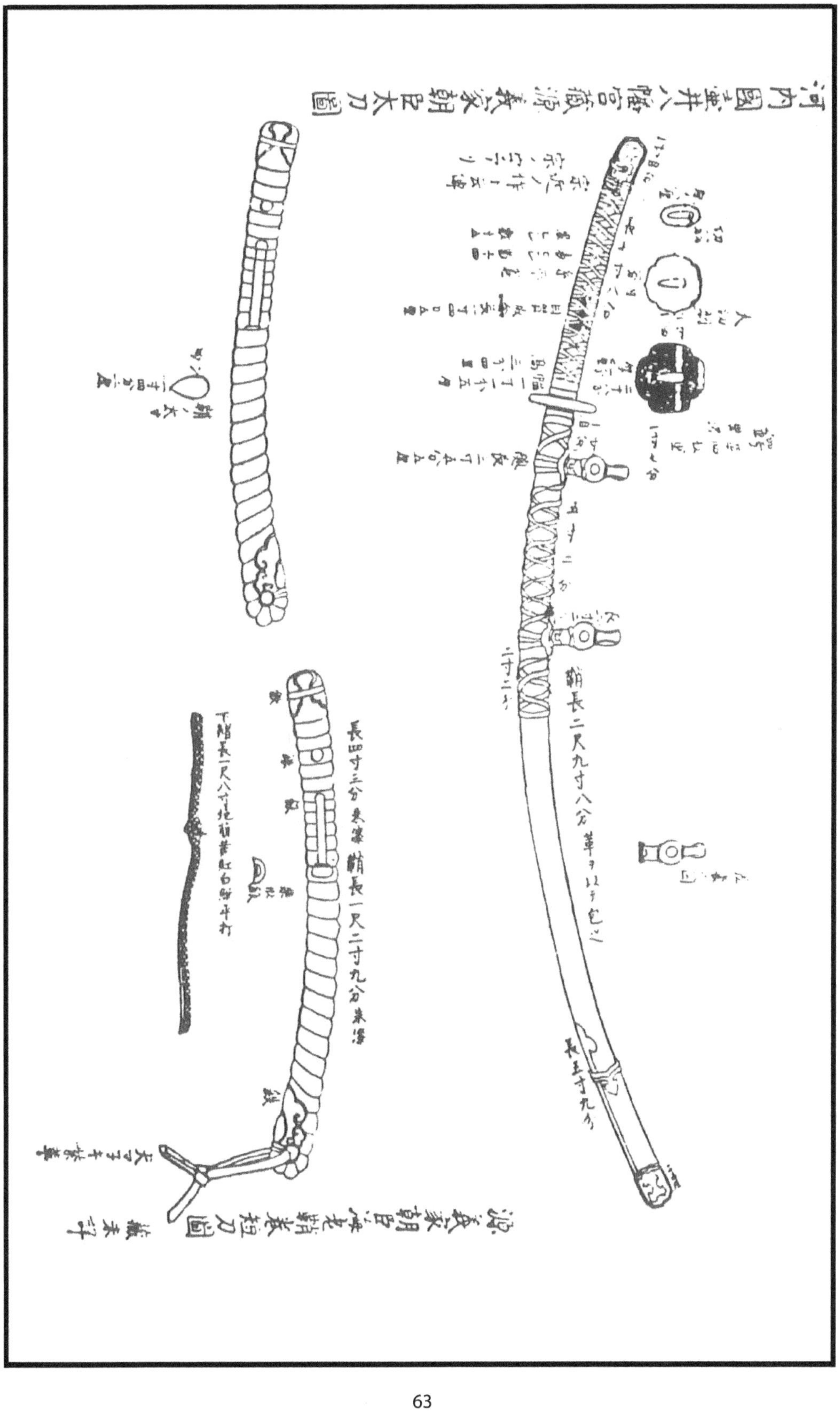
河内國壺井八幡宮蔵源義家朝臣太刀圖
鞘長二尺九寸八分

赤木短刀圖　相摸國箱根推現社藏　同藏源賴朝卿昨納太刀圖

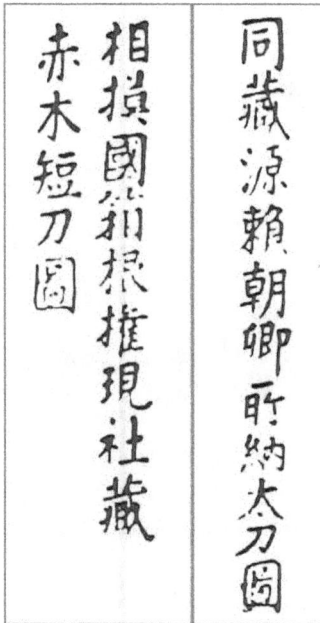

Figure 2.23 Tachi and Ken - Yoritomo Minamoto.

The desriptions read, "Drawing of short sword (ken) with bishopwood hilt, Collection of the Hakone Gongen Shrine, Sagami Province;" and, "Drawing of long sword donated by Lord Yoritomo Minamoto, same collection."

Minamoto no Yoritomo (源 頼朝, May 9, 1147 – February 9, 1199) was the founder and the first Shogun of the Kamakura Shogunate of Japan. He ruled from 1192 until 1199.

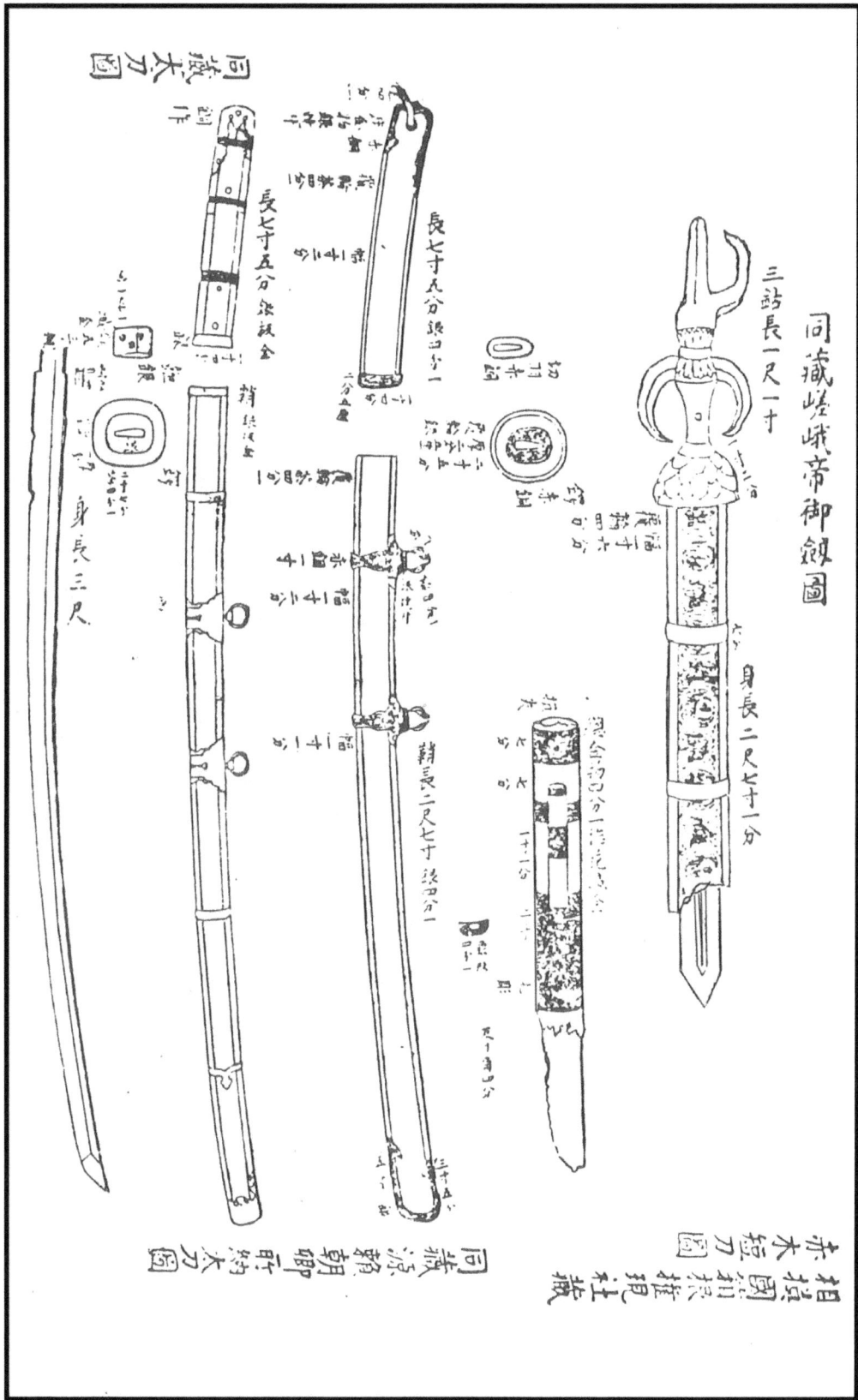

河內國天野山金剛寺藏
楠正成卿短刀圖
所彫後醍醐天皇

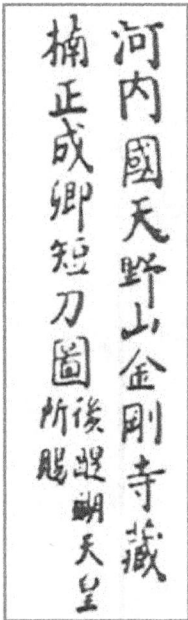

Figure 2.24 Wakizashi and Kozuka.

The description reads, "Drawings of three Kozuka (utility knife) handles, one Kozuka blade, and a short sword (wakizashi). All with the family crest of the Tokugawa Shogunate."

The Tokugawa shogunate, also known as the Tokugawa bakufu (徳川幕府) and the Edo bakufu (江戸幕府), was the last feudal Japanese military government which existed between 1603 and 1868. The heads of government were the shoguns, and each was a member of the Tokugawa clan. The Tokugawa shogunate ruled from Edo Castle and the years of shogunate became known as the Edo period. This time is also called the Tokugawa period or pre-modern (Kinsei (近世)).

源義家法楯之圖
ヒノ對シテ又無上法衛ヲ

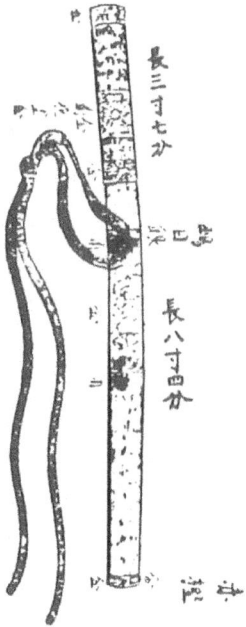

長三寸七分

長八寸四分

九寸二分

河内國柏原天野郷上金剛寺ノ什物短刀ハ則チ後醍醐天皇

伊豫國三島社藏高力左近大夫高長所納刀圖

Figure 2.25 Wakizashi - Mishima Shrine.

The description reads, "Drawing of sword donated by Sakon Dayu Takanaga Koriki, Collection of Mishima Shrine, Iyo Province."

The Kōriki clan (高力氏) was a samurai clan which briefly came to prominence during the Sengoku and early Edo periods. Kōriki Kiyonaga (1530-1608) was a hereditary retainer of the Tokugawa clan, who served Tokugawa Ieyasu as Bugyō of Sunpu and was made Daimyō of Iwatsuki Domain in Musashi Province in 1590.

His son, Kōriki Tadafusa (1583-1655) distinguished himself in combat during the Battle of Sekigahara and the Siege of Osaka and was transferred to Hamamatsu Domain (35,000 koku) in Tōtōmi Province in 1619.

These swords were donated to the Mishima Shrine by his son Kōriki Takanaga (1604-1676) who governed the Kōriki clan for a few short years before he was dispossessed for bad administration and exiled to Sendai in Mutsu Province in 1668. The clan subsequently sunk into obscurity and moved to the Shimōsa Province until the end of the Edo period.

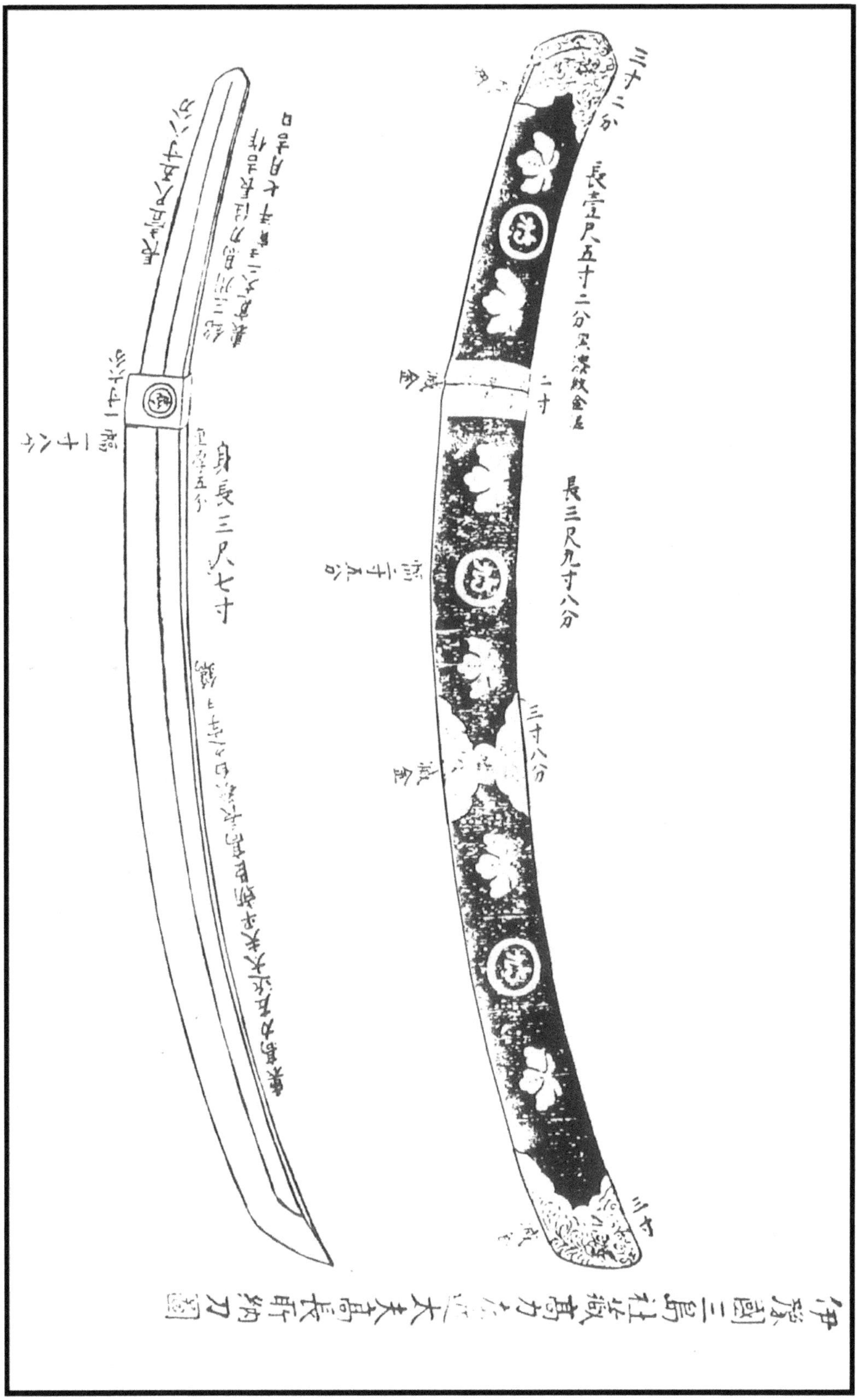
長三尺九寸八分
身長三尺七寸

信濃國諏訪社藏細切丸太刀圖　同藏平重衡卿所納太刀圖

Figure 2.26 Two Tachi - Shigehira Taira.

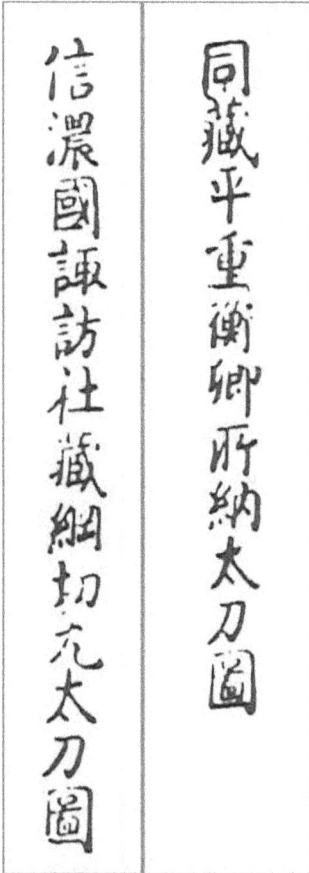

The description reads, "Drawing of long sword (tachi) named 'Kokomaru', Collection of Suwa Shrine, Shinano Province;" and, "Drawing of long sword (tachi) donated by Lord Shigehira Taira, same collection."

Taira no Shigehira (平 重衡) (1158–1185) was one of the sons of Taira no Kiyomori, and one of the Taira Clan's chief commanders during the Heian period of the 12th century. Following the Battle of Uji in 1180, Shigehira ordered the burning of Nara (see Siege of Nara).

After defeating Minamoto no Yukiie at the Battle of Sunomatagawa, Shigehira was named commander-in-chief of the Taira forces, and was given 13,000 men.

He was defeated and captured four years later at the Battle of Ichi-no-Tani, and then turned over to the monks of the Tōdai-ji, which he had burned. He was then beheaded by the monks in late 1185.

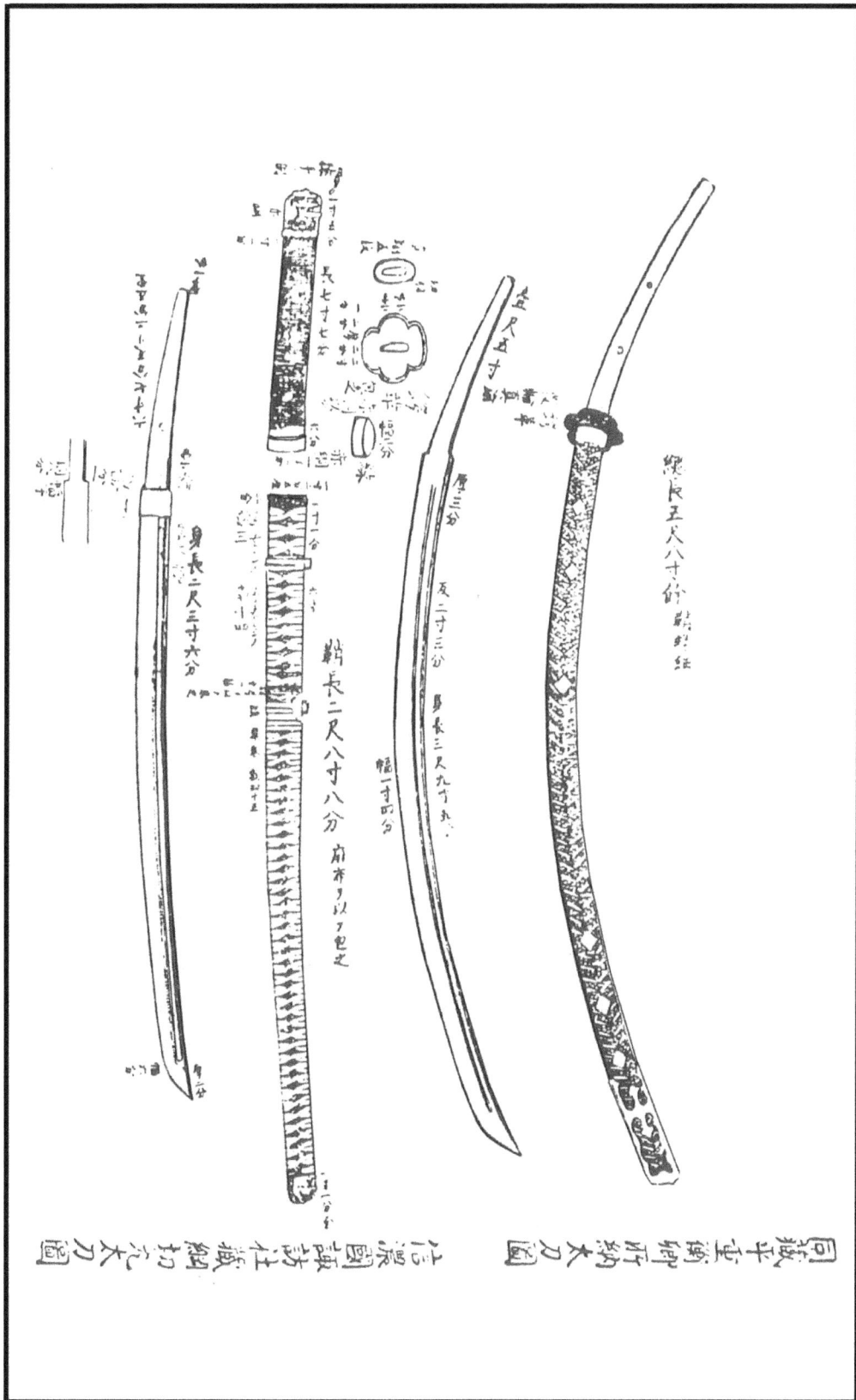

相摸國鎌倉荏柄天満宮藏短刀圖

Figure 2.27 Tachi and Tanto - Egara Tenmangu Shrine.

The description reads, "Drawing of long sword (tachi) and short sword (tanto), Collection of Egara Tenmangu Shrine, Kamakura, Sagami Province."

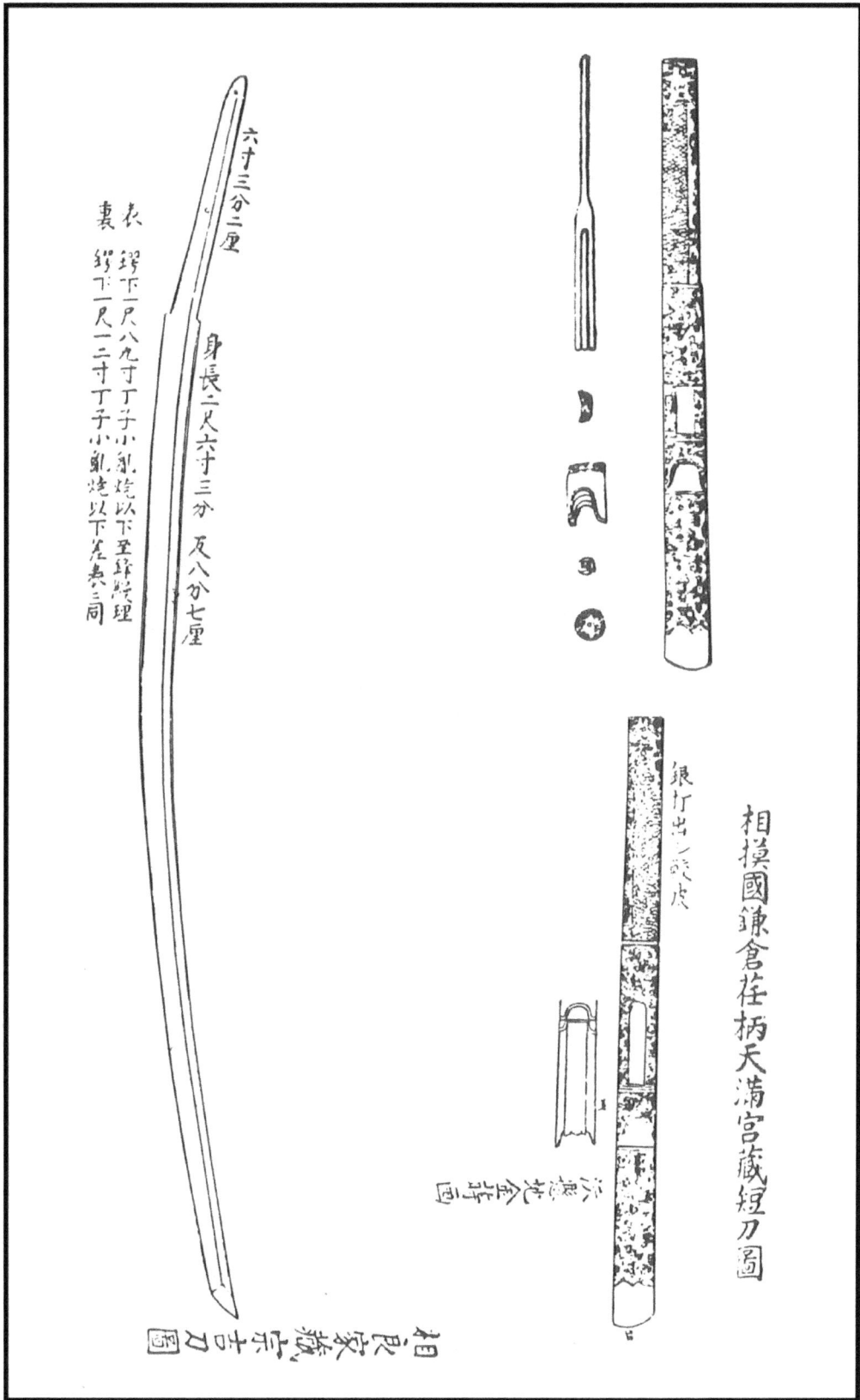

讃岐國高松海中所出劔圖

尾張國海東郡勝幡村堀地所獲短刀圖

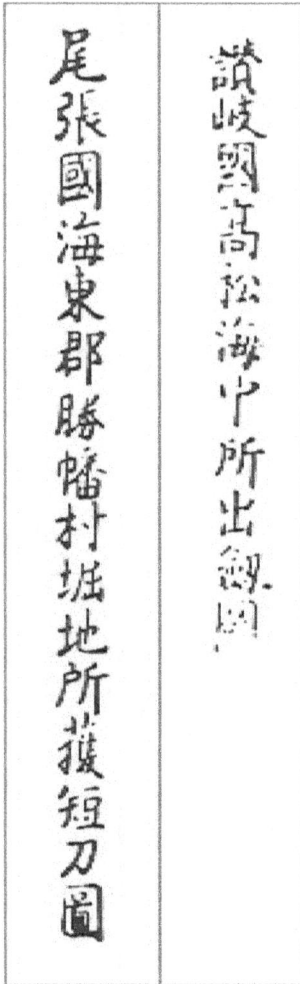

Figure 2.28 Wakizashi and Tanto.

The description reads, "Drawing of straight two-edge sword (tanto) retrieved from ocean offshore from Takamatsu, Sanuki Province;" and, "Drawing of short sword (wakizashi) unearthed in Katsuhata Village, Kaito District, Owari Province."

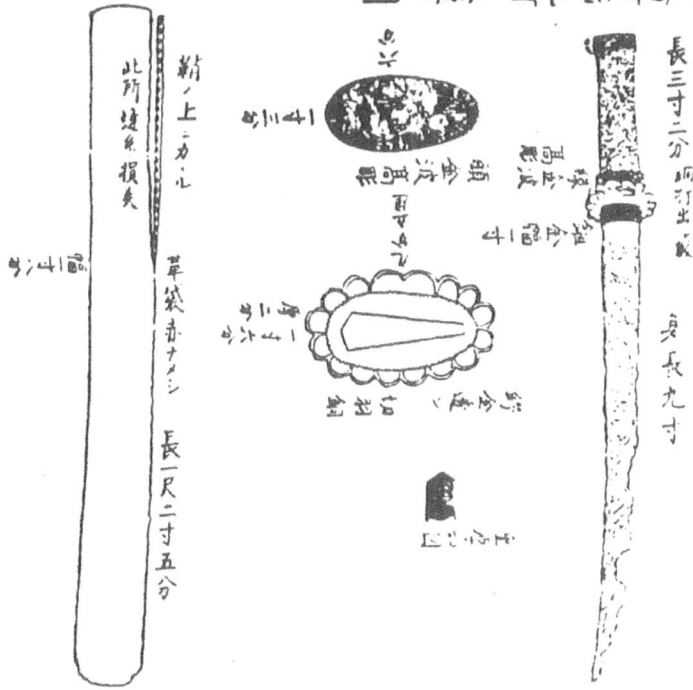

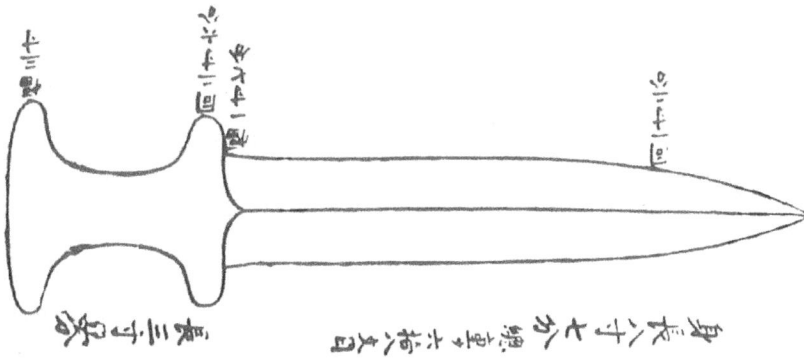

安德帝御剱圖　長門國赤間關阿彌陀寺藏

同藏能登守教經刀圖

Figure 2.29 Tachi and Ken - Noritsune Taira.

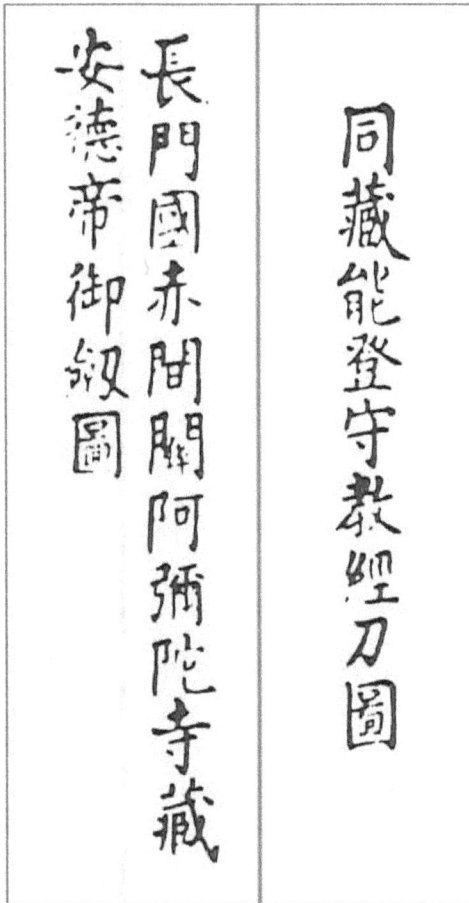

Descriptions read, "Drawing of straight two-edge (ken) sword belonging to Emperor Antoku, Collection of Amida Temple, Akamaseki, Nagato Province;" and, "Drawing of long sword (tachi belonging to Noritsune Taira, Lord of Noto, same collection."

Emperor Antoku (安徳天皇) (December 22, 1177 – March 24, 1185) was the 81st emperor of Japan, and his reign spanned the years from 1180 through 1185. During this time, the imperial family was involved in a bitter struggle between warring clans. Yoritomo, with his cousin Yoshinaka, led a force from the Minamoto clan against the Taira, who controlled the emperor. During the sea battle of Dan-no-ura in March 1185, a member of the royal household took Antoku and plunged with him into the water in the Shimonoseki Straits, drowning the child emperor rather than allowing him to be captured by the opposing forces.

Taira no Noritsune (平 教経) (1160–1185) fought in the Genpei War battles of Mizushima, Ichi-no-Tani, and Dan-no-ura alongside his brethren in clan Taira. Tradition holds that he died by drowning himself, at Dan-no-ura, while holding a Minamoto warrior under each arm. In the play,

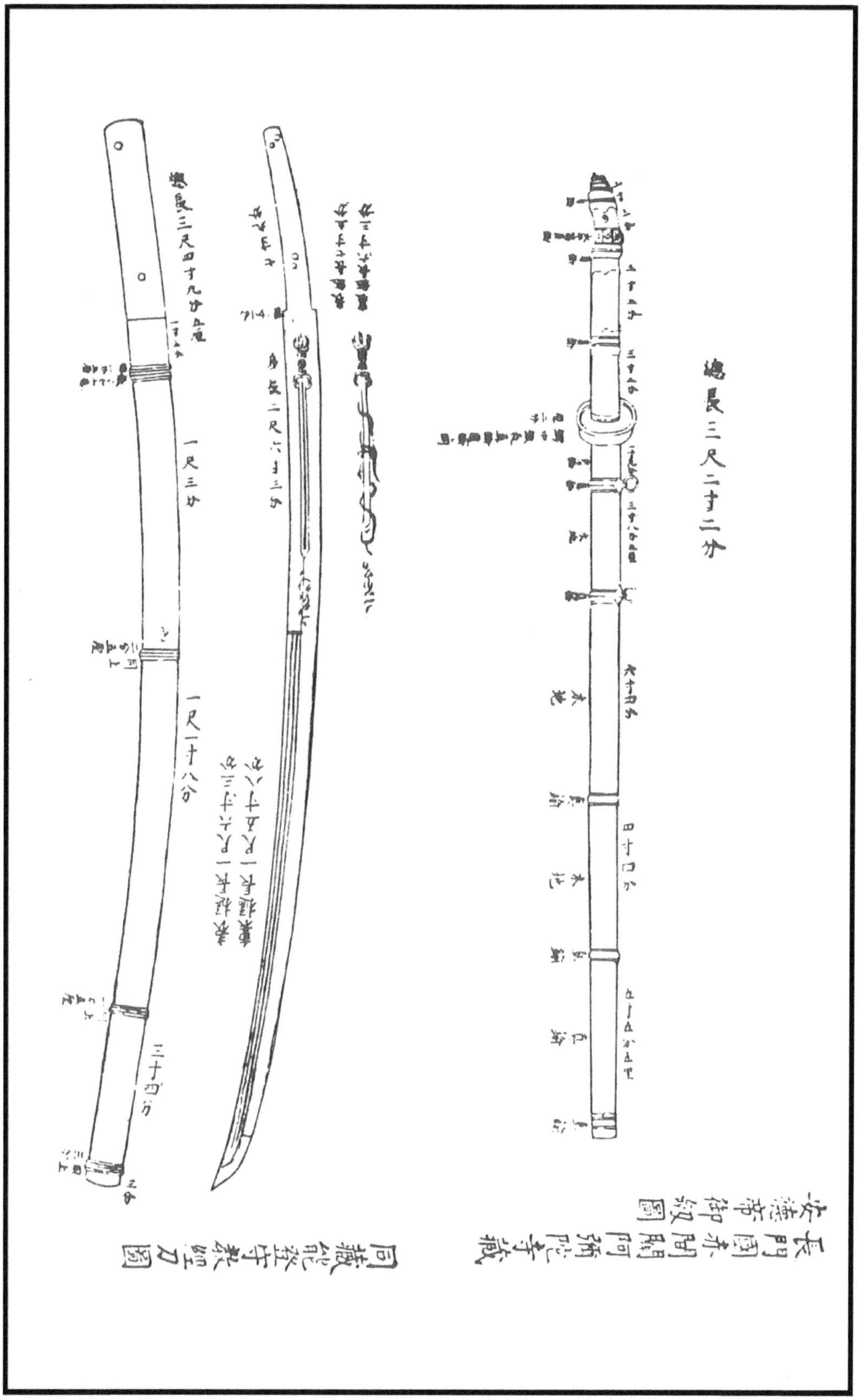

總長三尺四寸九分五厘

一尺三寸

一尺一寸八分

三十四分

身長二尺六寸三分

總長三尺二寸二分

同藏

或眾藏太刀圖

Figure 2.30 Tachi.

The description reads, "Drawing of long sword (tachi), private collection."

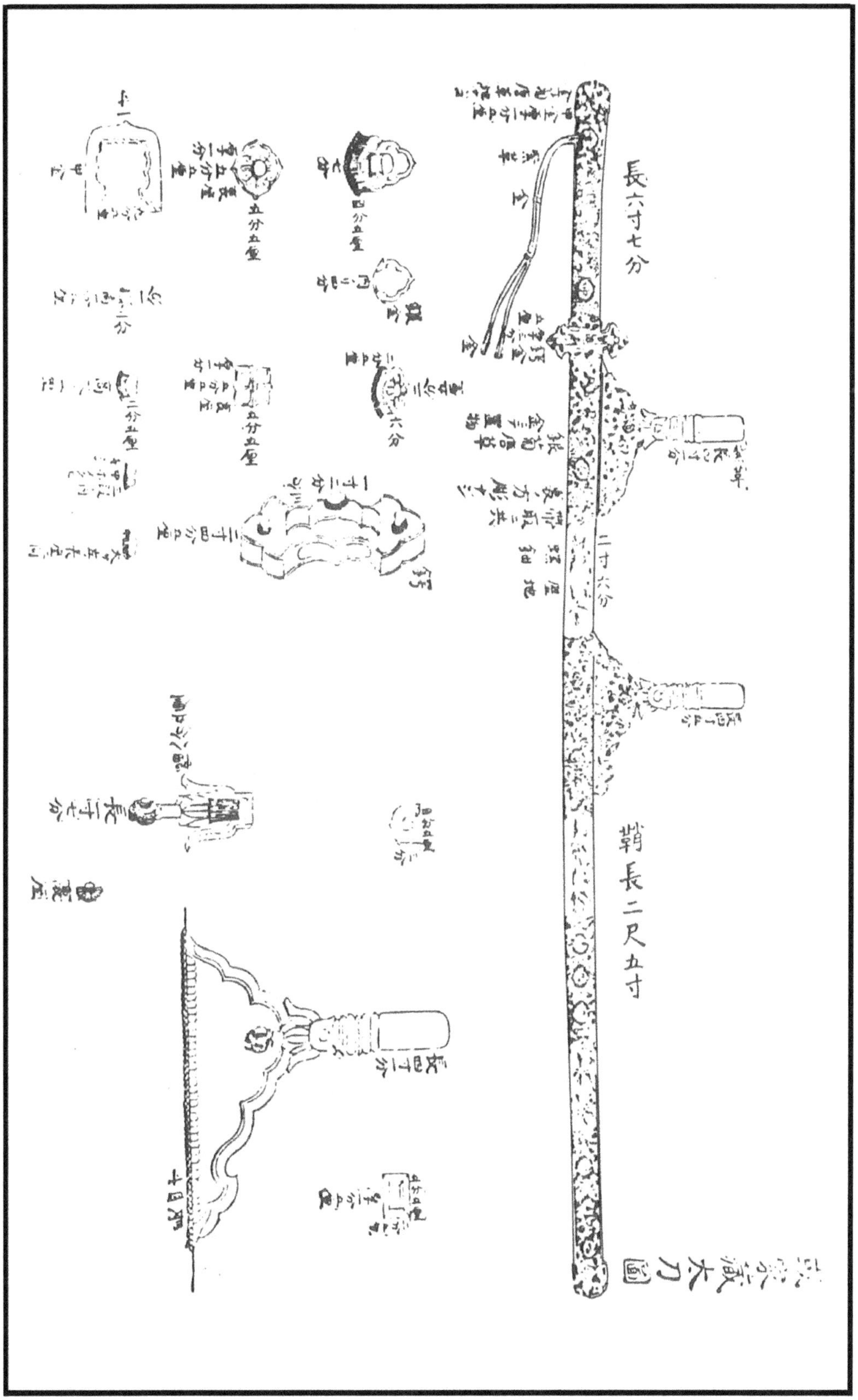
長六寸七分
鞘長二尺五寸
二寸六分

攝津國故住吉社藏神息歛圖

或家藏．太刀圖

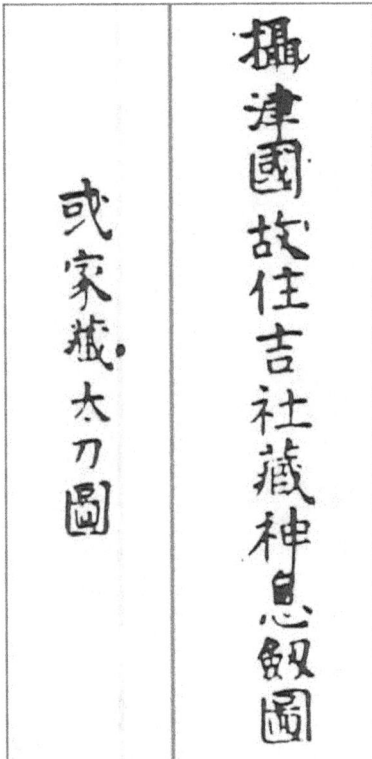

Figure 2.31 Two Tachi - Shinsoku.

The descriptions read, "Drawing of a long sword (tachi) crafted by Shinsoku, Collection of Sumiyoshi Shrine, Settsu Province;" and, "Drawing of long sword, Private collection."

Shinsoku (秋萬歳) (Active Period 806-810) is a very famous smith in the history of Japanese swords. One of the oldest legendary smiths. It said that before retirement, he spent 1000 days to make this tachi to present to the Sumiyoshi Shrine, then he became a priest at the Usa shrine in Buzen province.

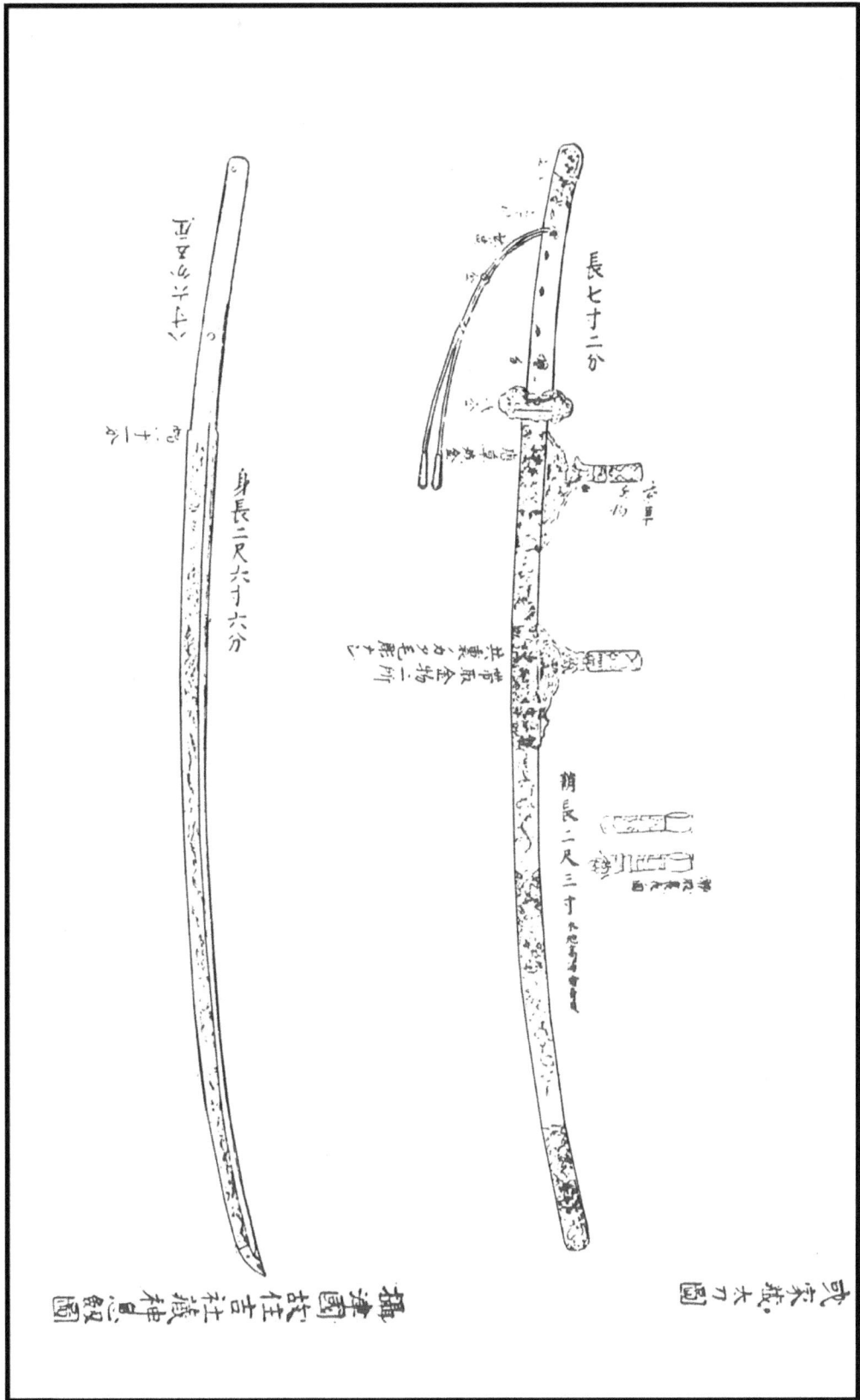

摂津國丹生山田照眼家栗花洛理左衛門家蔵太刀圖

Figure 2.32 Tachi.

The description reads, "Drawing of long sword (tachi), Collection of farmer Rizaemon Tsuyu in Niuyamada, Settsu Province."

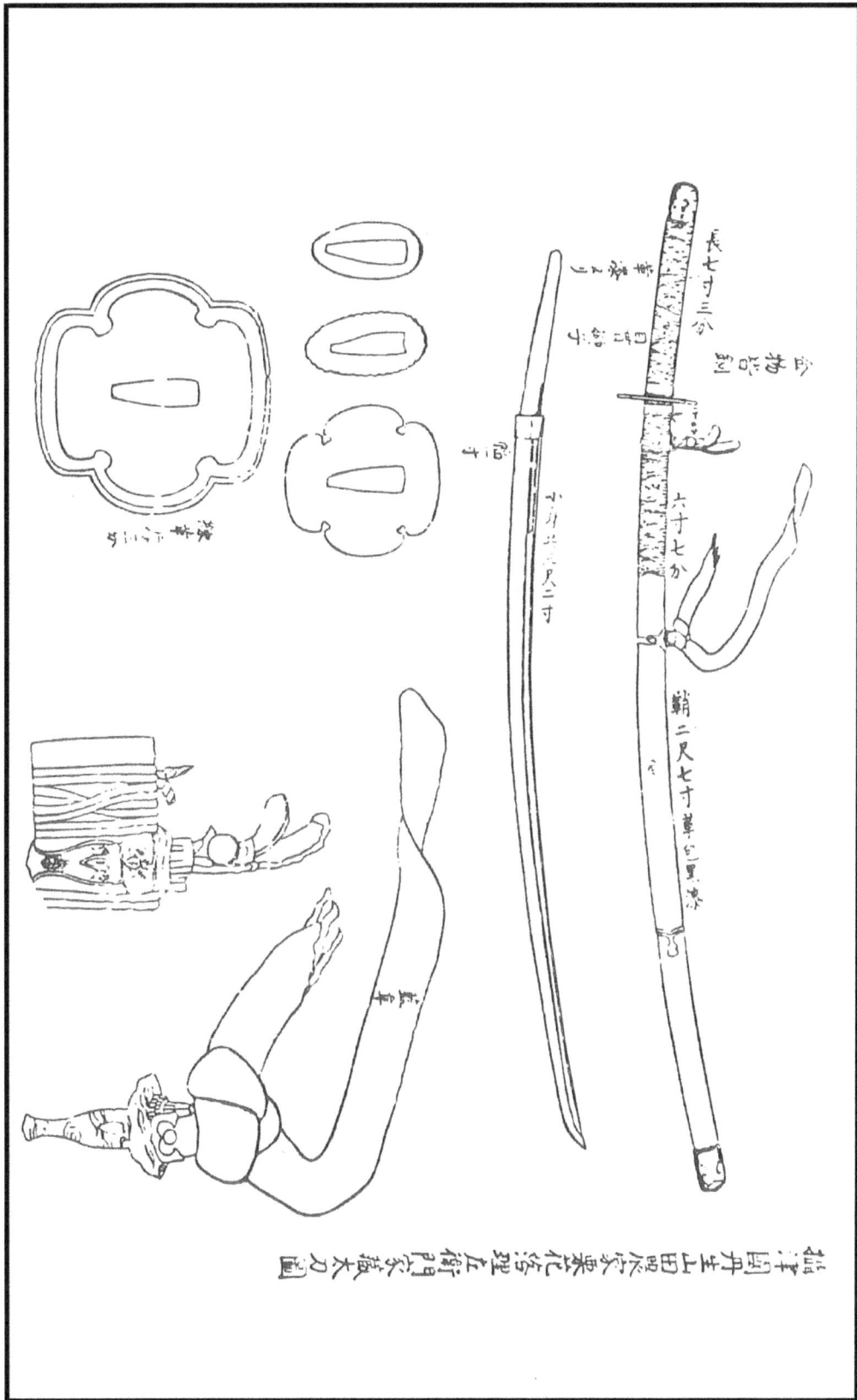

武藏國新坐郡新倉村堀地所獲短刀金具圖藏未許

Figure 2.33 Tsuba and Parts.

The description reads, "Drawing of metal sword fittings (tsuba and parts) unearthed from Niikura Village, Niiza District, Musashi Province; Collection unknown."

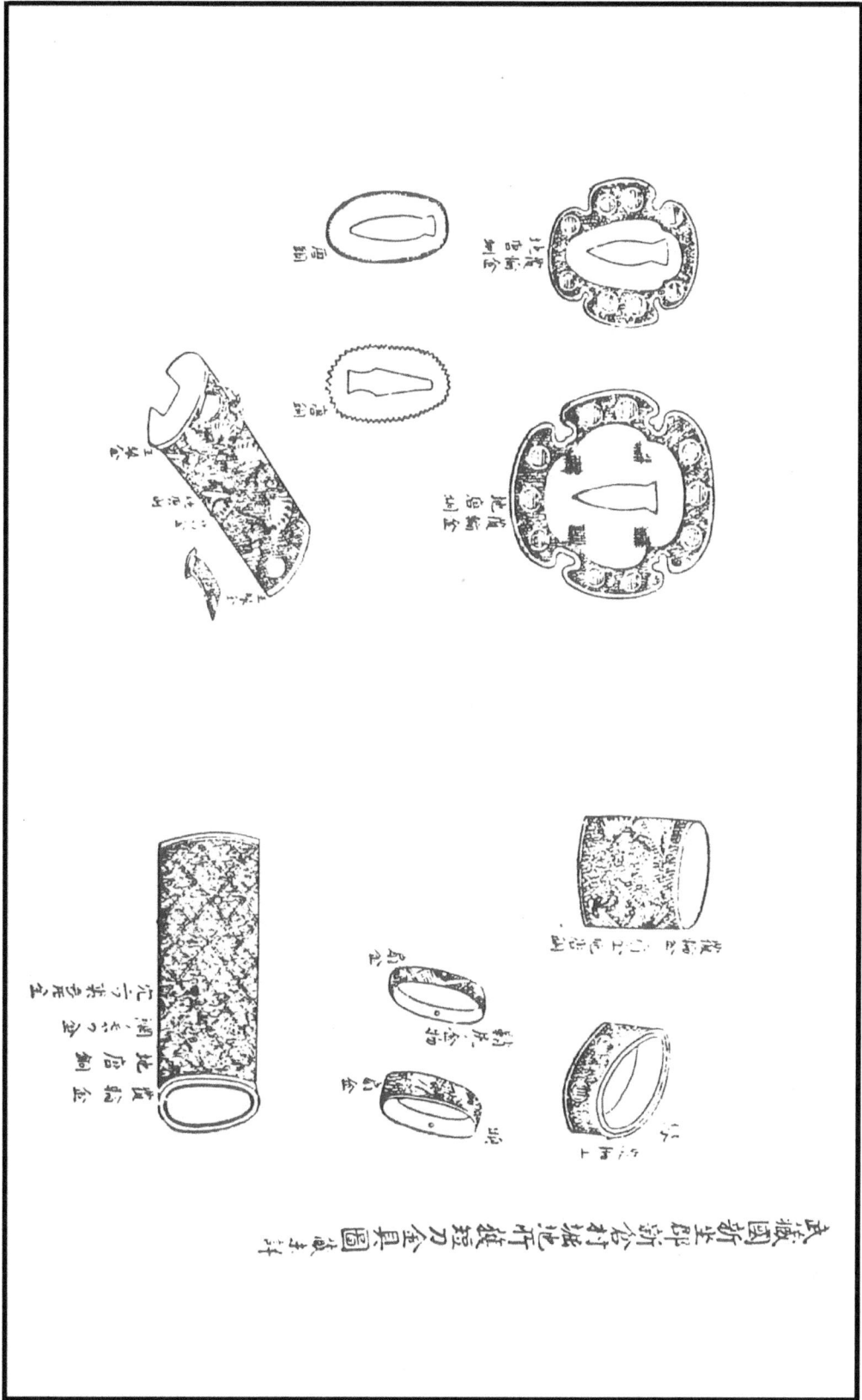

或家藏柄鍔圖
泊信ヲリ傳来十二

Figure 2.34 Tsuka and Tsuba.

The description reads, "Drawing of hilt (tachi tsuka) and hand guards (tsuba), Private collection [illegible]."

山城國本能寺薙刀劔圖

Figure 2.35 Three Tanto - Honno-ji Temple.

The description reads, "Drawing of sword, Collection of Honno-ji Temple, Yamashiro Province."

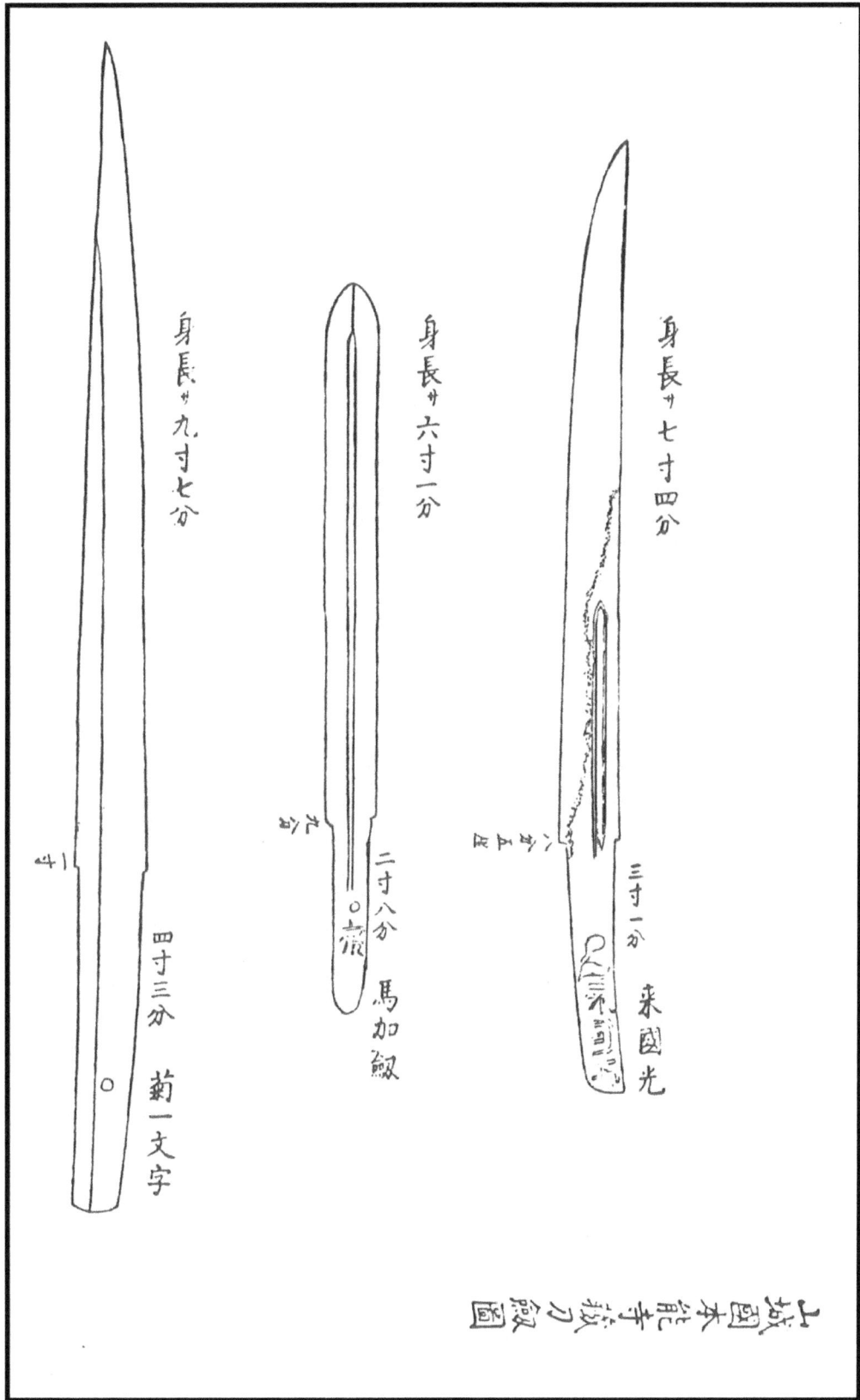

身長サ九寸七分

身長サ六寸一分

身長サ七寸四分

四寸三分　菊一文字

二寸八分　馬加敏

三寸一分　来國光

陸奥國白川郡大村堀地所發刀圖

Figure 2.36 Ancient Ken.

Drawing of sword (ancient ken) unearthed from Omura Village, Shirakawa District, Mutsu Province

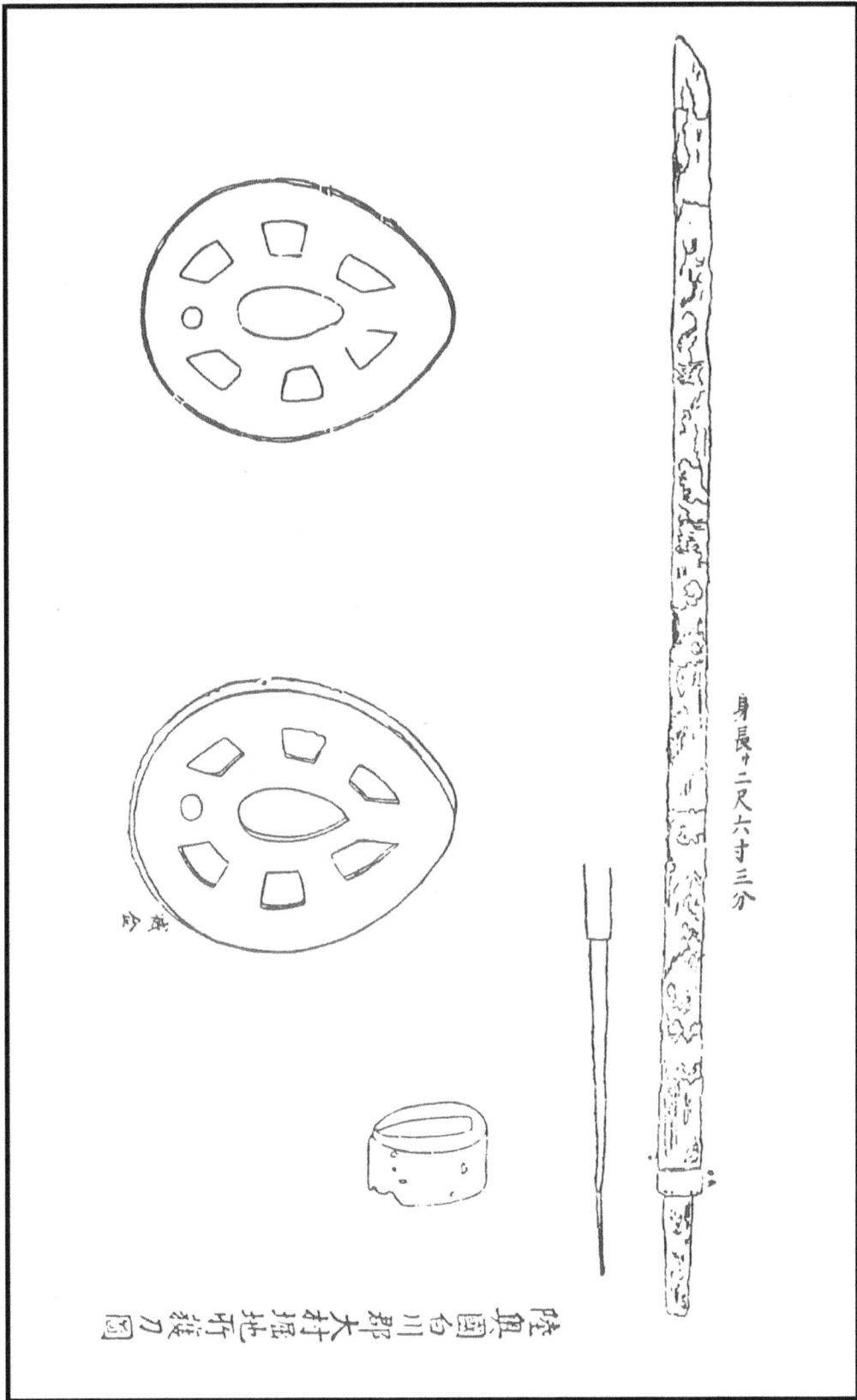

身長ゝ二尺六寸三分

陸角図合三躬大井通利所蔵
図刀雜并芋坪

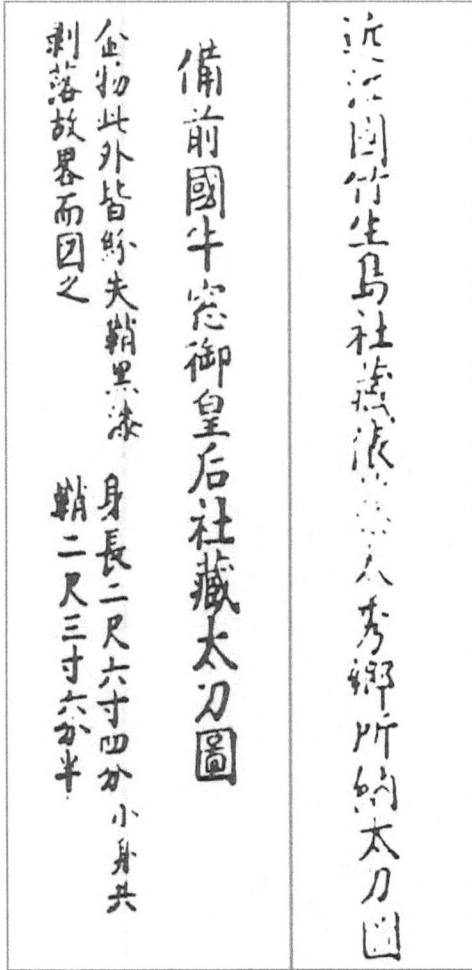

Figure 2.37 Tachi and Tachi Koshirae - Chikubushima Shrine.

The descriptions read, "Drawing of long sword donated by Toda Hidesato Tawara, Collection of Chikubushima Shrine, Omi Province;" and, "Drawing of long sword parts (koshirae) from Gokogo Shrine, Ushimado, Bizen Province – All but metal fittings [illegible]; Black lacquer scabbard…Length: 2 "shaku", 6 "sun" 4 "bu" [approximately 79.2 cm] (including tang) Omitted due to peeling; Scabbard: 2 "shaku", 3 "sun", 6 "bun" and a half [approximately 71 cm]"

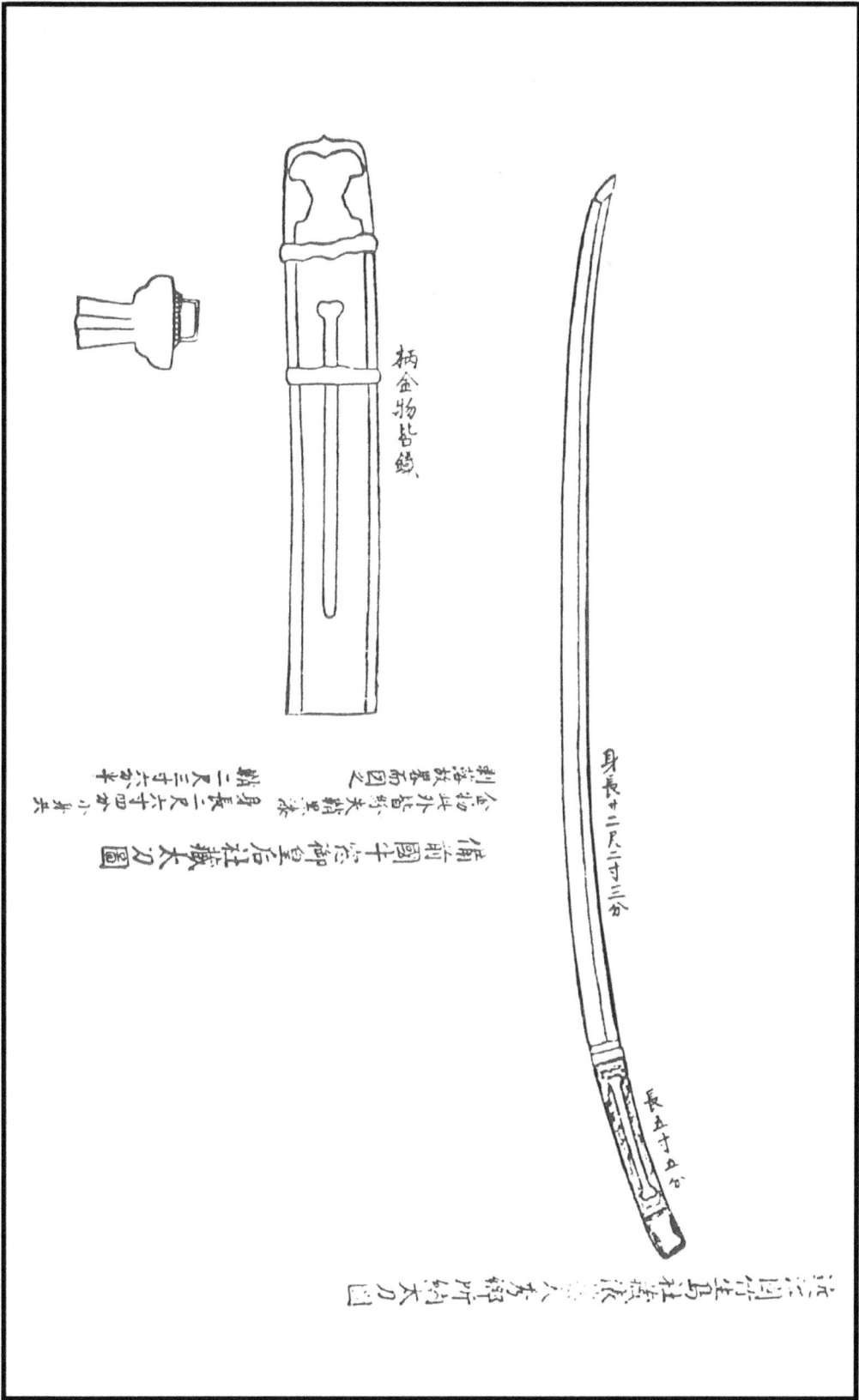

柄金物皆鋦、

身長二尺二寸三分

長五寸五分

此太刀長二尺二寸三分反四分此所蔵相州正宗造之圖

備前長船兼光作
以此太刀試罪人四人
同時截断云々
身長小サシ尺ニテ寸ハ
朝康公小サシ尺目ヲ以
截レリ

武蔵國多摩郡御嶽山社藏寶壽丸太刀圖

Figure 2.38 Tachi with Horimono - Mitakesan Shrine.

The descriptions reads, "Drawing of long sword with 'Horimono', Collection of Mitakesan Shrine, Tama District, Musashi Province."

Horimono (彫り物, 彫物 literally carving, engraving), are the engraved images or carvings on the blade of a Japanese sword. In this carving, the dragon winding around the sword is called the kurikara, and is a depiction of the sword of Fudō Myō-ō, a central deity in Japanese mythology. The other carving is of the same sword without the dragon. Traditionally, both swords represent wisdom cutting through ignorance.

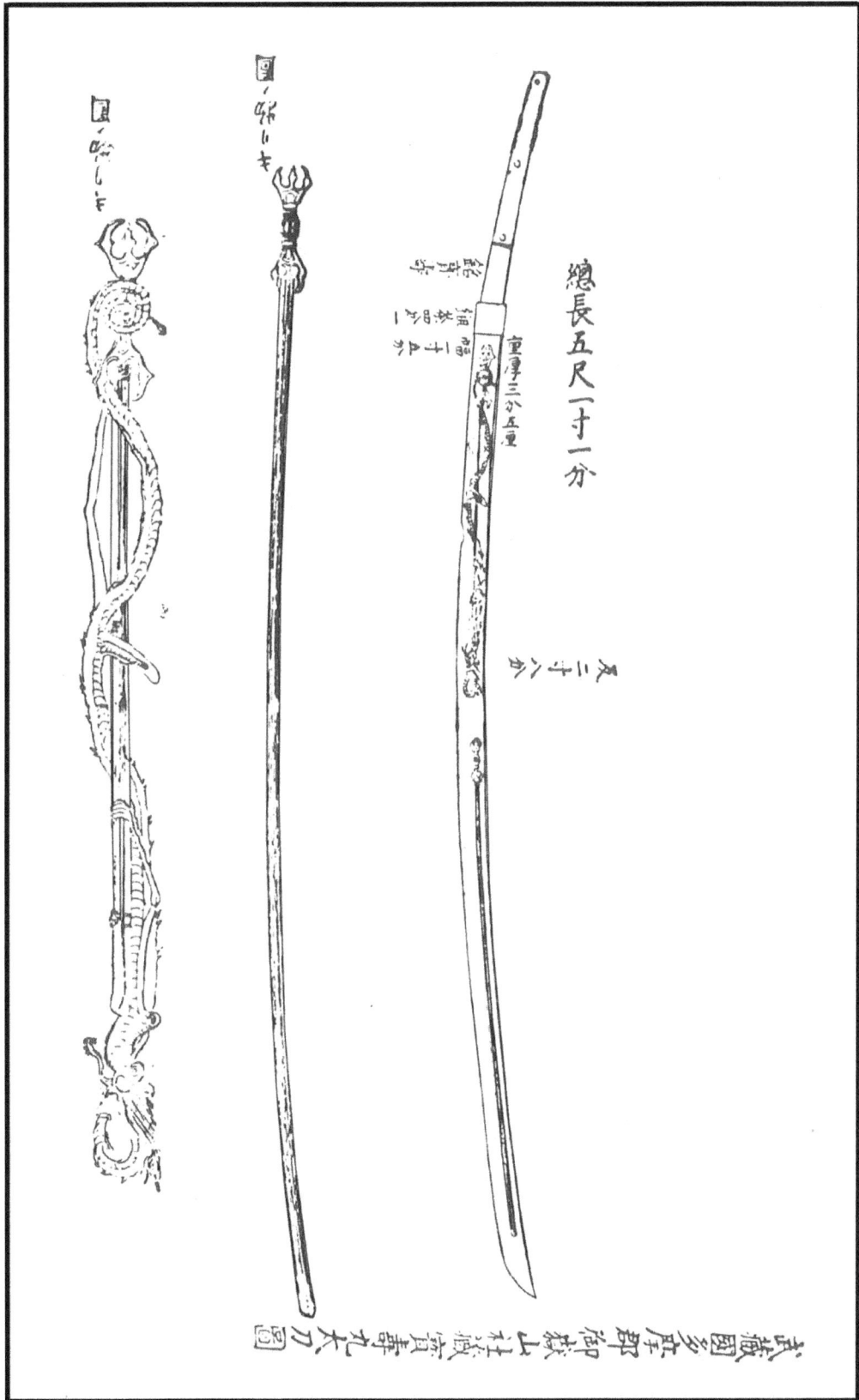

山城國六角堂蔵劔圖

Figure 2.39 European Style Sword - Rokkaku-do Temple.

The description reads, "Drawing of straight (European style) two-edge sword, Collection of Rokkaku-do Temple, Yamashiro Province."

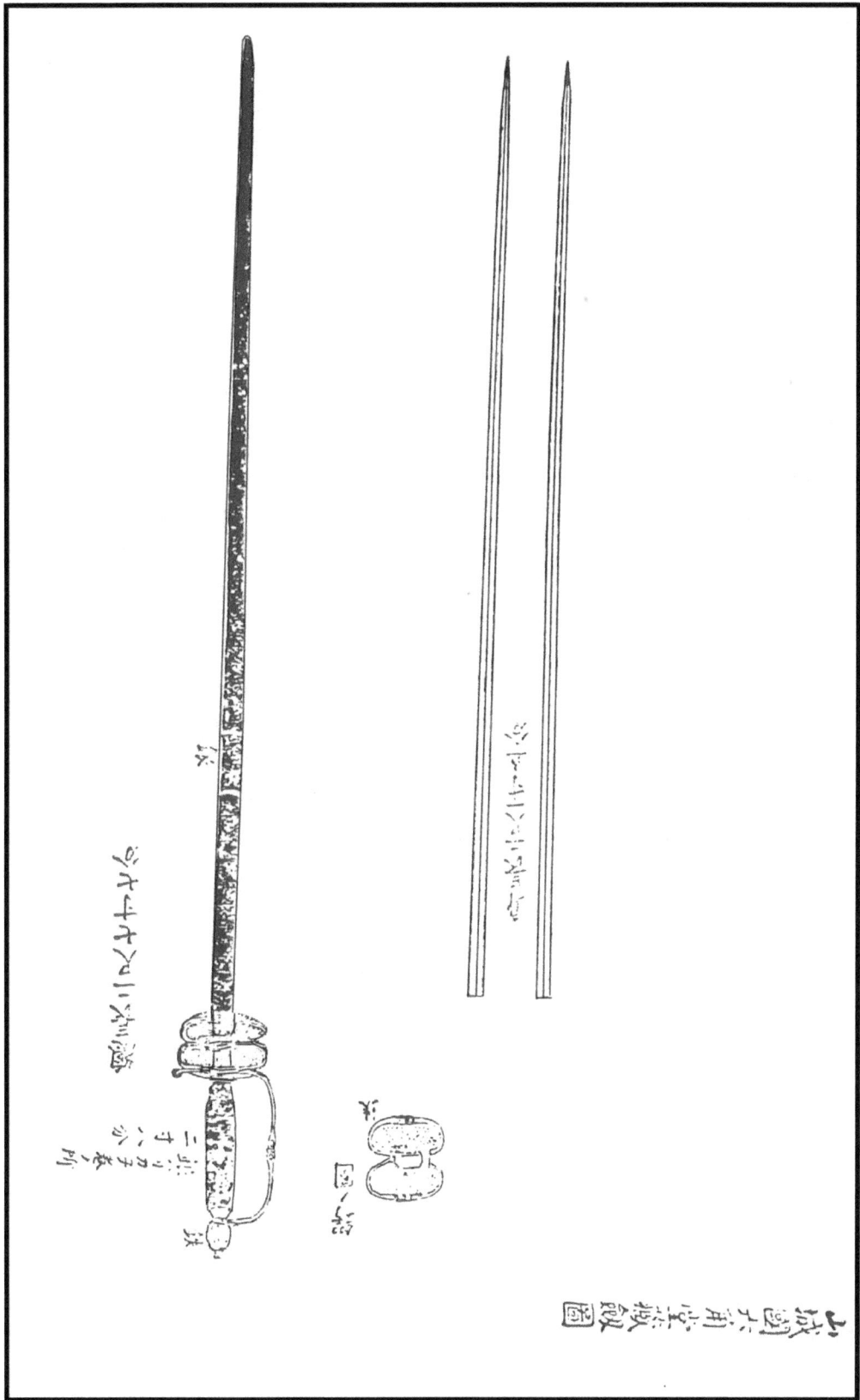

山城國本能寺藏織田信長公刀圖

Figure 2.40 Katana - Oda Nobunaga.

The description reads, "Drawing of long sword (katana) belonging to Lord Nobunaga Oda, Collection of Honno-ji Temple, Yamashiro Province."

Oda Nobunaga (織田 信長) (June 23, 1534 – June 21, 1582) was a Daimyo (warlord) of Japan in the late 16th century. He is accreditted with initiating the unification of Japan near the end of the Warring States period. He lived a life of continuous military conquest, eventually conquering a third of Japan before his death in a 1582 coup. His successors were Toyotomi Hideyoshi, a loyal Oda supporter who was the first to unify all of Japan and was thus the first ruler of the whole country since the Ōnin War, and later Tokugawa Ieyasu, who was to consolidate his rule under a shogunate, which ruled Japan until the Meiji Restoration in 1868. Nobunaga is remembered in Japan as one of the most brutal figures of the Warring States period and was recognized as one of Japan's greatest rulers. Nobunaga was the first of three unifiers during the Warring States period, followed by Toyotomi Hideyoshi and Tokugawa Ieyasu. Oda Nobunaga was well on his way to the complete conquest and unification of Japan when Akechi Mitsuhide, one of his generals, forced Nobunaga to commit suicide in Honnō-ji in Kyoto. Akechi declared himself master over Nobunaga's domains, but was quickly defeated by Hideyoshi.

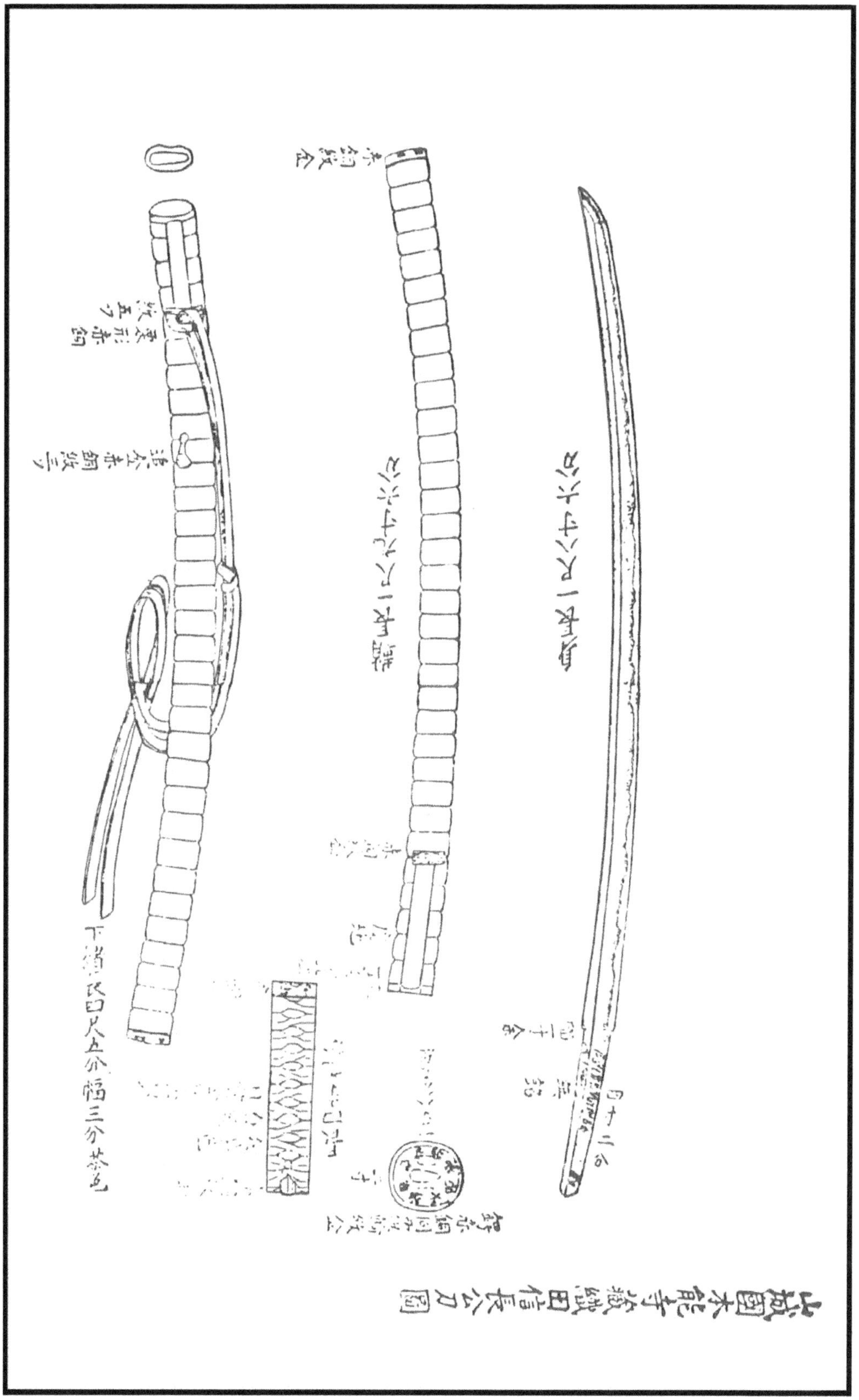
山城國本能寺藏織田信長公刀圖

大坂商家西村庄兵衛藏義政公鍔圖　高松家臣楠正助藏正成卿短刀圖

Figure 2.41 Wakizashi and Handguard - Masashige Kusunoki.

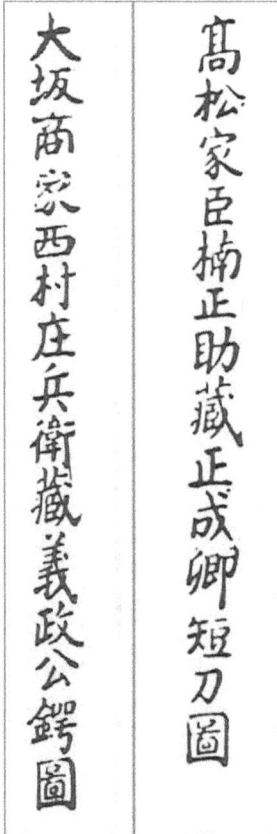

Descriptions read, "Drawing of short sword (wakizashi) belonging to Lord Masashige Kusunoki, Collection of Masasuke Kusunoki, retainer of the Takamatsu Clan;" and, "Drawing of handguard (European style) belonging to Lord Yoshimasa, Collection of the Osaka merchant Shohei Nishimura."

Kusunoki Masashige (楠木 正成, 1294 – July 4, 1336) was a 14th-century samurai who fought for Emperor Go-Daigo in his attempt to wrest rulership of Japan away from the Kamakura shogunate and is remembered as the ideal of samurai loyalty. Kusunoki Masashige is most famous for following the emperor's orders and knowingly marching his army into almost certain death. The battle, which took place at Minatogawa in modern-day Chūō-ku, Kobe, was a tactical disaster. Kusunoki and his army were completely surrounded, down to only 73 of the original 700 horsemen, where he died from wounds sustained in battle along with his brother Masasue, 11 close clan members, and 60 others. According to legend, his last words were *Shichisei Hōkoku!* (七生報國: "Would that I had seven lives to give for my emperor!")

Ashikaga Yoshimasa (足利 義政, January 20, 1436 – January 27, 1490) was the 8th shogun of the Ashikaga shogunate who reigned from 1449 to 1473 during the Muromachi period of Japan. Yoshimasa was the son of the sixth shogun Ashikaga Yoshinori.

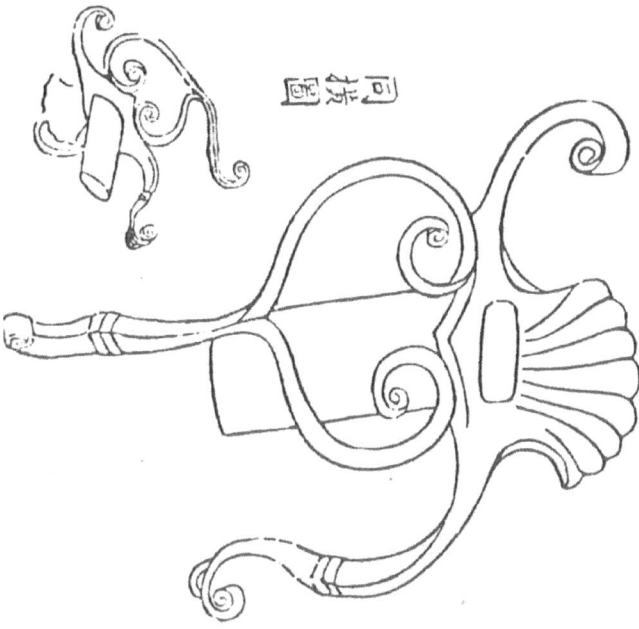

可抜圖

大坂高津西村庄兵衛藏養良公靈
圖

二寸九分

高松家臣柚助藏正成卿短刀
圖

同藏義政公短刀図

Figure 2.42 Tanto.

The description reads, "Drawing of short sword (tanto) belonging to Lord Yoshimasa, same collection as previous page."

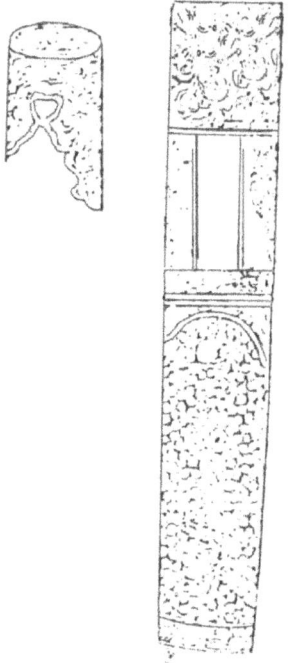

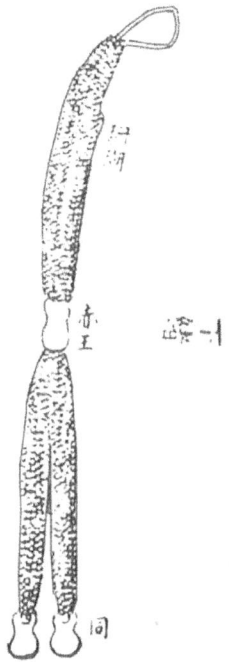

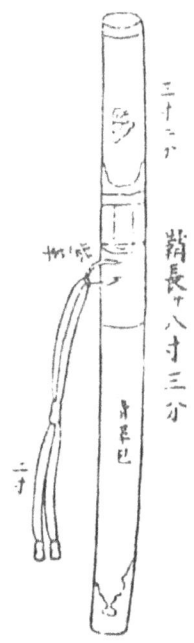

Figure 2.43 Tanto Accoutrements.

The description reads, "Drawing of short sword (tanto) accoutrements and blade belonging to Lord Yoshimasa, same collection as previous page." Same sword as in previous drawing.

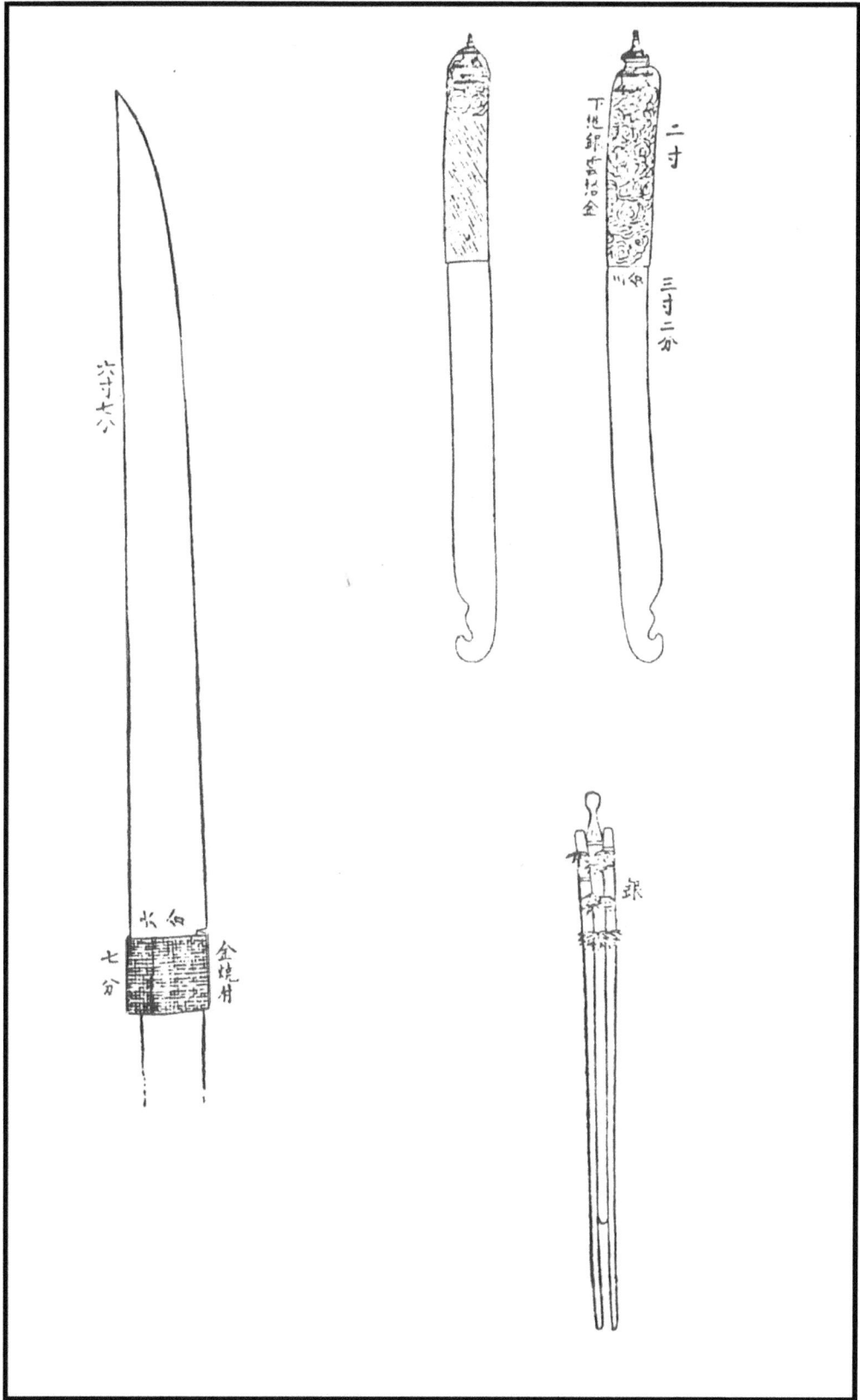

六寸七分

二寸

三寸二分

下地銀古鍍金

水d

七分

金焼付

銀

Figure 2.44 Tanto Storage Box.

The description reads, "Drawing of short sword (tanto) storage box belonging to Lord Yoshimasa, same collection as previous page." Same sword as in previous drawing.

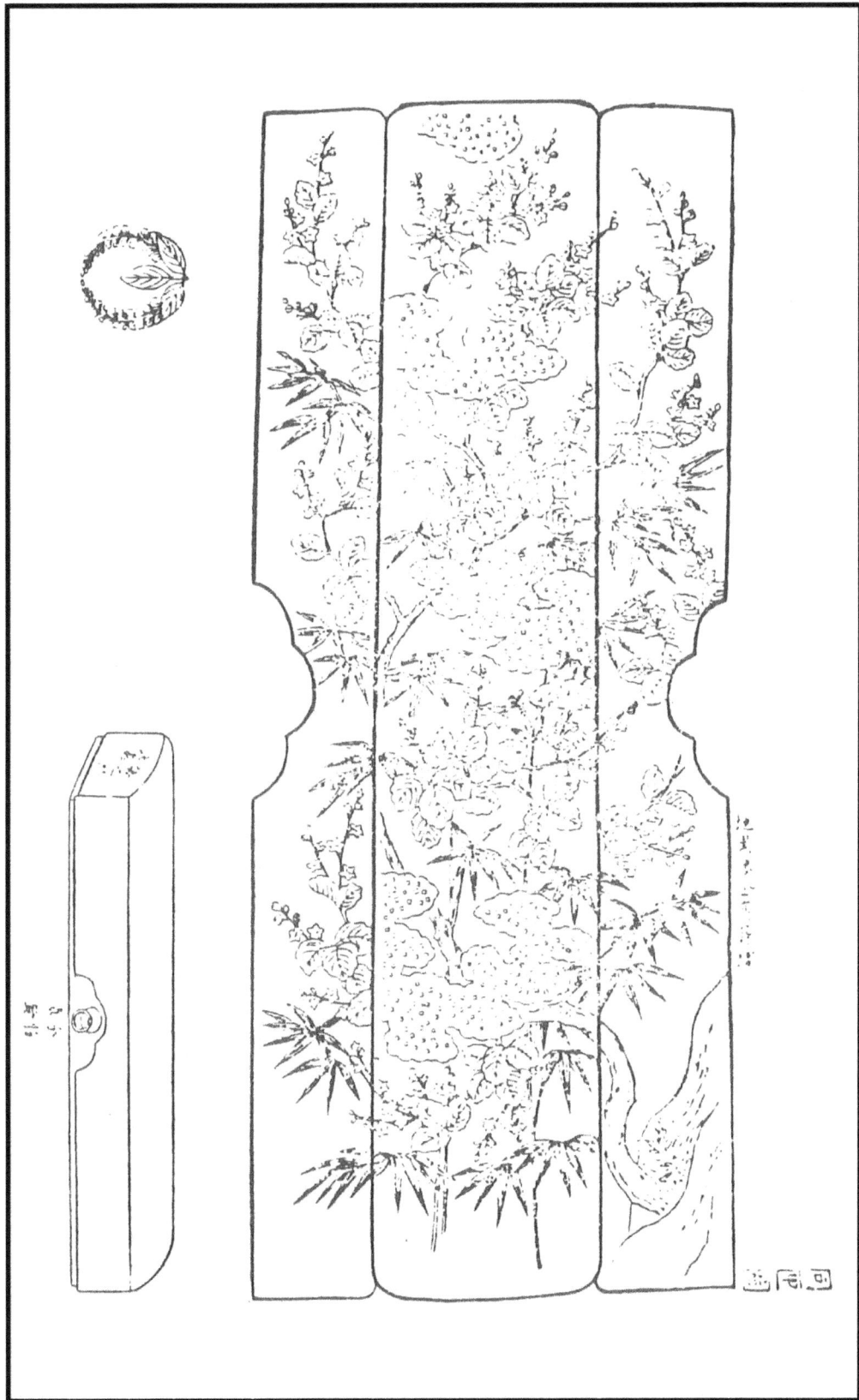

同袋圖

河内國柱本社藏劔圖

大和國吉野櫻奉坊尖徹理源大師割地劔圖

Figure 2.45 Ceremonial Swords - Morimoto Shrine.

Descriptions read, "Drawing of straight two-edge sword 'Rigen Taishi Warichi', Collection of Sakura Motobo Temple, Yoshino, Yamato Province;" and, "Drawing of straight two-edge sword, Collection of Morimoto Shrine, Kawachi Province;" and, "Drawing of bag from same collection."

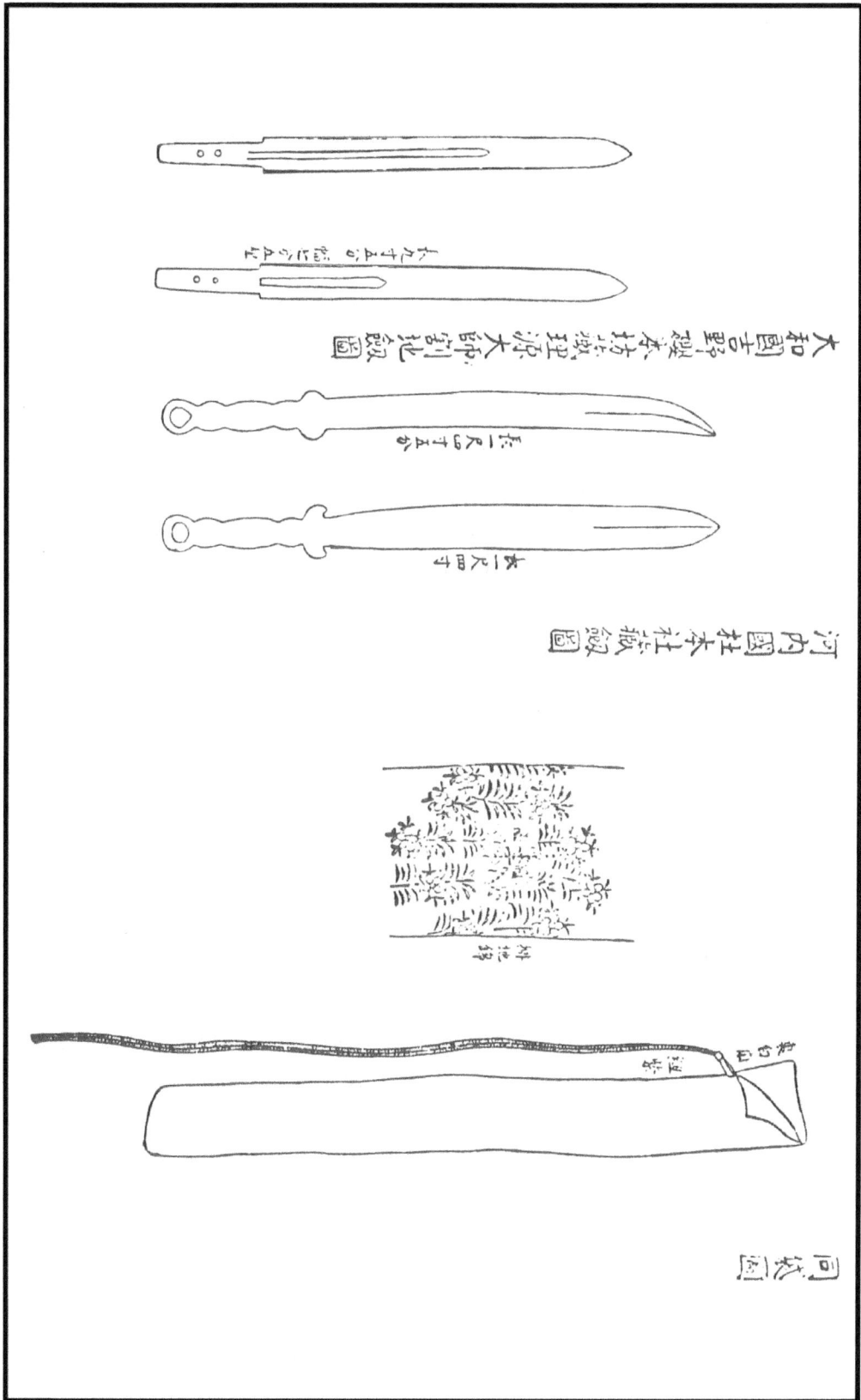

大
和
國
吉
野
郡
鐵
本
杜
御
理
源
大
師
刃
社
劍
國

長
一
尺
九
寸
五
分

長
一
尺
四
分

河
内
國
本
社
藏
劍
國

神
社
劍

柏
原
田
口

圖
友
可

大和國吉野山櫻本坊藏護摩刀圖

Figure 2.46 Tachi - Nagayoshi.

The description reads, "Drawing of long sword (tachi), Collection of Sakura Motobo Temple, Yoshinoyama, Yamato Province."

This sword was made by Nagayoshi (長吉). He worked from bun-mei 1469 to mei-o 1492. Considered one of the greatest swordsmiths of his time, and, in addition to his swords, he was particularly famous for his mastery of horimono (blade carvings).

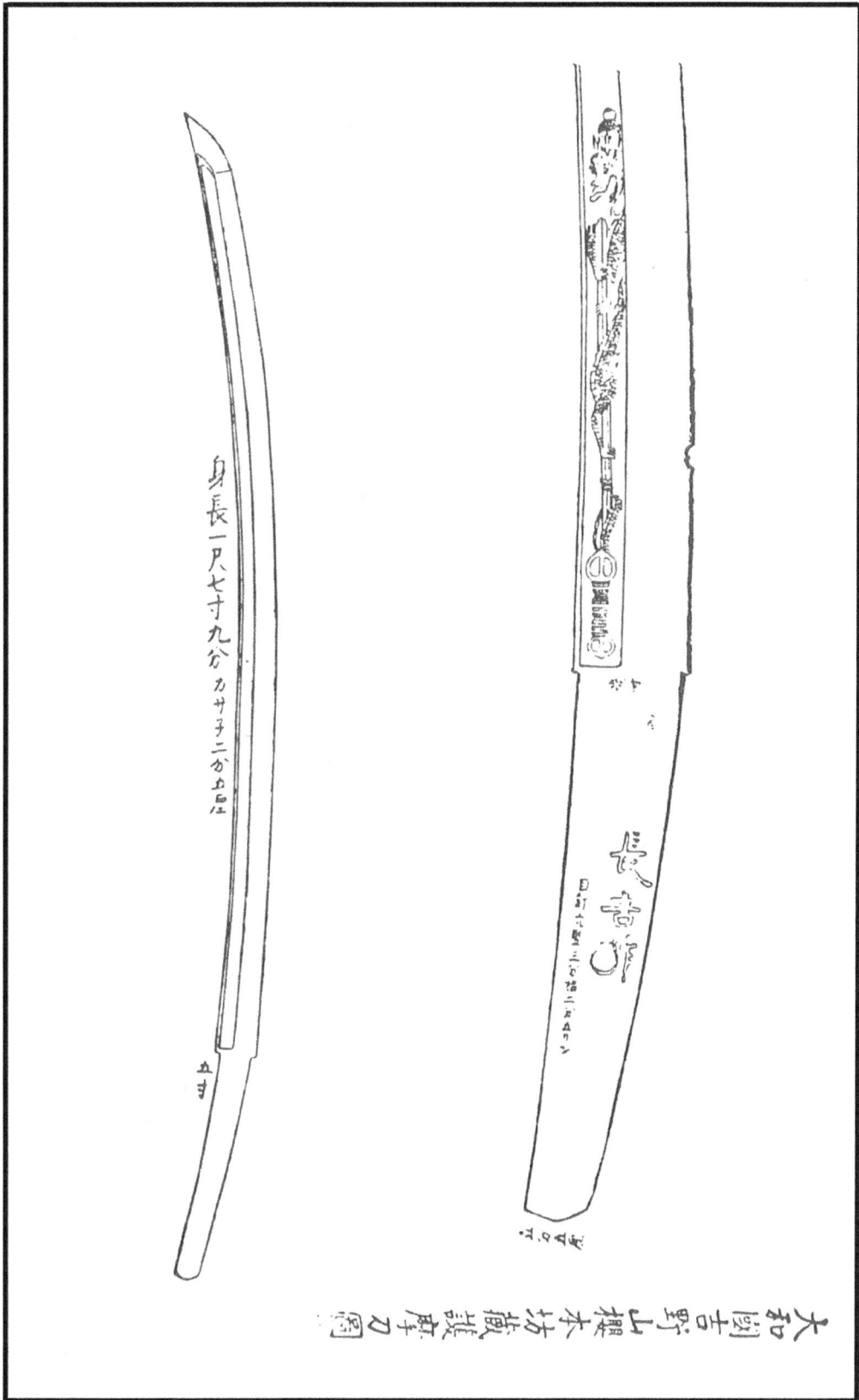

身長一尺七寸九分 カサネ二分五厘

大和國吉野山槻木坊梯職彫手刀圖

山城國本能寺藏大太刀圖

Figure 2.47 O-Dachi - Honno-ji Temple.

The description reads, "Drawing of extra-long sword (o-dachi), Collection of Honno-ji Temple, Yamashiro Province.

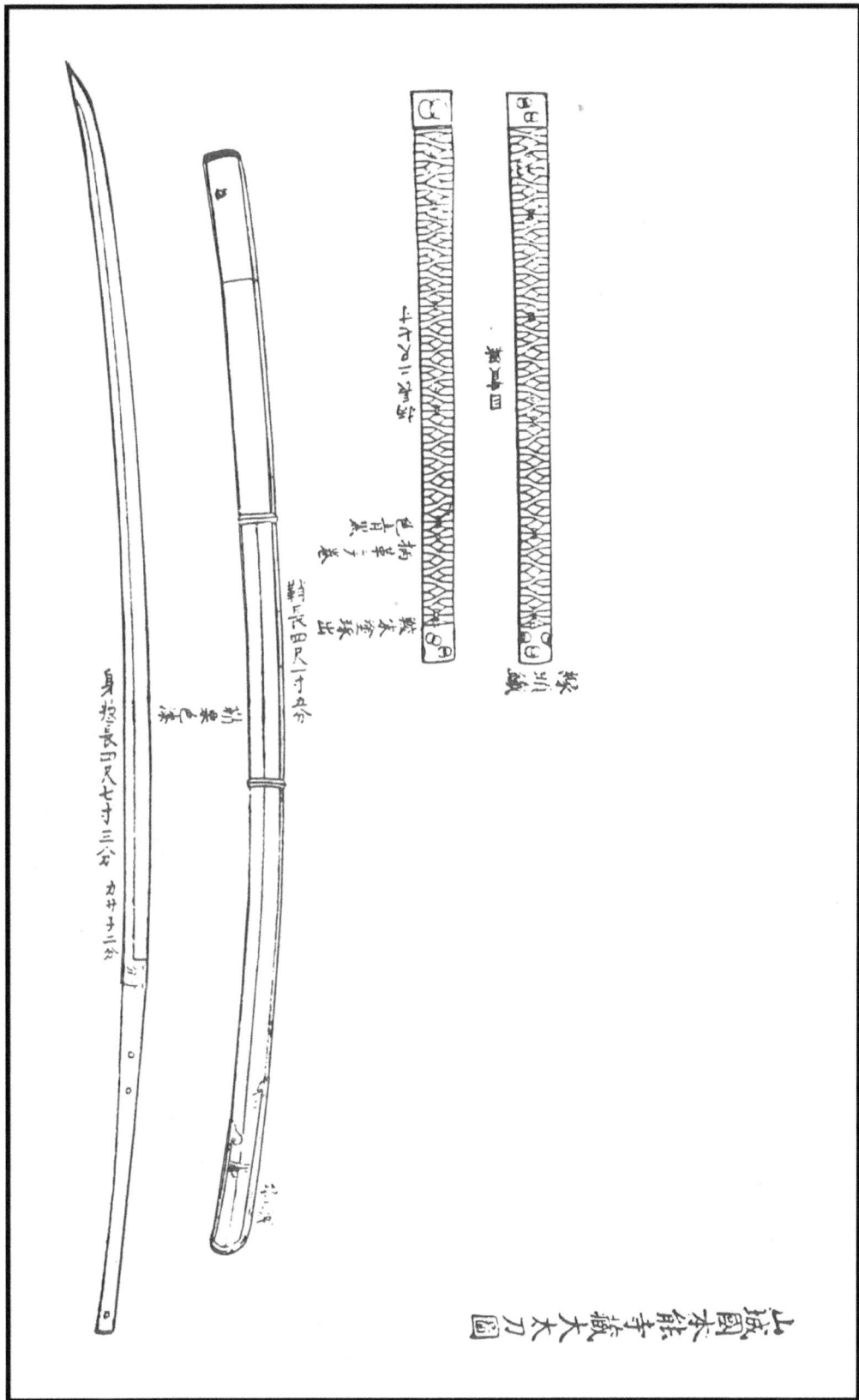

大和國吉野山櫻本坊藏村上彦四郎鍔圖

Figure 2.48 Tsuba - Hikoshiro Murakami.

The description reads, "Drawing of hand guard belonging to Hikoshiro Murakami, Collection of Sakura Motobo Temple, Yoshinoyama, Yamato Province." Murakami Hikoshiro Yoshiteru (村上義光)(d. 1333), noted for his faithfulness and dedication, died while defending prince Morinaga.

Here is an excerpt from Richard Gordon Smith's book, Ancient Tales and Folklore of Japan, describing Hikoshiro's death:

"In an attempt to help the prince escape, after having been already wounded three times that day in battle, he switched armor with the prince, saying, 'Give me your armor, and let me pretend that I am your Highness. I will show our enemies how a prince can die.'"

"Changing clothes hastily, and donning the prince's armor, Murakami, bleeding badly from his wounds, and already more dead than alive with weakness from the loss of blood, regained the wall, and struggling up the last steps he reached a point where he could see and be seen by the whole of the enemy."

"'I am Prince Morinaga!' he shouted. 'Fate is against me, though I am in the right. Sooner or later Heaven's punishment will come down on you. Until then my curses upon you, and take a lesson as to how a prince can die, emulating it, if you dare, when your time comes!'"

"With this Murakami Hikoshiro Yoshiteru drew his short sword across his abdomen, and, seizing his quivering entrails, he flung them into the midst of his enemies, his dead body falling directly afterwards."

"His head was taken to the Regent in Kioto as the head of Prince Morinaga, who escaped to plot in the future."

To the right is a depiction of Murakami Hikoshiro Yoshiteru standing in the middle of battle, treading on the neck of one of his assailants on the ground. A second being hurled over his right shoulder.

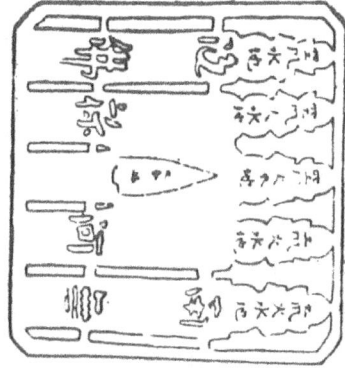

大和國吉野山櫻木坊藏村上天信日出繪圖

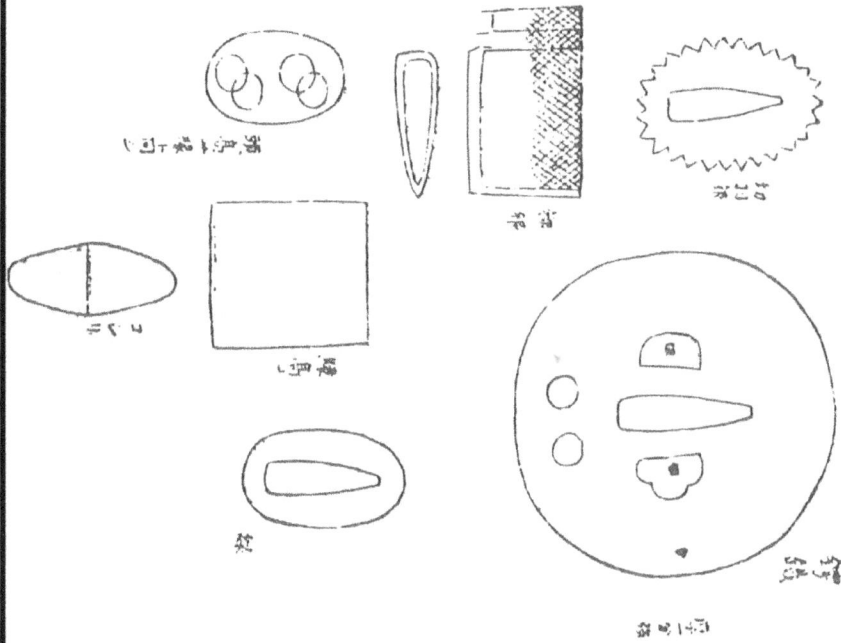

越後國一宮彌彦明神社藏 太刀圖

Figure 2.49 O-Dachi - Yahiko Myojin Shrine.

The description reads, "Drawing of extra-long sword (o-dachi), Collection of Ichinomiya Yahiko Myojin Shrine, Echigo Province."

身長七尺四十二分

幅寸八分

小身長三尺一寸八分

肥後國阿蘇宮阿蘇神社藏

太刀圖

此御寸法實ハ大小ナリ十六年八月出之
此御太刀大永十六年八月造畢

陸奥國白川郡舩田村堀地所獲太刀圖

Figure 2.50 Ancient Long Sword.

The description reads, "Drawing of long sword (Ancient period) unearthed from Funada Village, Shirakawa District, Mutsu Province."

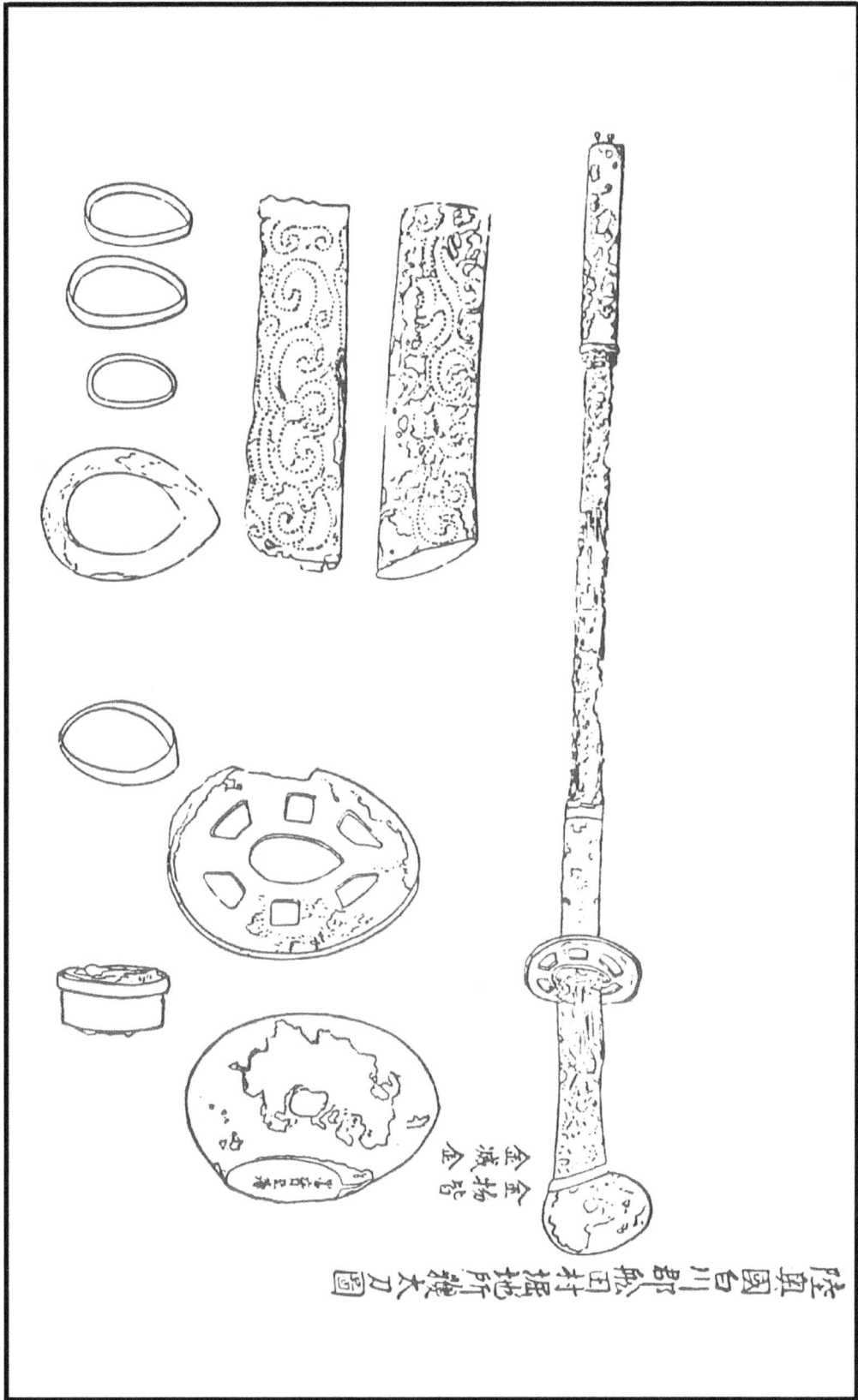

陸
奥
国
白
河
郡
舟
田
村
福
島
勝
之
助
所
蔵
太
刀
図

金
象
嵌
金
具

金
鍍
物
全
部

陸奥國白川郡舩田村堀地所搜太刀圖

Figure 2.51 Ancient Long Sword Mountings.

The description reads, "Drawing of long sword (Ancient period) mounts unearthed from Funada Village, Shirakawa District, Mutsu Province (same as previous picture)."

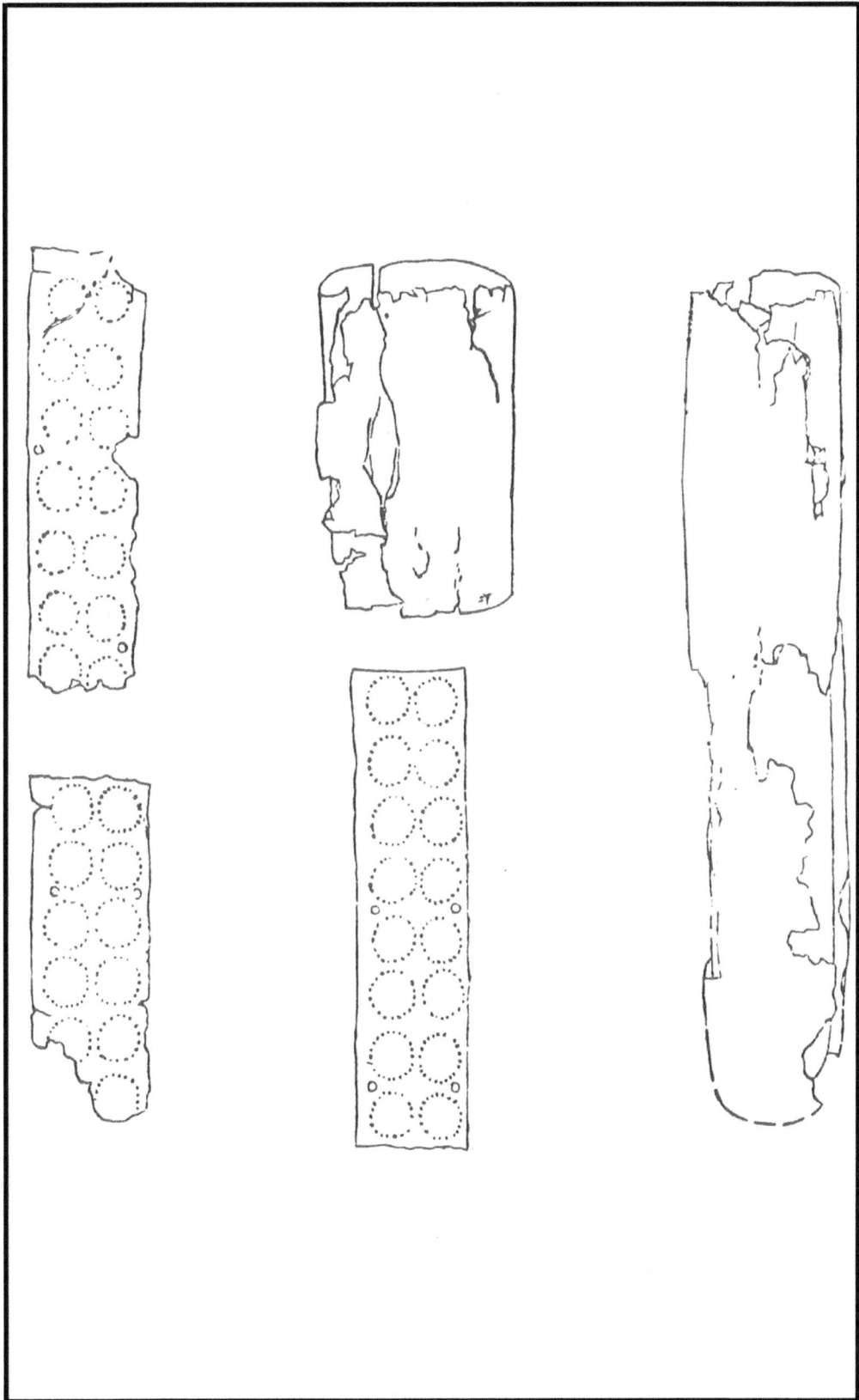

河
内
國
譽
田
八
幡
宮
藏
劔
圖

蜷
川
氏
藏
劔
圖

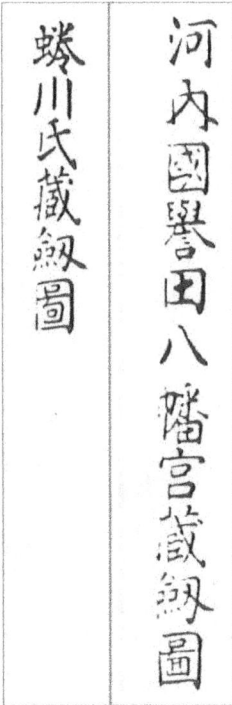

Figure 2.52 Two Ken - Konda Hachimangu Shrine.

Descriptions read, "Drawing of straight two-edge sword (ken), Collection of Konda Hachimangu Shrine, Kawachi Province;" and, Drawing of straight two-edge sword (ken), Collection of Ninakawa."

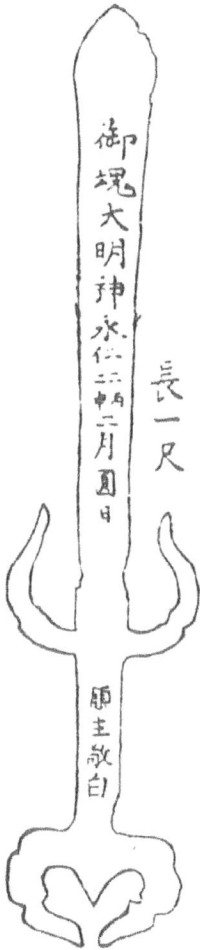

蜷川氏藏劔圖

御魂大明神水位三帳二月圓日

長一尺

願主敬白

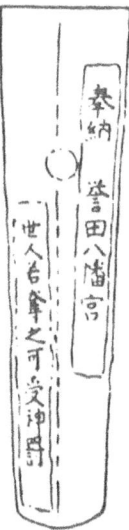

奉納
誉田八幡宮
一世人若筆之可愛神剣

河内國誉田八幡宮藏劔圖

長一尺二分　幅七分

肥後國阿蘇大宮司惟絲螢丸太刀圖

河内國譽田八幡宮蔵刀圖

Figure 2.53 Tachi - Konda Hachimangu Shrine.

Descriptions read, "Drawing of long sword (tachi) 'Hotarumaru', property of Aso High Priest Koresumi, Higo Province;" and, "Drawing of sword, Collection of Konda Hachimangu Shrine, Kawachi Province."

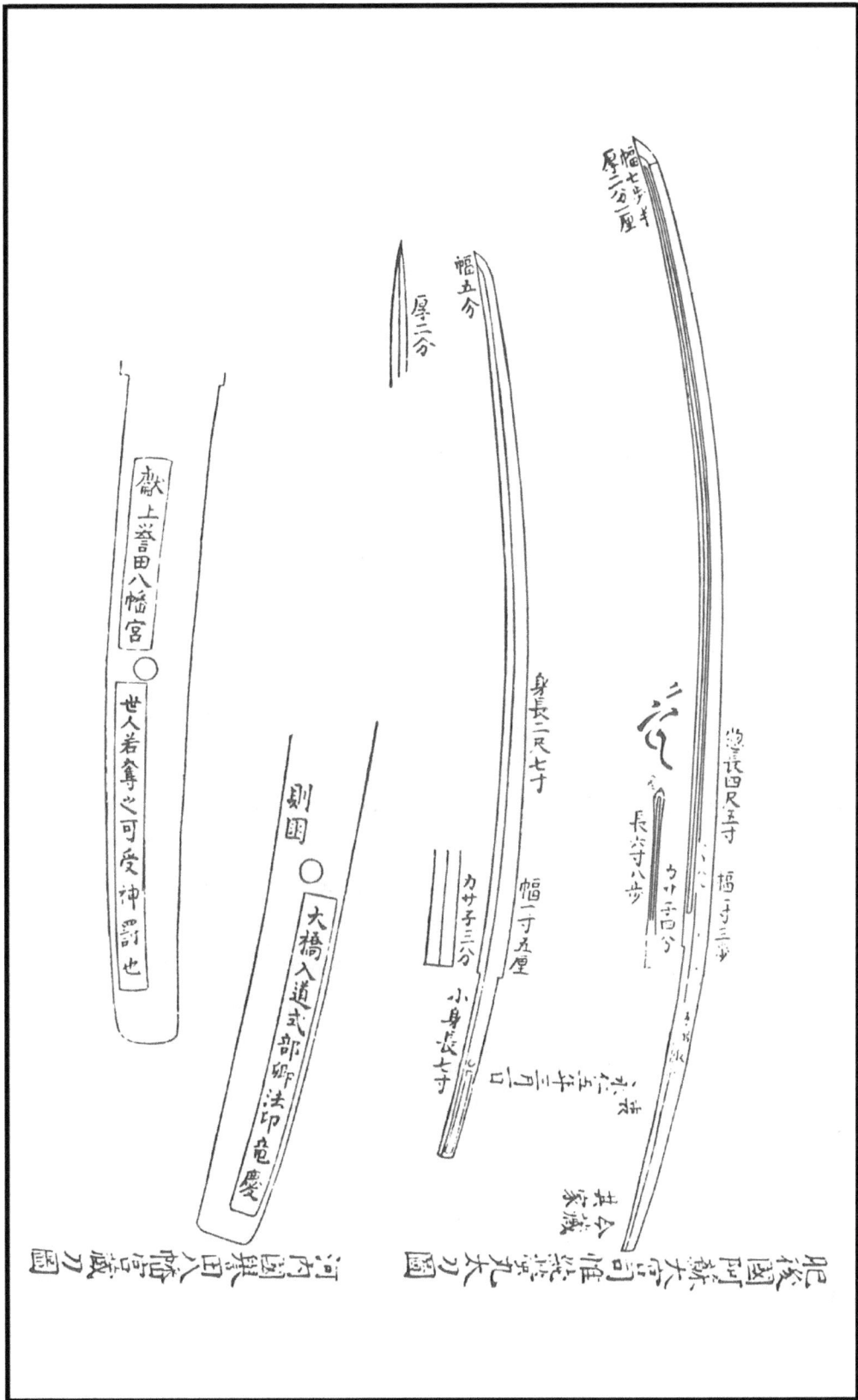

献上誉田八幡宮

世人若奪之可受神罰也

則国

大橋入道武部卿法印竜慶

厚三分

幅五分

身長二尺七寸

幅一寸五厘

カサ子三分

小身長七寸

幅七歩半
厚三分二厘

長六寸八分

学説四尺五寸　幅一寸三歩

河内國愛宕山藏小鍛治宗近太刀圖

梶原景時刀圖

武藏國荏原郡馬込村萬福寺藏

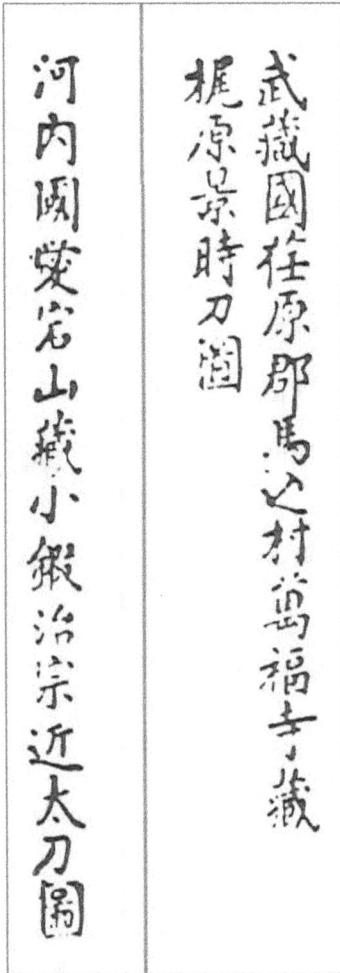

Figure 2.54 Two Tachi - Kajiwara Kagetoki.

Descriptions read, "Drawing of sword belonging to Kagetoki Kajiwara, Collection of Manpuku-ji Temple, Magome Village, Ebara District, Musashi Province;" and, "Drawing of long sword crafted by sword smith Munechika, Collection of Atagosan, Kawachi Province."

Kajiwara Kagetoki (梶原 景時) (c.1162 – February 6, 1200) was a spy for Minamoto no Yoritomo in the Genpei War, and a warrior against the Taira. He came to be known for his greed and treachery.

Originally from Suruga province, Kajiwara entered the Genpei War fighting under Oba Kagechika, against the Minamoto. After the Taira victory at Ishibashiyama in 1181, he was sent to pursue the fleeing Minamoto no Yoritomo. Having discovered him, Kajiwara switched sides, leading his forces in another direction, and turning to Yoritomo's cause.

Sanjō Munechika (c. 987) was a forerunner of the Yamashiro tradition, and the earliest identified smith working in Kyoto.

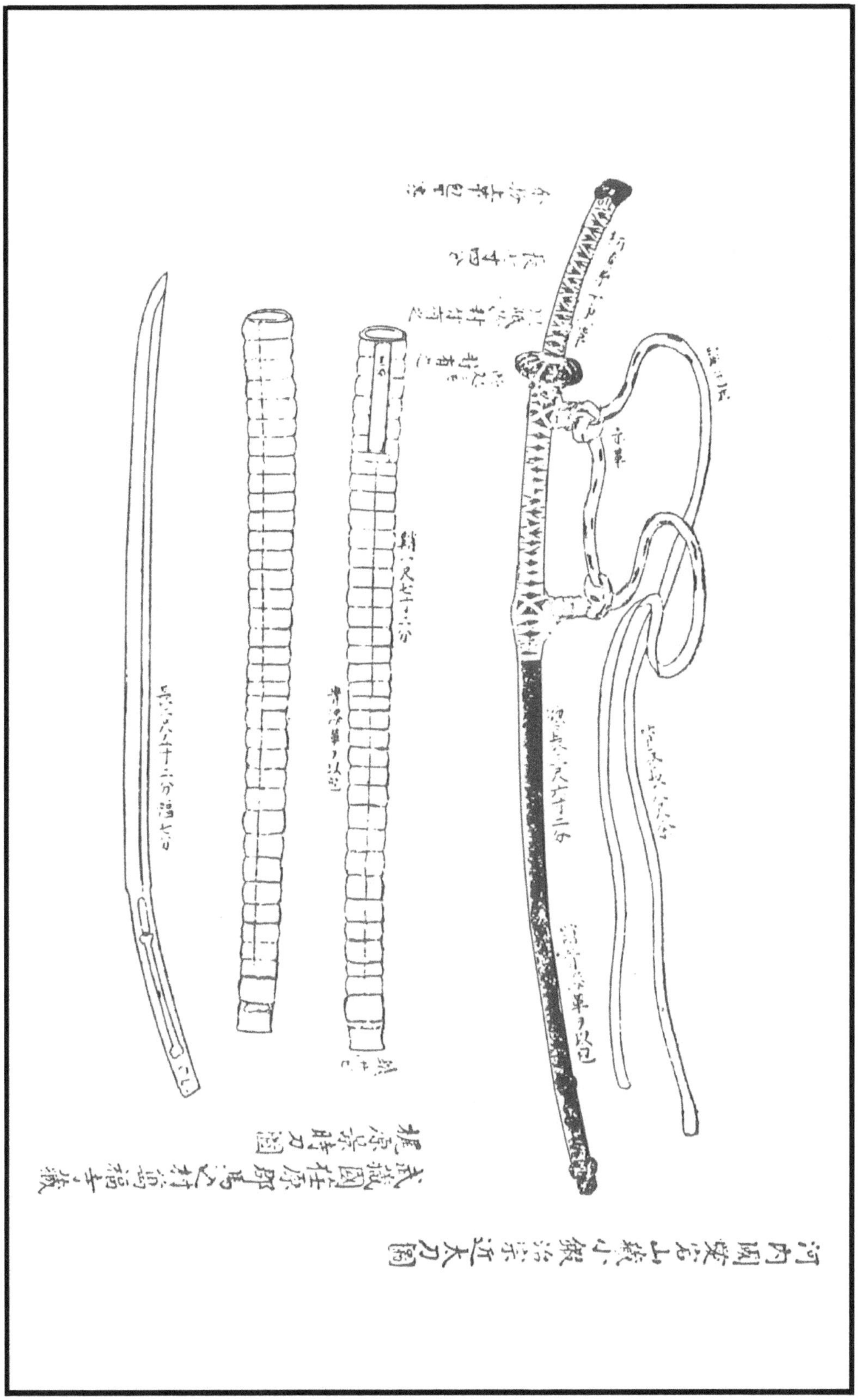

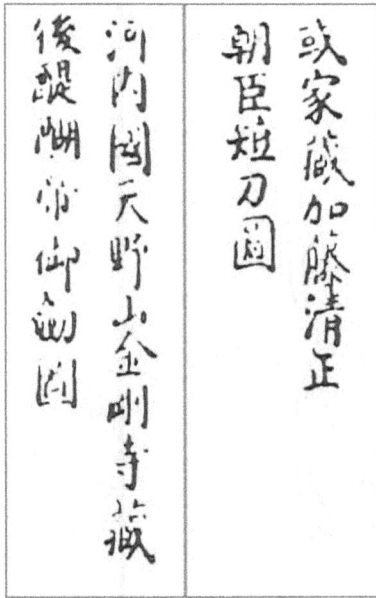

Figure 2.55 Tanto and Wakizashi - Amanosan Kongo-ji Temple.

Descriptions read, "Drawing of sword belonging to Court Noble Kiyomasa Kato, Private collection;" and, "Drawing of straight two-edge sword belonging to Emperor Godaigo, Collection of Amanosan Kongo-ji Temple, Kawachi Province."

Katō Kiyomasa (加藤 清正, July 25, 1561 – August 2, 1611) was a Japanese daimyō of the Azuchi-Momoyama and Edo period. His court title was Higo-no-kami. His child name was Yashamaru, and first name was Toranosuke.

Emperor Go-Daigo (後醍醐天皇 Go-Daigo-tennō) (November 26, 1288 – September 19, 1339) was the 96th emperor of Japan, according to the traditional order of succession.

Post-Meiji historians construe Go-Daigo's reign to span 1318–1339; however, pre-Meiji accounts of his reign considered the years of his reign to encompass only between 1318–1332. Pre-Meiji scholars also considered Go-Daigo a pretender Emperor in the years from 1336 through 1339.

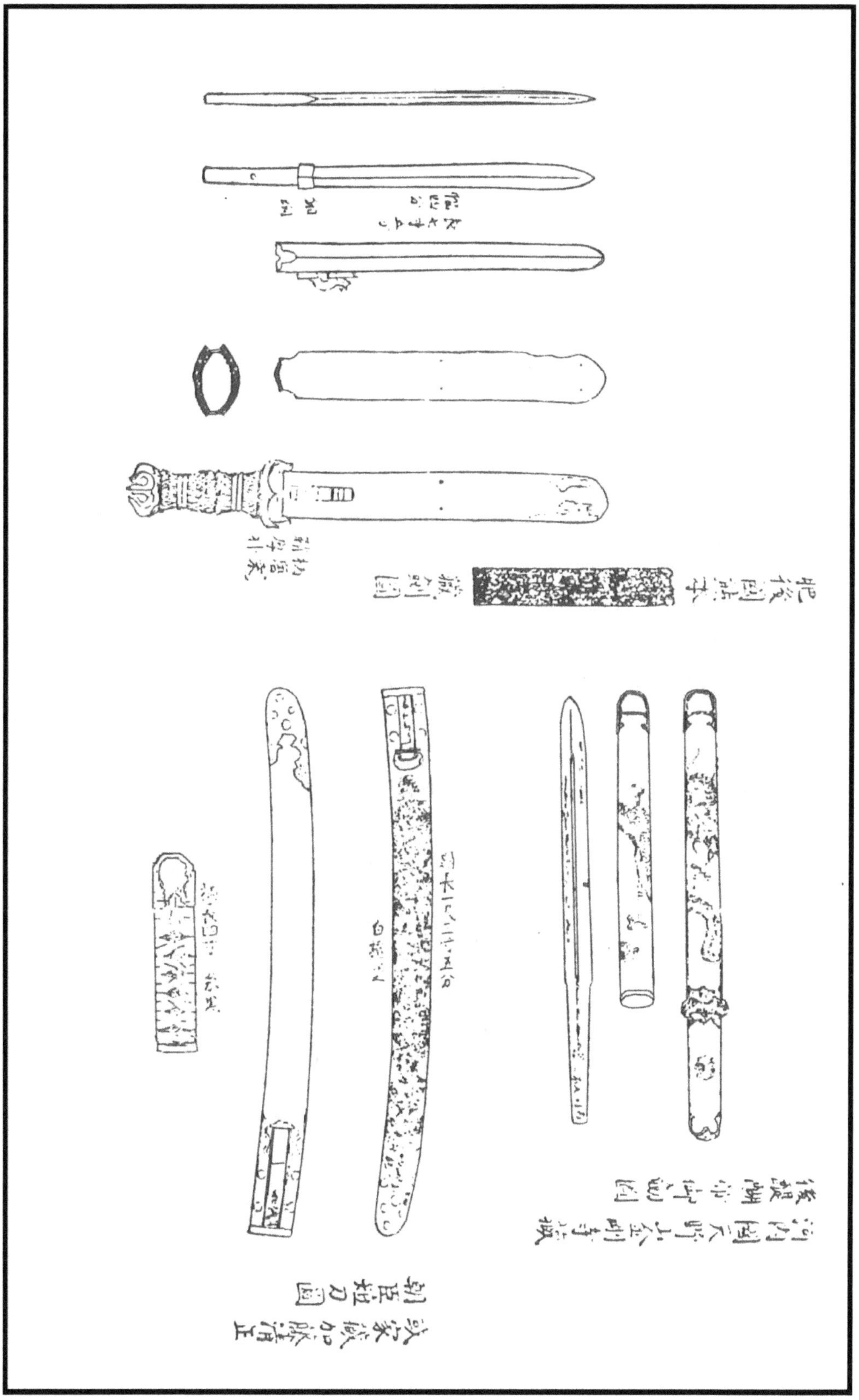

大和國法隆寺藏七躍之劍圖

Figure 2.56 Ken - Horyu-ji Temple.

The description reads, "Drawing of Seven Heavenly Bodies Sword, Collection of Horyu-ji Temple, Yamato Province."

This sword is considered an incarnation drawn from Chinese mythology and incorporated in Japanese Shintoism. The carvings (horimono) on the blade are the symbols of various heavenly bodies. According to Chinese tradition, the heavens are divided into four houses of seven major heavenly bodies each, corresponding respectively to the four directions and four seasons of east, or spring; south, summer; west, autumn; and north, winter.

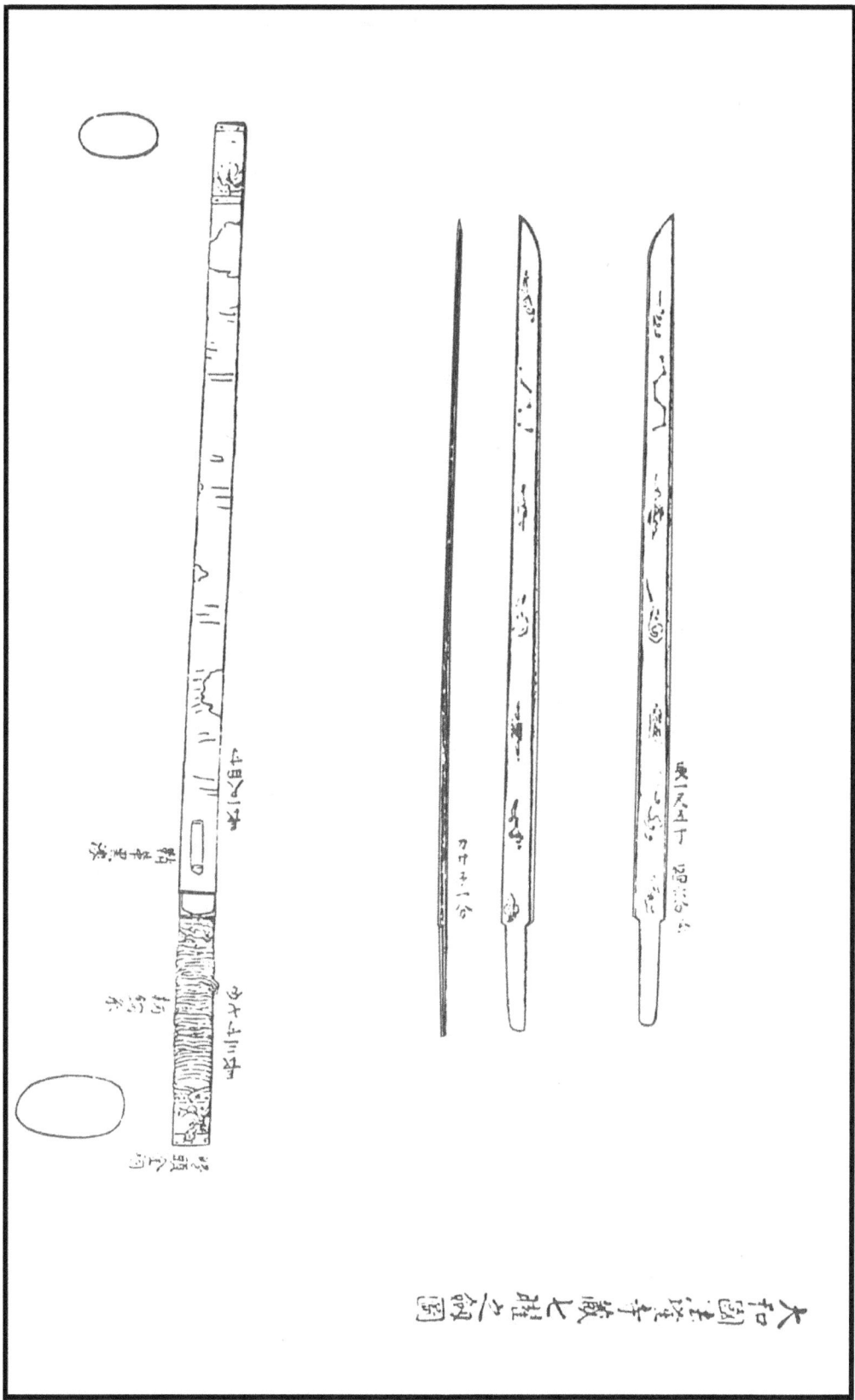

山城國六條　八幡宮藏刀圖

Figure 2.57 Katana - Hachimangu Shrine.

The description reads, "Drawing of sword (katana) with a cloisonné handle and scabbard (tsuka and saya), Collection of Hachimangu Shrine, Rokujo, Yamashiro Province."

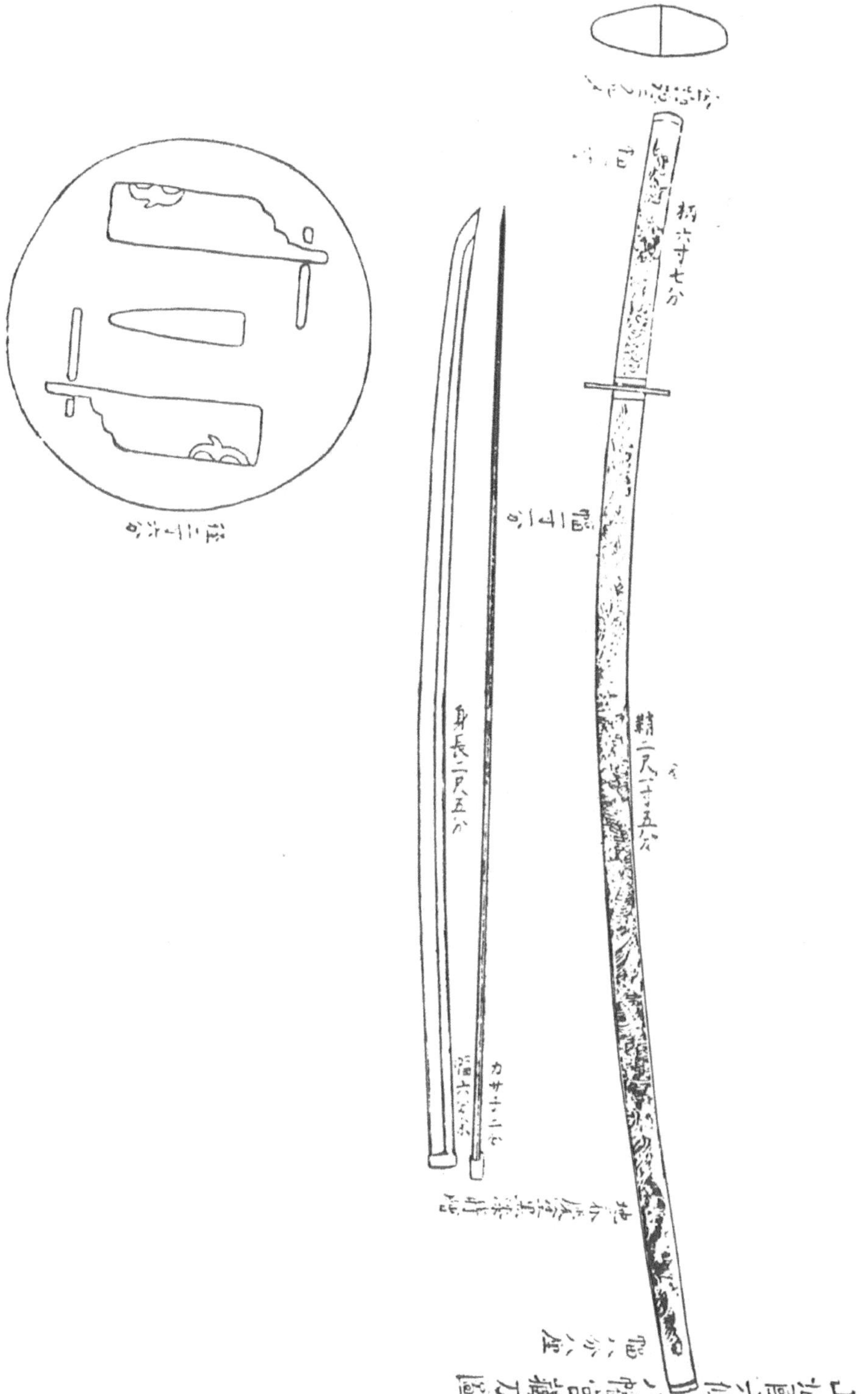
山城國六條八幡宮藏刀圖
柄六寸七分
鞘二尺一寸五分
身長二尺五分

山城國佛光寺寸院大善院藏
武田信玄鍔圖

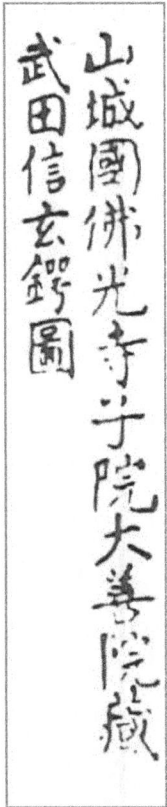

Figure 2.58 Tsuba and Accessories - Bukko-ji Daizen-in Temple.

The description reads, "Drawing of hand guard (tsuba) and accessories belonging to Shingen Takeda, Collection of Bukko-ji Daizen-in Temple, Yamashiro Province."

Takeda Shingen (**武田 信玄**, December 1, 1521 – May 13, 1573), of Kai Province, was a pre-eminent daimyo in feudal Japan with exceptional military prestige in the late stage of the Sengoku period.

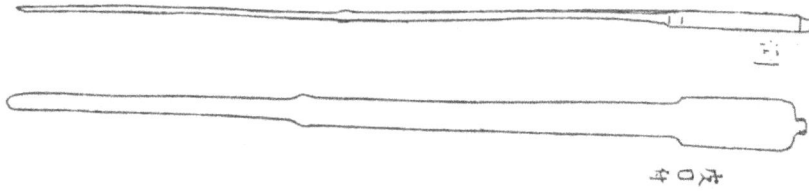

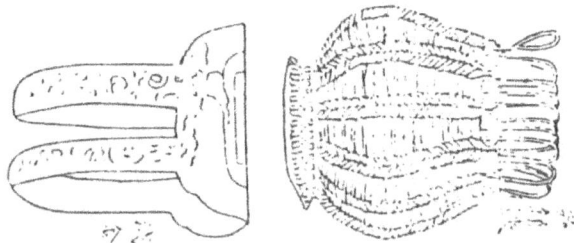

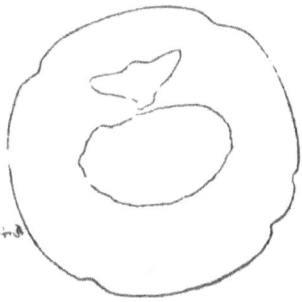

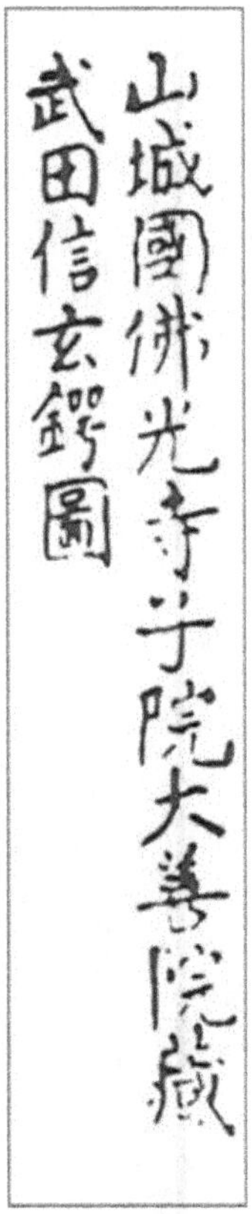

山城國佛光寺子院大善院藏

武田信玄鍔圖

Figure 2.59 Tachi - Bukko-ji Daizen-in Temple.

The description reads, "Drawing of long sword (tachi) and accessories belonging to Shingen Takeda, Collection of Bukko-ji Daizen-in Temple, Yamashiro Province (same as previous picture)."

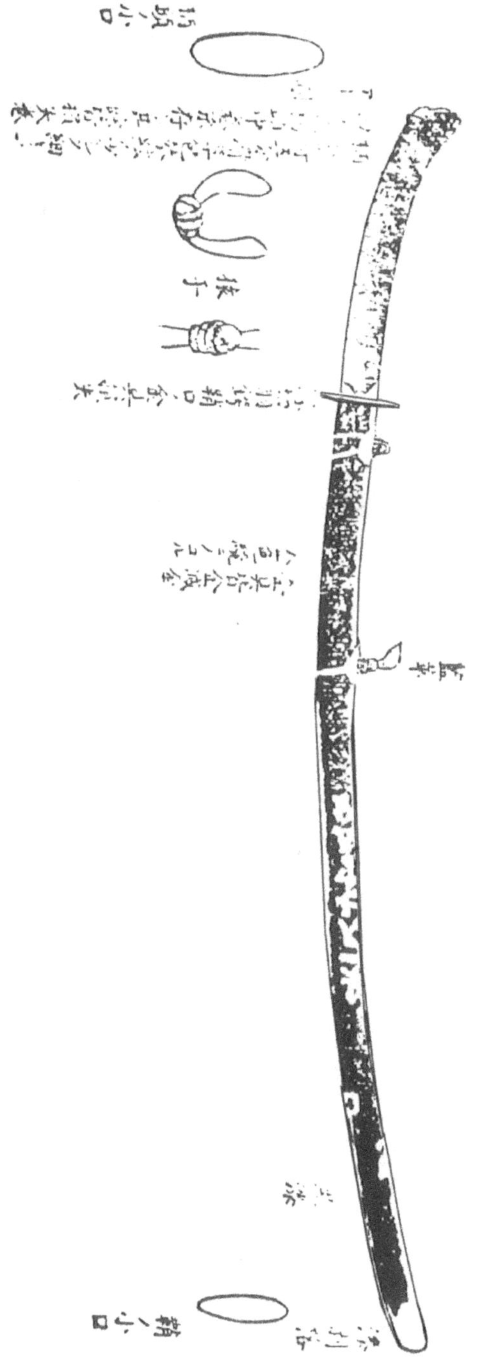

紀伊國高野山龍光院藏劔圖

Figure 2.60 Ken - Koyasan Ryuko-in Temple.

The description reads, "Drawing of straight two-edge sword (ken), Collection of Koyasan Ryuko-in Temple, Kii Province."

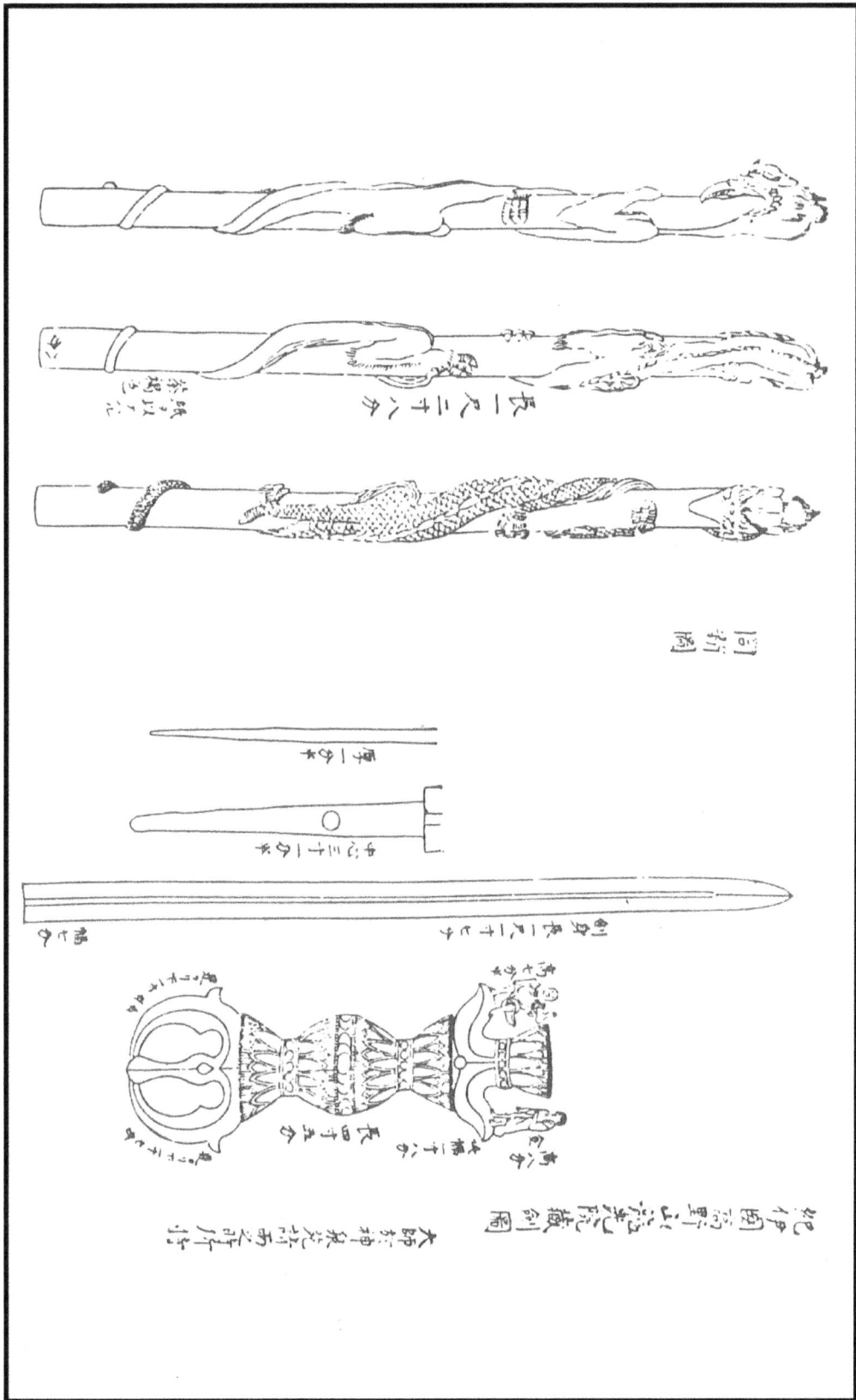

摂津國河邉郡多田庄神吉秀山満願寺蔵
辛壽九太刀圖

Figure 2.61 Tachi named Kojumaru.

The description reads, "Drawing of long sword 'Kojumaru', Collection of Shinshuzan Mangan-ji Temple, Tada Manor, Kawabe District, Settsu Province."

This sword is said to have been used by Nakamitsu Fujiwara in the Heian period (c. 960) to kill his son Kojumaru. Tradition holds that Minamoto no Mitsunaka's son Bijomaru was sent to a temple to become a priest, but the boy spent all his time practicing with his sword. Greatly angered, Mitsunaka ordered his faithful retainer Nakamitsu to kill Bijomaru, but Nakamitsu could not bear to do it. Instead, he sacrificed his only son, Kojumaru. When he learned what had happened, Bijomaru converted and became a well-known priest, founding a temple in Kojumaru's honor, and Nakamitsu named the sword after his son.

柄長六寸一分

鞘長二尺二寸三分

身長一尺八寸一分

播磨國清水寺藏田村丸劍太刀圖 三

Figure 2.62 Ken - Kiyomizu Temple.

The description reads, "Drawing of long swords (ken) owned by Tamuramaru, Collection of Kiyomizu Temple, Harima Province (3 swords)."

Sakanoue no Tamuramaro (坂上 田村麻呂, 758 – June 17, 811) was a general and shogun of the early Heian Period of Japan. He was the son of Sakanoue no Karitamaro.

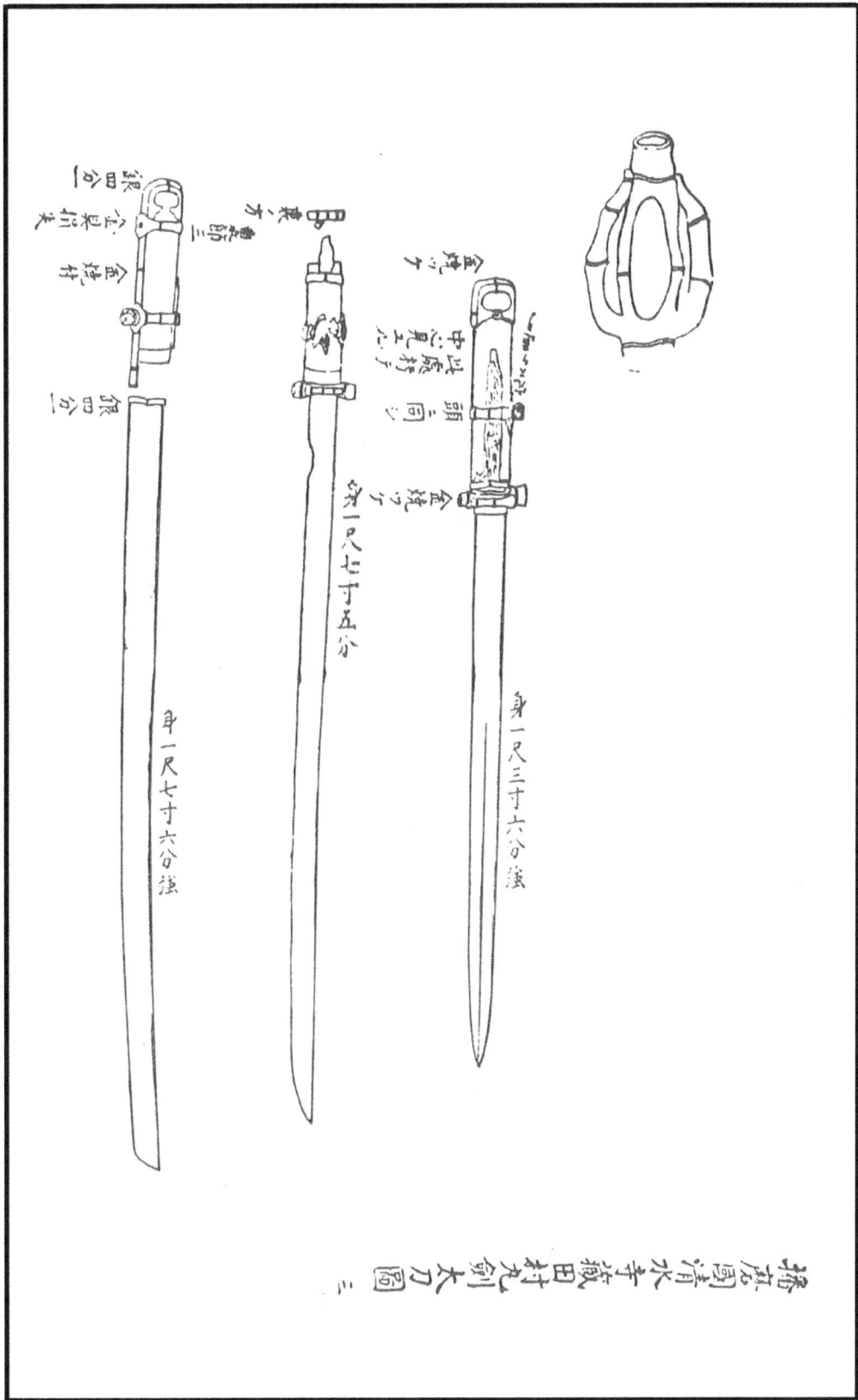

伊豆國三嶋社藏北条宗川節太刀金具圖

Figure 2.63 Tachi and Accessories - Mishima Shrine.

The description reads, "Drawing of long sword (tachi) and metal fittings donated by the Hojo Family, Collection of Mishima Shrine, Izu Province."

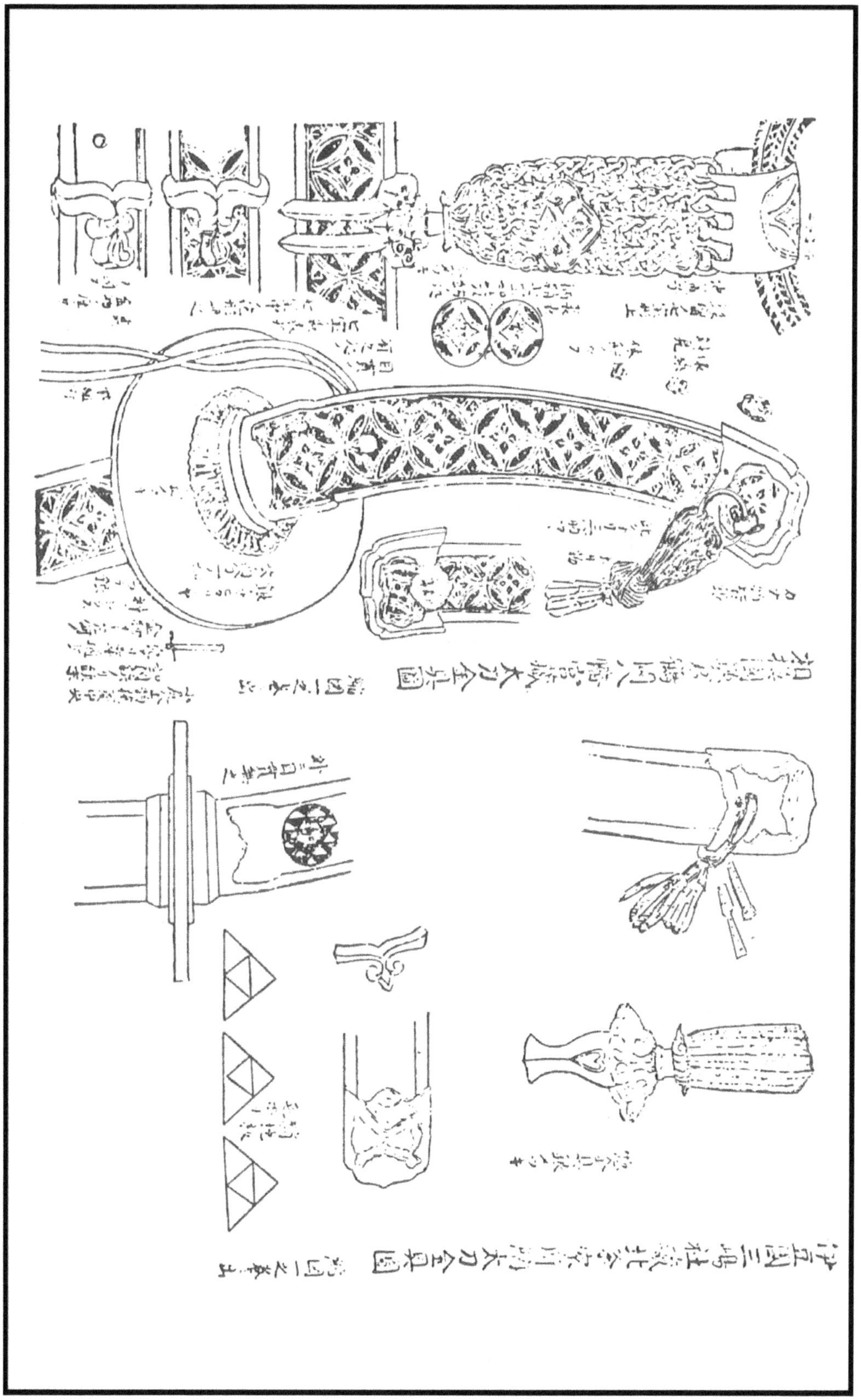

伊豫國三島社藏平重盛公太刀金具圖

Figure 2.64 Tachi and Fittings - Mishima Shrine.

The description reads, "Drawing of long sword (tachi) and metal fittings belonging to Lord Shigemori Taira, Collection of Mishima Shrine, Iyo Province."

Taira no Shigemori (平 重盛, 1138 – September 2, 1179) was the eldest son of the Taira clan patriarch, Taira no Kiyomori. He took part in the Hōgen and Heiji rebellions. He died of illness in 1179.

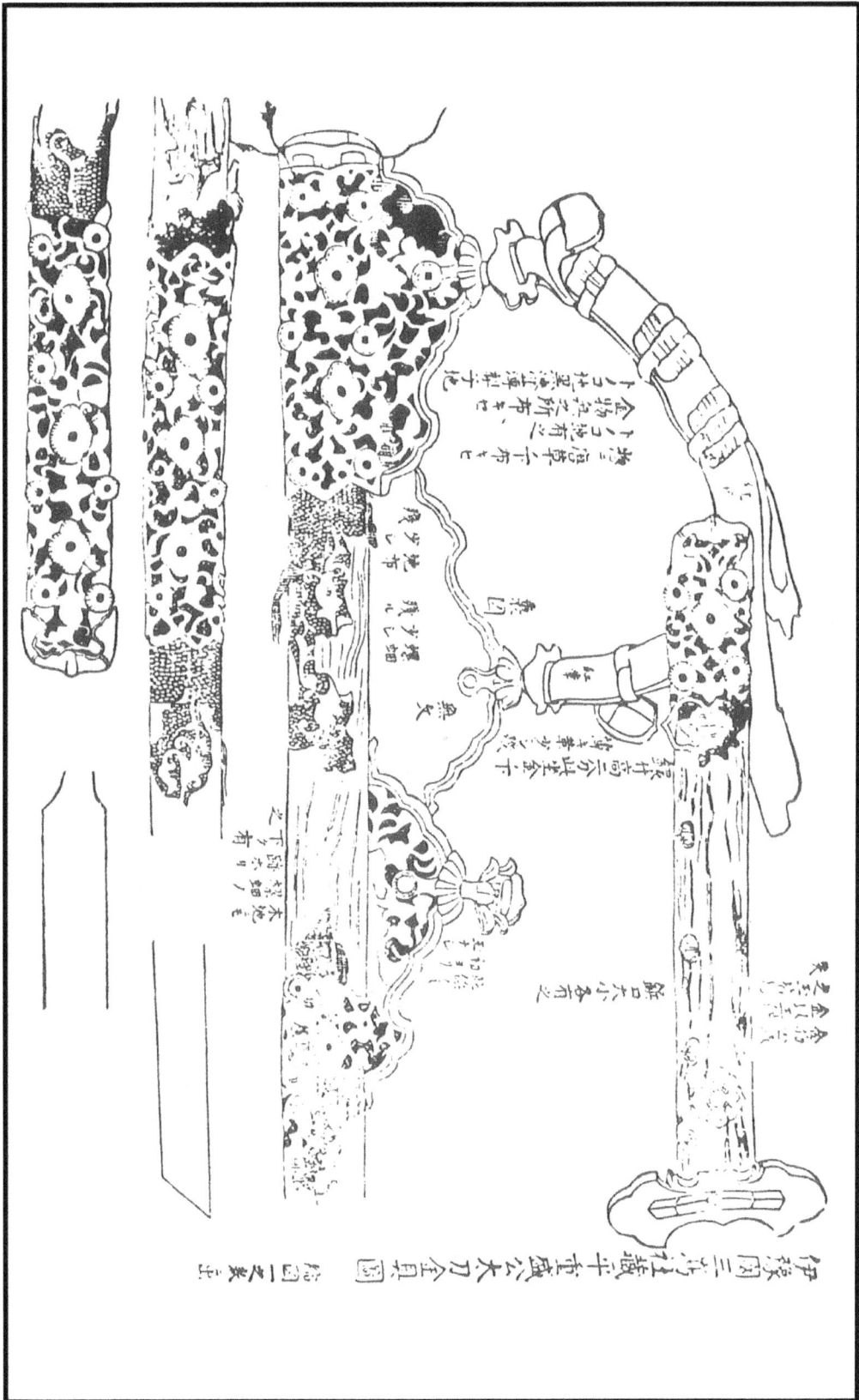

同藏大塔宮所納太刀金具圖

Figure 2.65 Tachi and Fittings - Mishima Shrine.

The description reads, "Drawing of long sword (tachi) and metal fittings donated by Prince Moriyoshi, same collection as previous page."

Prince Moriyoshi (護良親王 Moriyoshi Shinnō) (1308 – August 12, 1335) was a son of Emperor Go-Daigo and Minamoto no Chikako executed by Ashikaga Tadayoshi in 1335.

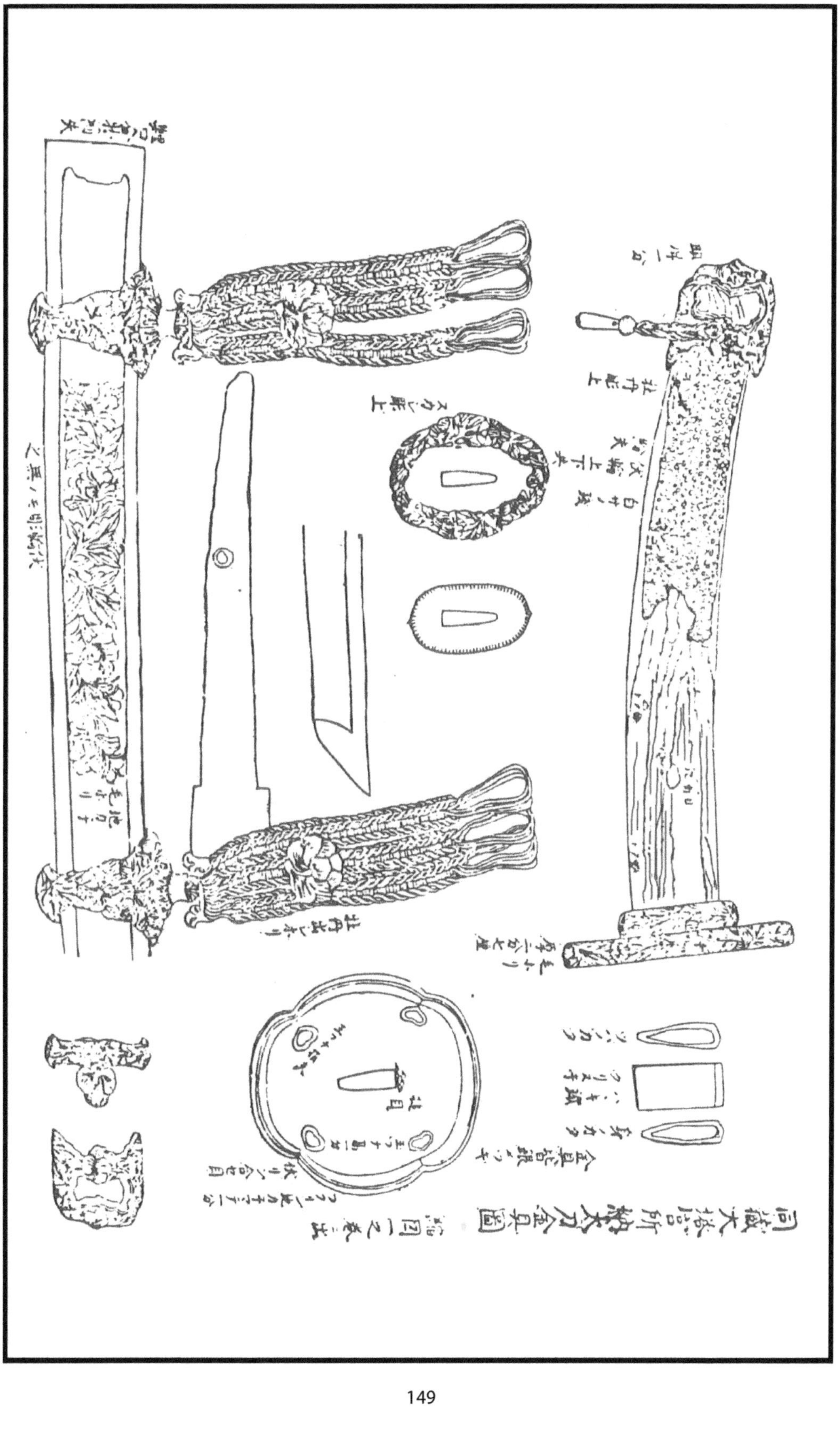

相模國鎌倉鶴岡八幡宮藏太刀金具圖 縮圖一之表三出

Figure 2.66 Tachi and Fittings - Tsurugaoka Hachimangu Shrine.

The description reads, "Drawing of long sword (tachi) and metal fittings, Collection of Tsurugaoka Hachimangu Shrine, Kamakura, Sagami Province; Appearing in miniature copy."

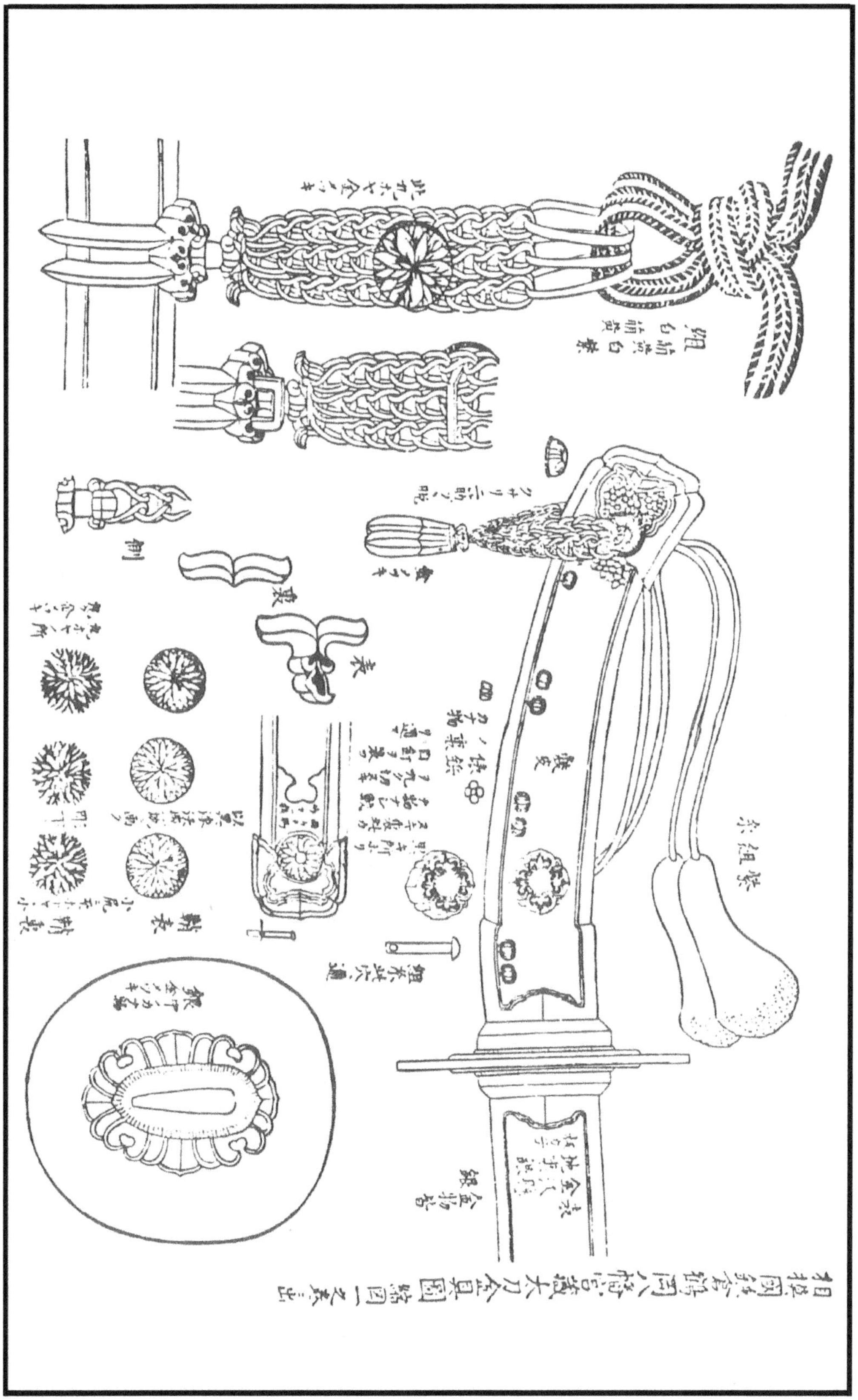

由良家蔵太刀図

Figure 2.67 Tachi.

The description reads, "Drawing of long sword (tachi), Collection of Yura Family."

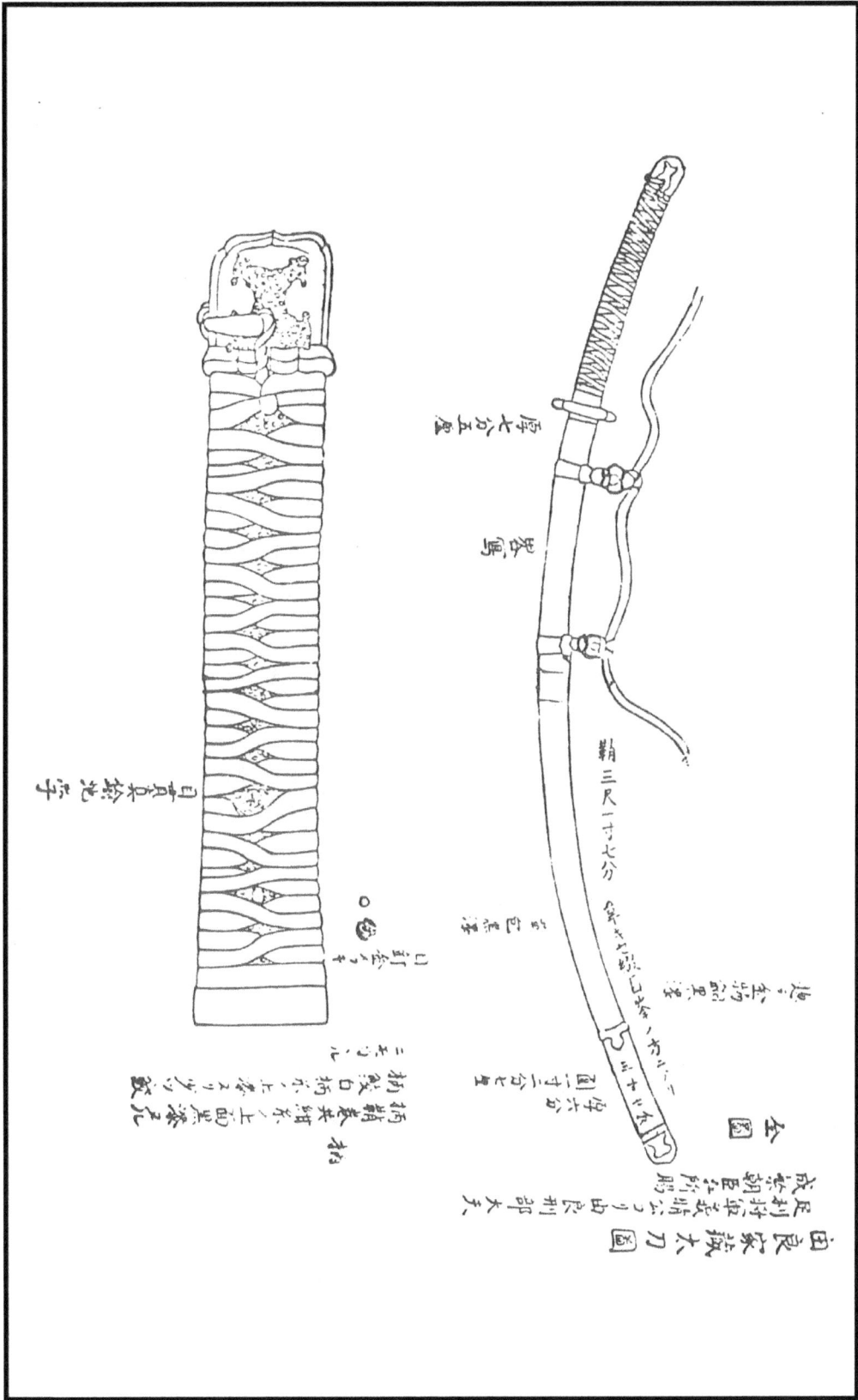

由良家藏太刀圖

Figure 2.68 Tachi Fittings.

The description reads, "Drawing of long sword (tachi) fittings, Collection of Yura Family (same collection as previous picture)."

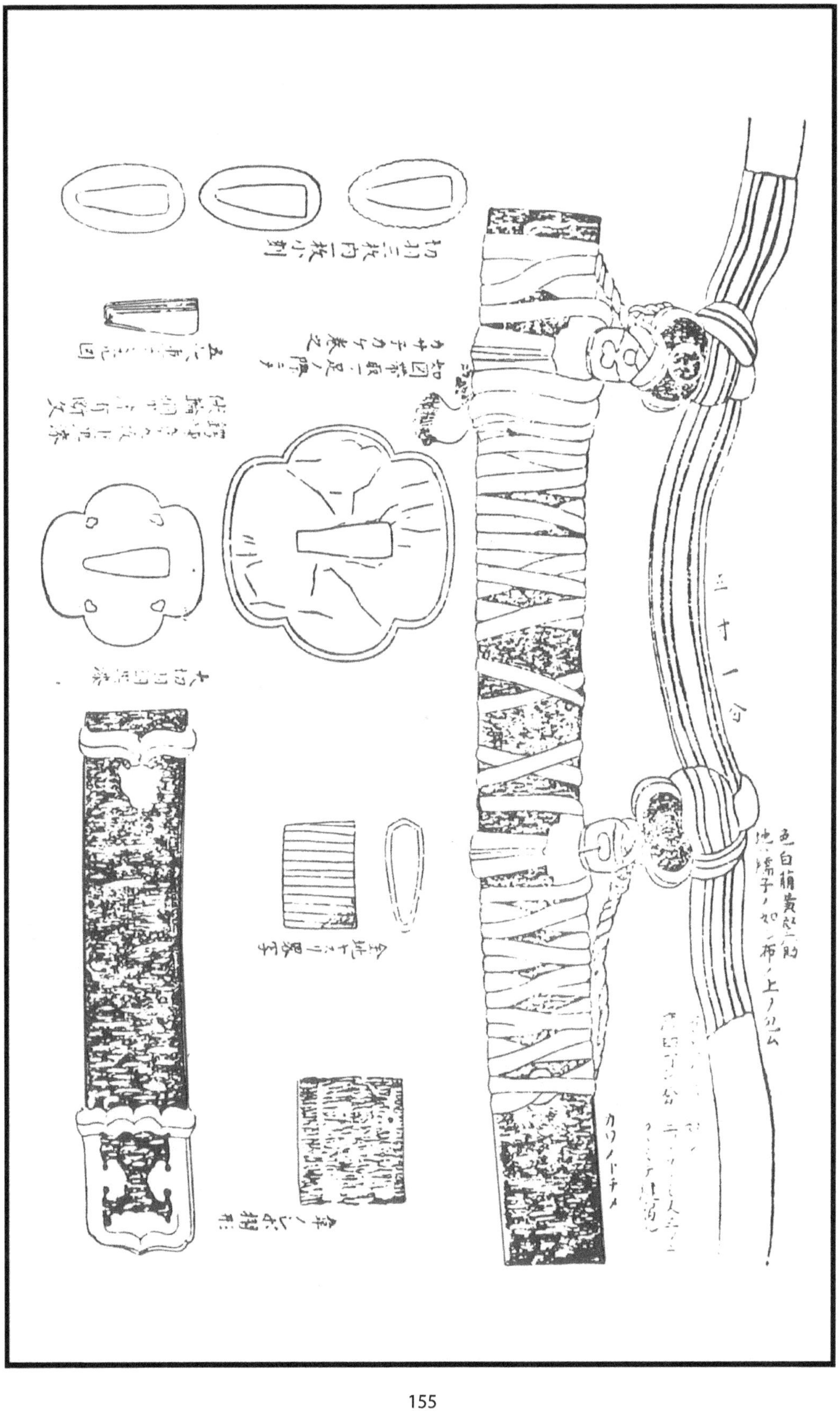

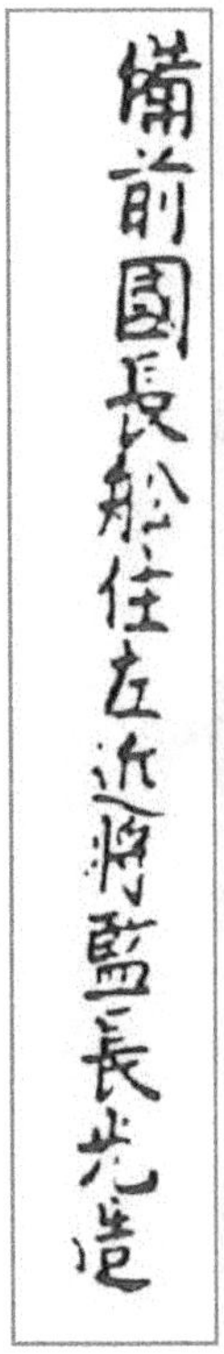

備前國長船住左近将監長光造

Figure 2.69 Tachi by Nagamitsu.

The description reads, "Crafted by Sakon Shokan Nagamitsu, sword smith of Osafune, Bizen Province."

Nagamitsu was the son of Bizen Mitsutada who was the founder of the Bizen Osafune School. The current thinking is that there were two generations of smiths who used the name Nagamitsu. The first generation was productive in about the Bunei and Koan eras (1264-1287). The Nidai who is thought to be the smith who signed Sakon Shokan Nagamitsu is represented by works from the Einin and Shoan eras (1293-1301).

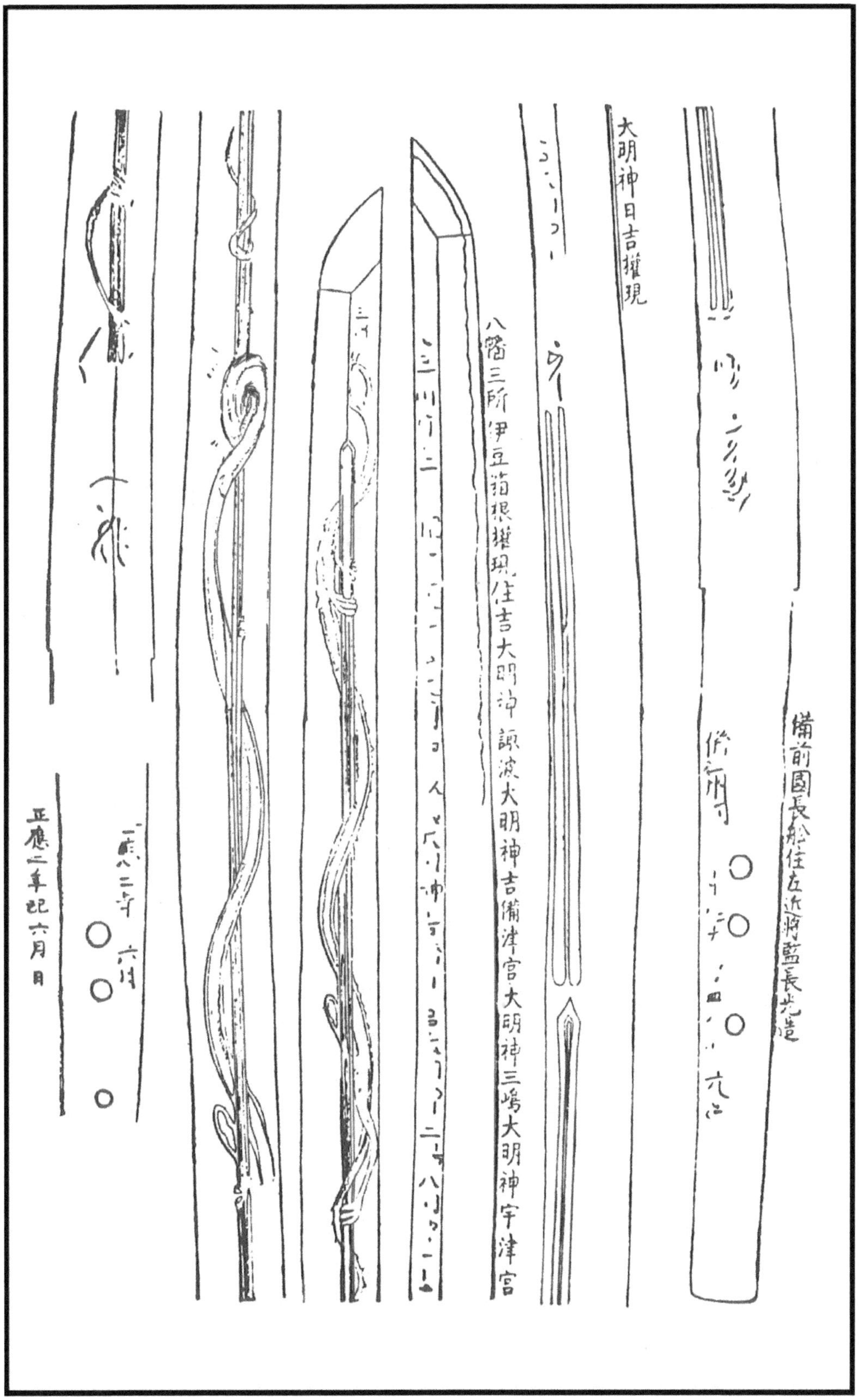
備前國長船住左近將監長光造
大明神日吉權現
八幡三所伊豆箱根權現住吉大明神諏波大明神吉備津宮大明神三嶋大明神宇津宮
正應二年記六月日

大和國東大寺八幡宮蔵競馬太刀圖

Figure 2.70 Wooden Tachi - Hachimangu Shrine of Todai-ji Temple.

The description reads, "Drawing of wooden sword used in horse racing, Collection of Hachimangu Shrine of Todai-ji Temple, Yamato Province."

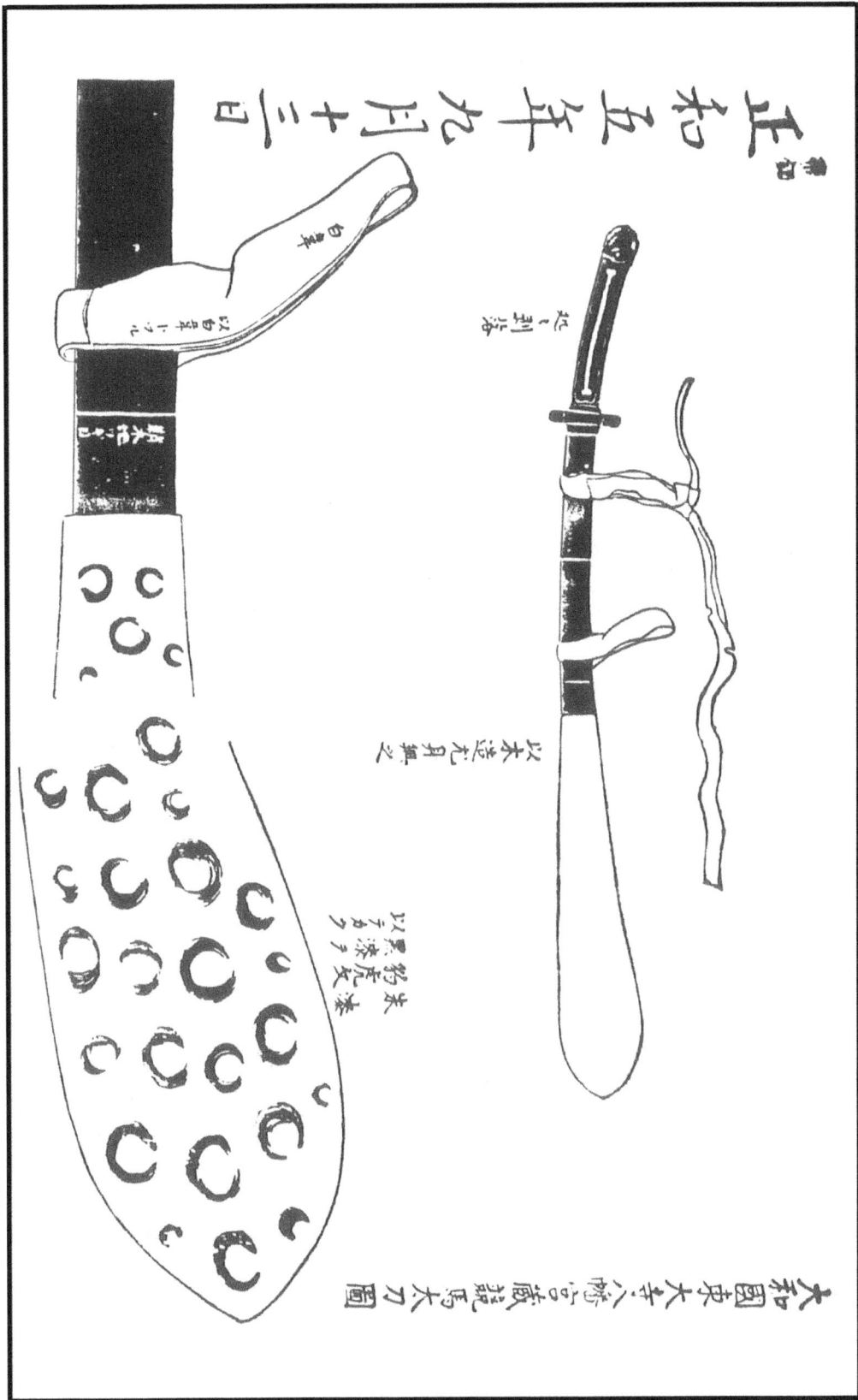

正
和
五
年
九
月
三
十
日

大
和
國
吏
大
神
八
幡
宮
の
蔵
造
黒
馬
大
刀
圖

大和國東大寺八幡宮藏競馬太刀圖

Figure 2.70 Wooden Tachi Tsuka - Hachimangu Shrine of Todai-ji Temple.

The description reads, "Drawing of wooden sword hilt (tsuka) used in horse racing, Collection of Hachimangu Shrine of Todai-ji Temple, Yamato Province (same collection as previous picture)."

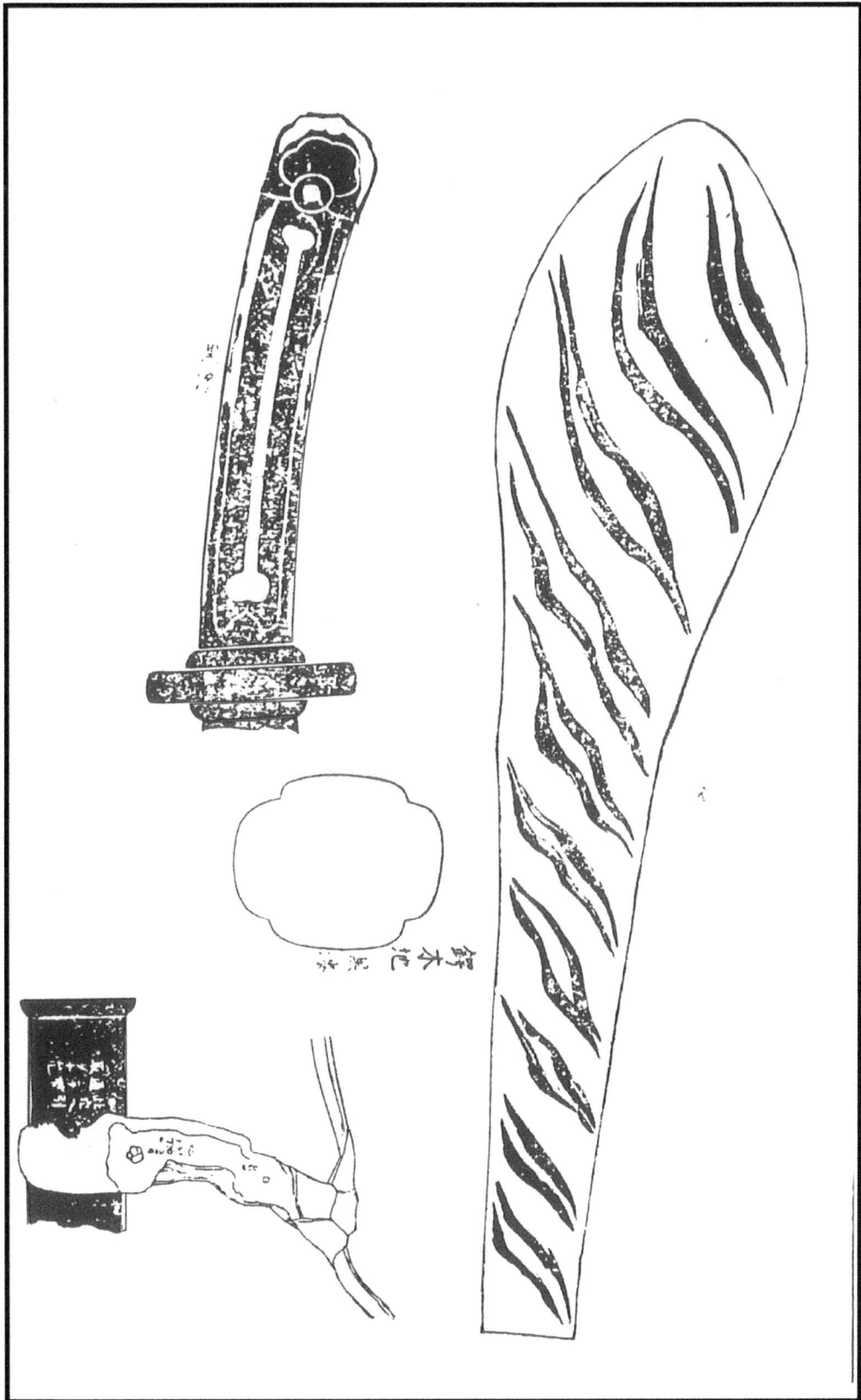

大坂商家藏楠正成卿短刀圖

Figure 2.72 Tanto - Masashige Kusunoki.

The description reads, "Drawing of short sword (tanto) belonging to Lord Masashige Kusunoki, Collection of an Osaka merchant."

As mentioned earlier, Kusunoki Masashige (楠木 正成, 1294 – July 4, 1336) was a 14th-century samurai who fought for Emperor Go-Daigo in his attempt to wrest rulership of Japan away from the Kamakura shogunate and is remembered as the ideal of samurai loyalty.

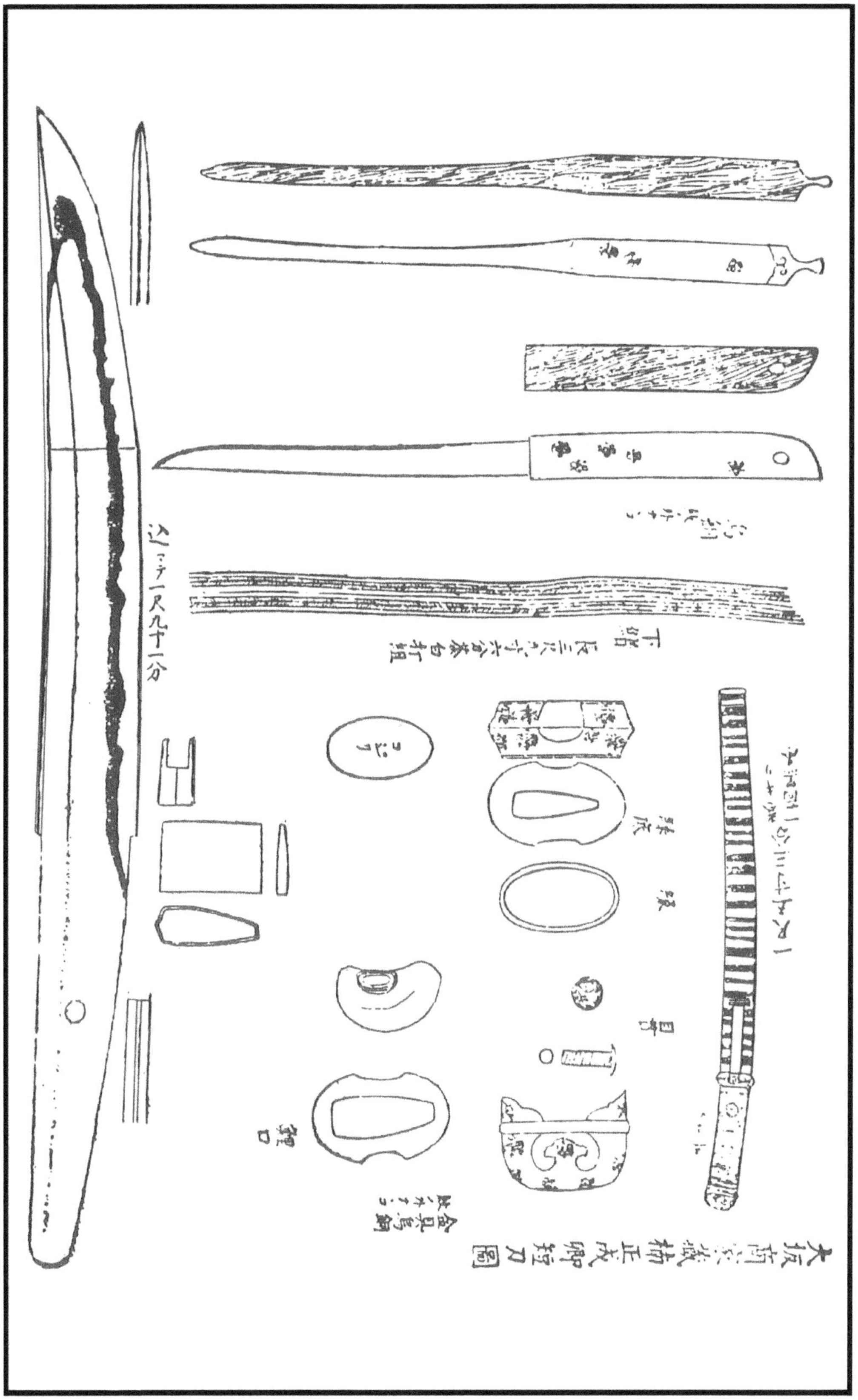

不動尊劍圖　攝津國住吉郡吾彦山大聖寺中坊不動院藏

Figure 2.73 Ken for Fudo - Abikosan Taishoji Nakabo Fudo-in Temple.

The description reads, "Drawing of straight two-edge sword (ken) for statue of Buddhist deity Fudo, Collection of Abikosan Taishoji Nakabo Fudo-in Temple, Sumiyoshi District, Settsu Province."

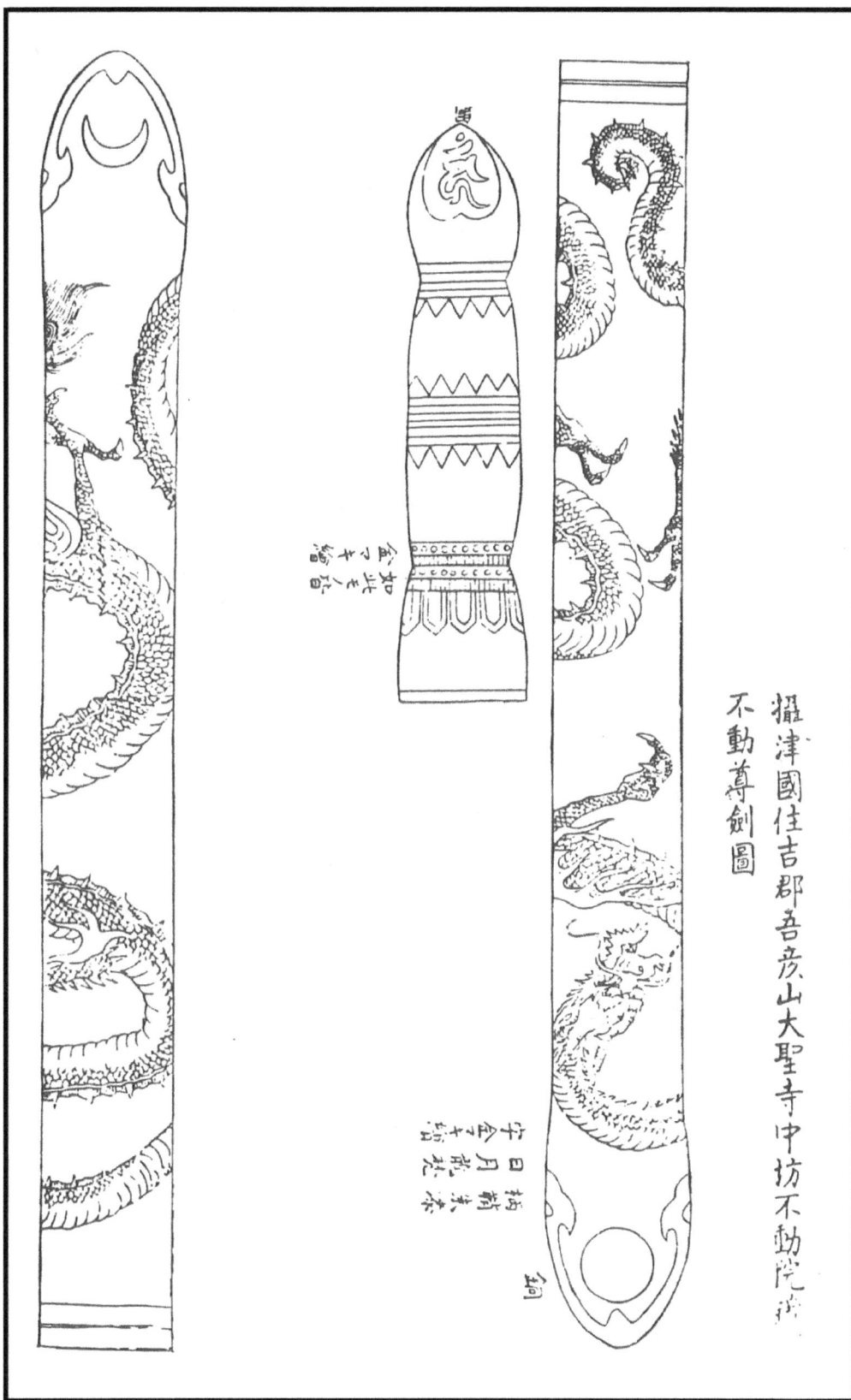

摂津國住吉郡吾彦山大聖寺中坊不動院僧

不動尊剣図

摂津國住吉郡吾彦山大聖寺中坊不動院蔵

雲次剣圖

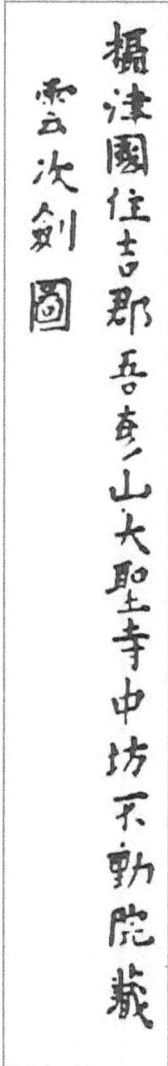

Figure 2.74 Ken - Abikosan Taishoji Nakabo Fudo-in Temple.

The description reads, "Drawing of a straight two-edge sword (ken) crafted by sword smith Unji, Collection of Abikosan Taishoji Nakabo Fudo-in Temple, Sumiyoshi District, Settsu Province."

Unji Bun-Po first signed Kuniyoshi then in 1312 he became Unji "Order Under Heaven." Worked with his brother, Kunitomo to produce a sword for Emperor Go-Daigo, whereafter they were allowed their school and Imperial reference in their names.

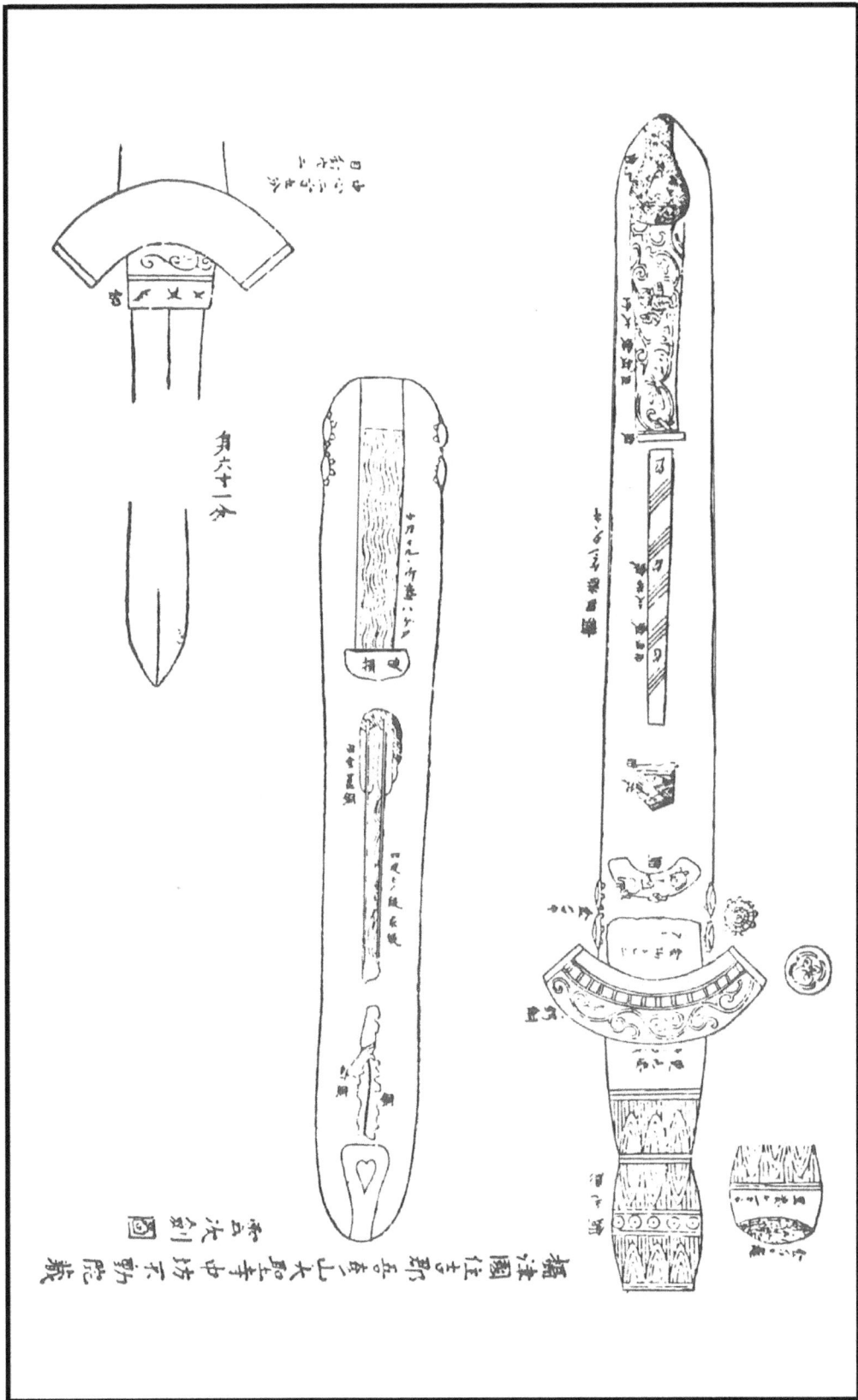

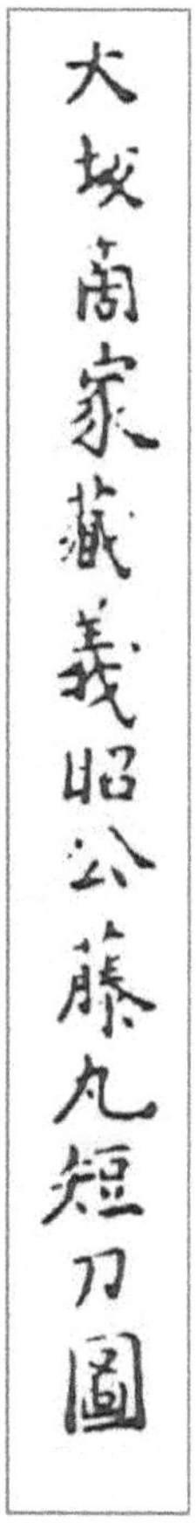

大坂商家蔵義昭公藤丸短刀圖

Figure 2.75 Wakizashi - Fujimaru.

The description reads, "Drawing of short sword (wakizashi) 'Fujimaru' belonging to Lord Yoshiakira, Collection of an Osaka merchant."

Ashikaga Yoshiaki (足利 義昭, December 5, 1537 – October 19, 1597) was the 15th shogun of the Ashikaga shogunate in Japan who reigned from 1568 to 1573. His father, Ashikaga Yoshiharu was the twelfth shogun, and his brother, Ashikaga Yoshiteru was the thirteenth shogun.

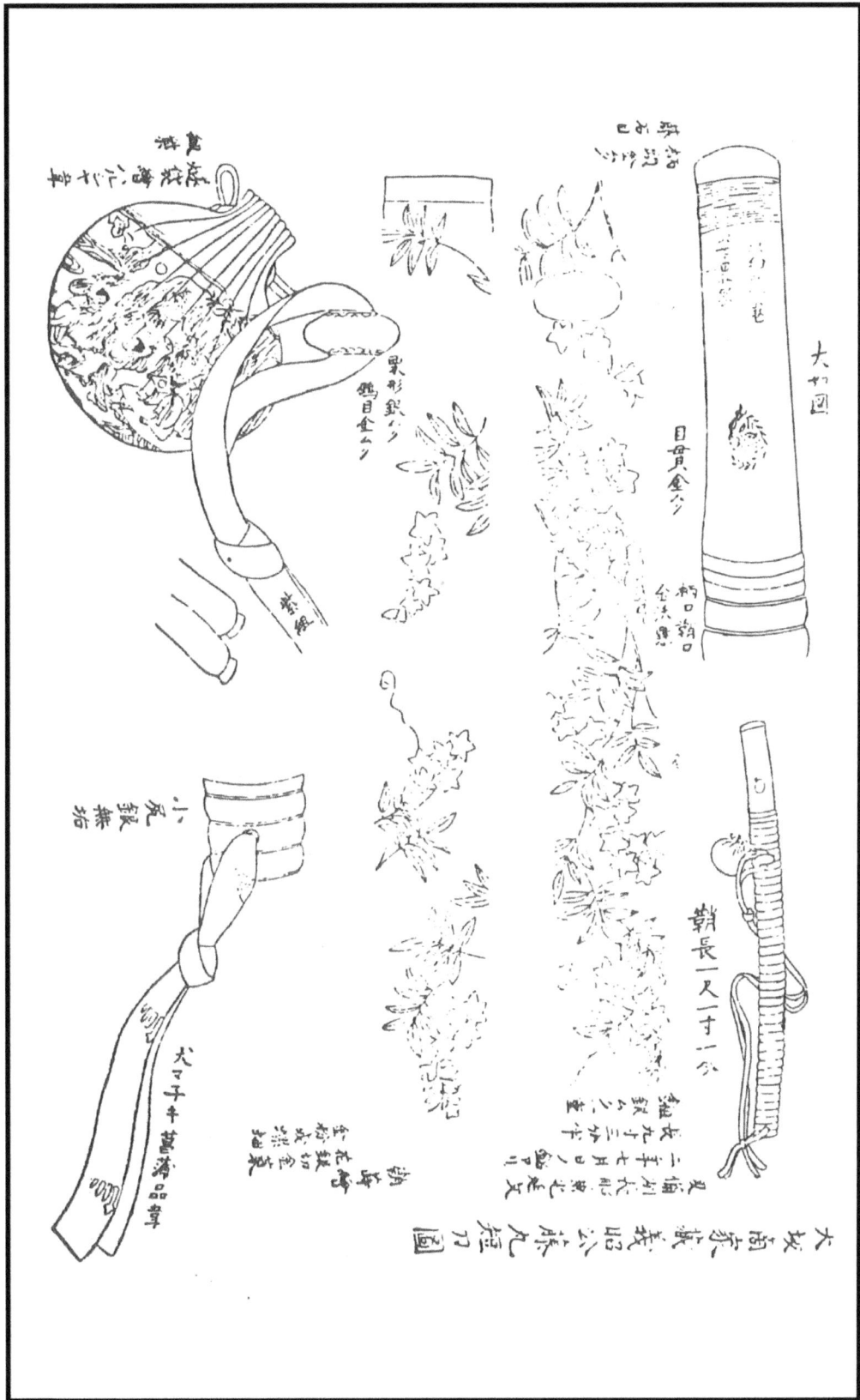

大坂商家蔵義昭公藤丸短刀圖

Figure 2.76 Tachi - Yoshiakira.

The description reads, "Drawing of long sword (tachi) belonging to Lord Yoshiakira, Collection of an Osaka merchant (same collection as previous picture)."

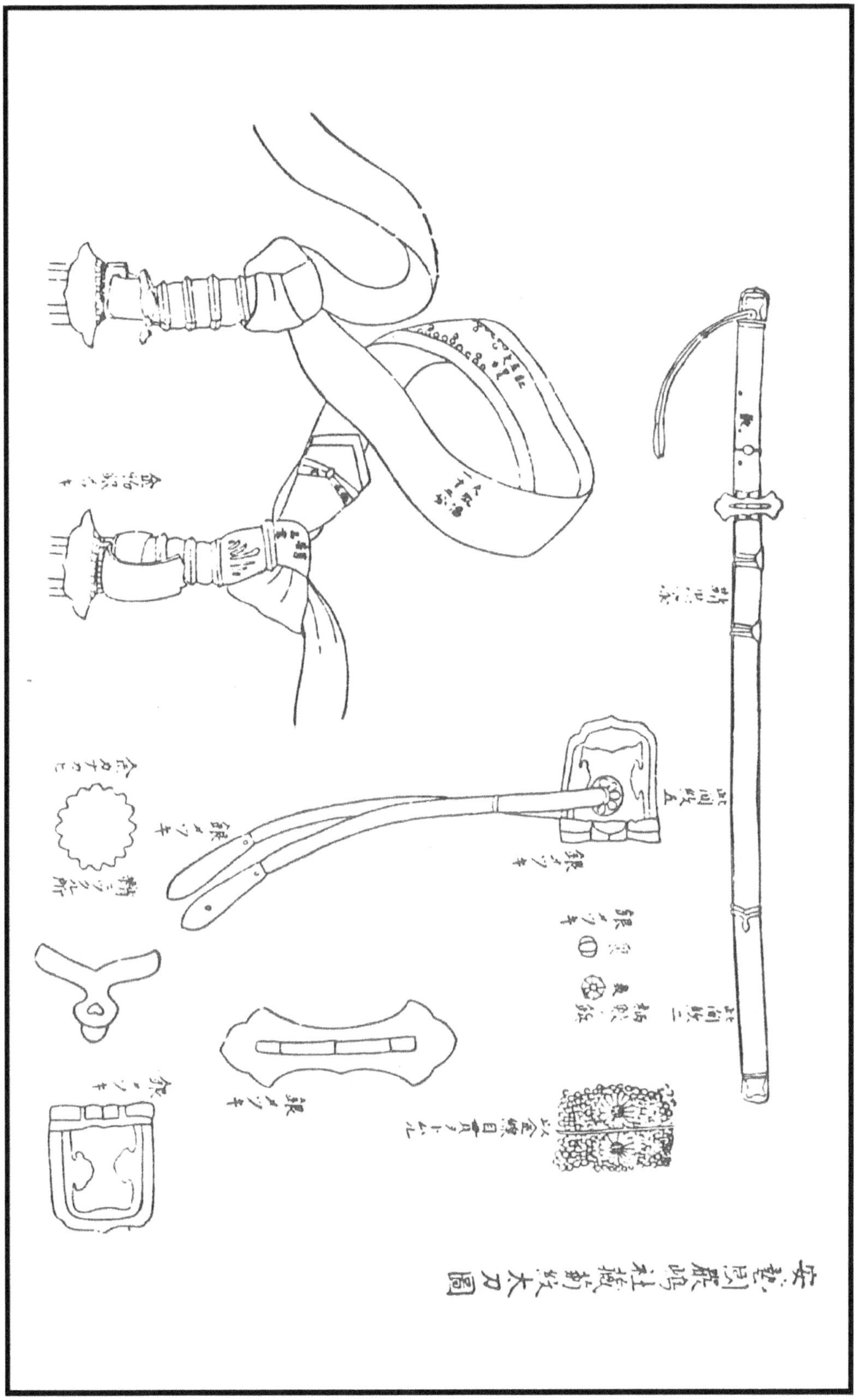

鬼丸太刀金具図

Figure 2.77 Tachi and Fittings.

The description reads, "Drawing of long sword 'Onimaru' and metal fittings."

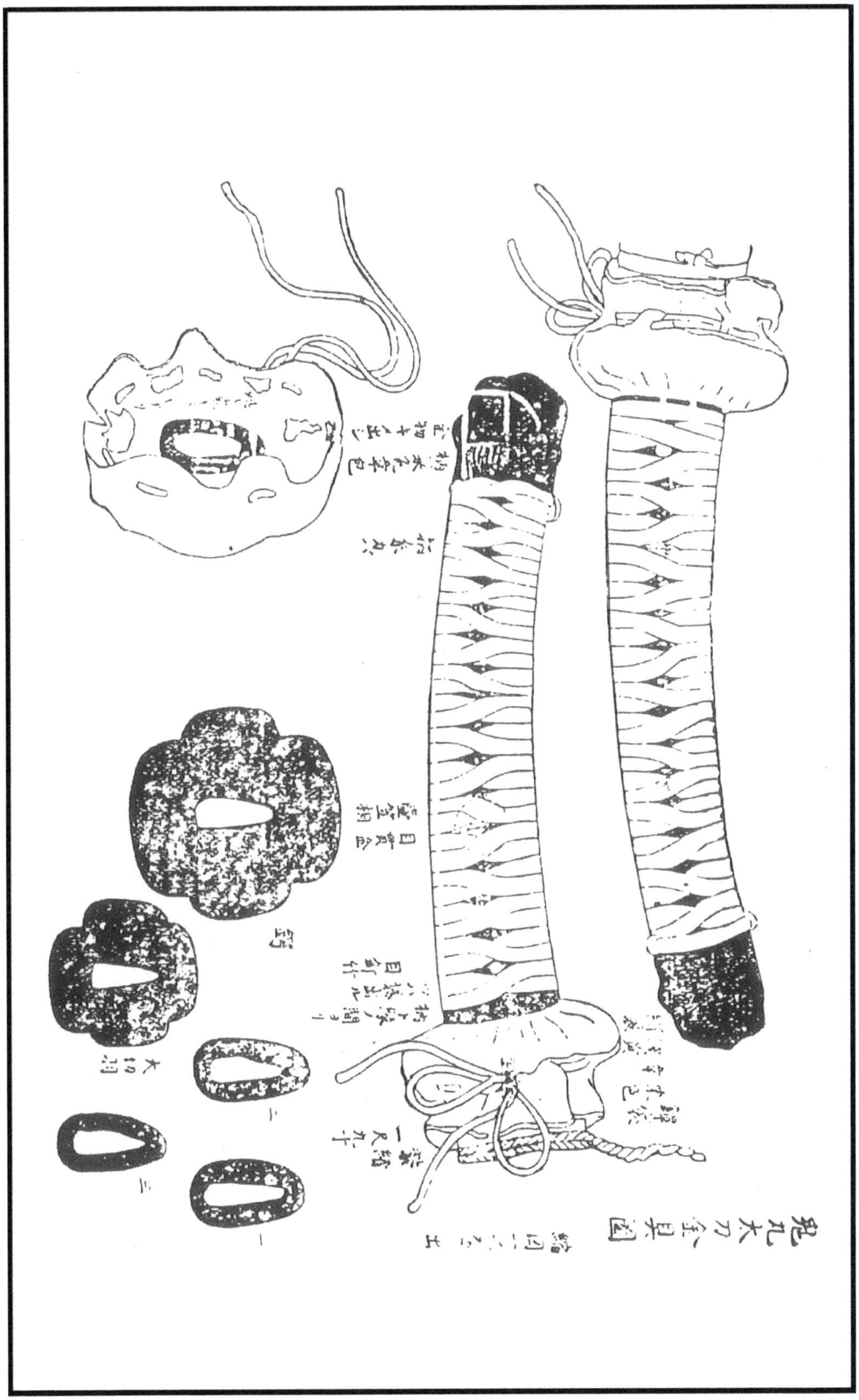

鬼丸太刀金具図

Figure 2.78 Tachi and Fittings.

The description reads, "Drawing of long sword 'Onimaru' and metal fittings (same sword as previous picture)."

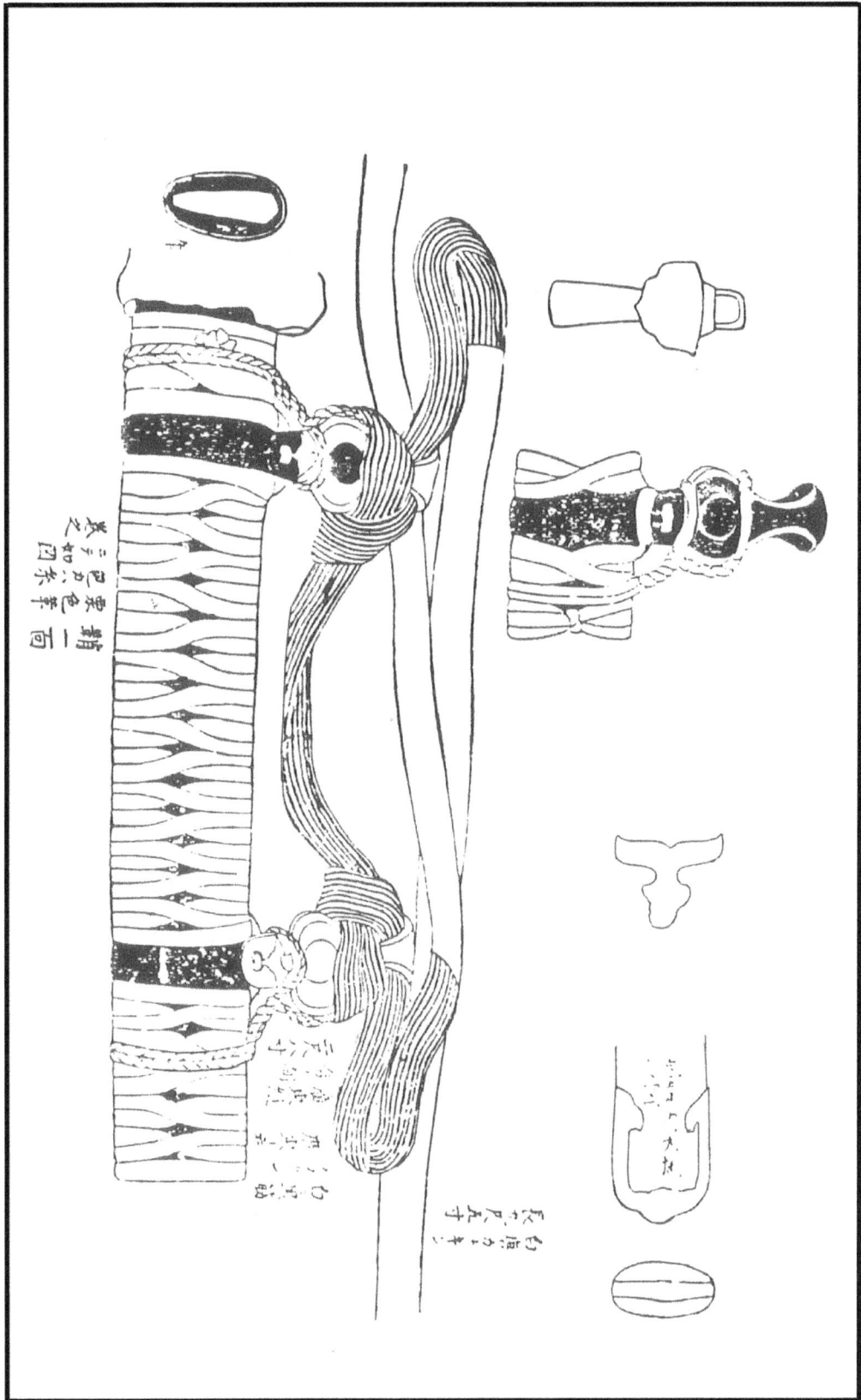

Figure 2.79 Tsuba and Fittings - Takauji Ashikaga.

The description reads, "Drawing of hand guard (tsuba) and metal fittings belonging to Lord Takauji Ashikaga, Collection of Kakubei Sakamoto, retainer of the Aizu Clan; Donated by Prince Moriyoshi."

Ashikaga Takauji (足利 尊氏, 1305 – June 7, 1358) was the founder and first shogun of the Ashikaga shogunate. His rule began in 1338, beginning the Muromachi period of Japan, and ended with his death in 1358. He was a descendant of the samurai of the (Minamoto) Seiwa Genji line (meaning they were descendants of Emperor Seiwa) who had settled in the Ashikaga area of Shimotsuke Province, in present day Tochigi Prefecture.

According to famous Zen master and intellectual Musō Soseki, who enjoyed his favor and collaborated with him, Takauji had three qualities. First, he kept his cool in battle and was not afraid of death. Second, he was merciful and tolerant. Third, he was very generous with those below him.

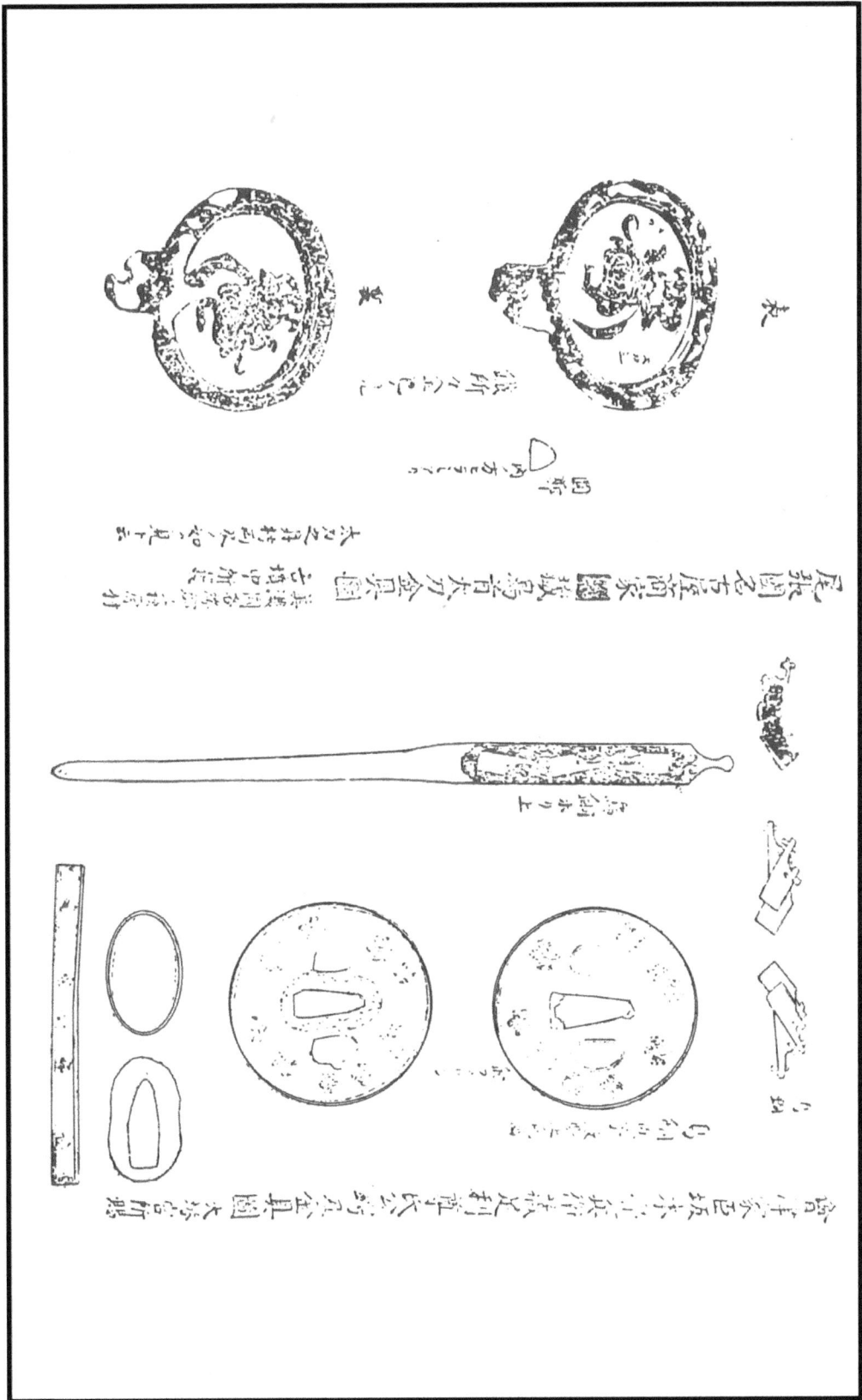

Figure 2.80 Saya and Fittings.

The description reads, "Drawing of scabbard (saya) and metal fittings belonging to Lord Takauji Ashikaga, Collection of Kakubei Sakamoto, retainer of the Aizu Clan; Donated by Prince Moriyoshi (same collection as previous picture)."

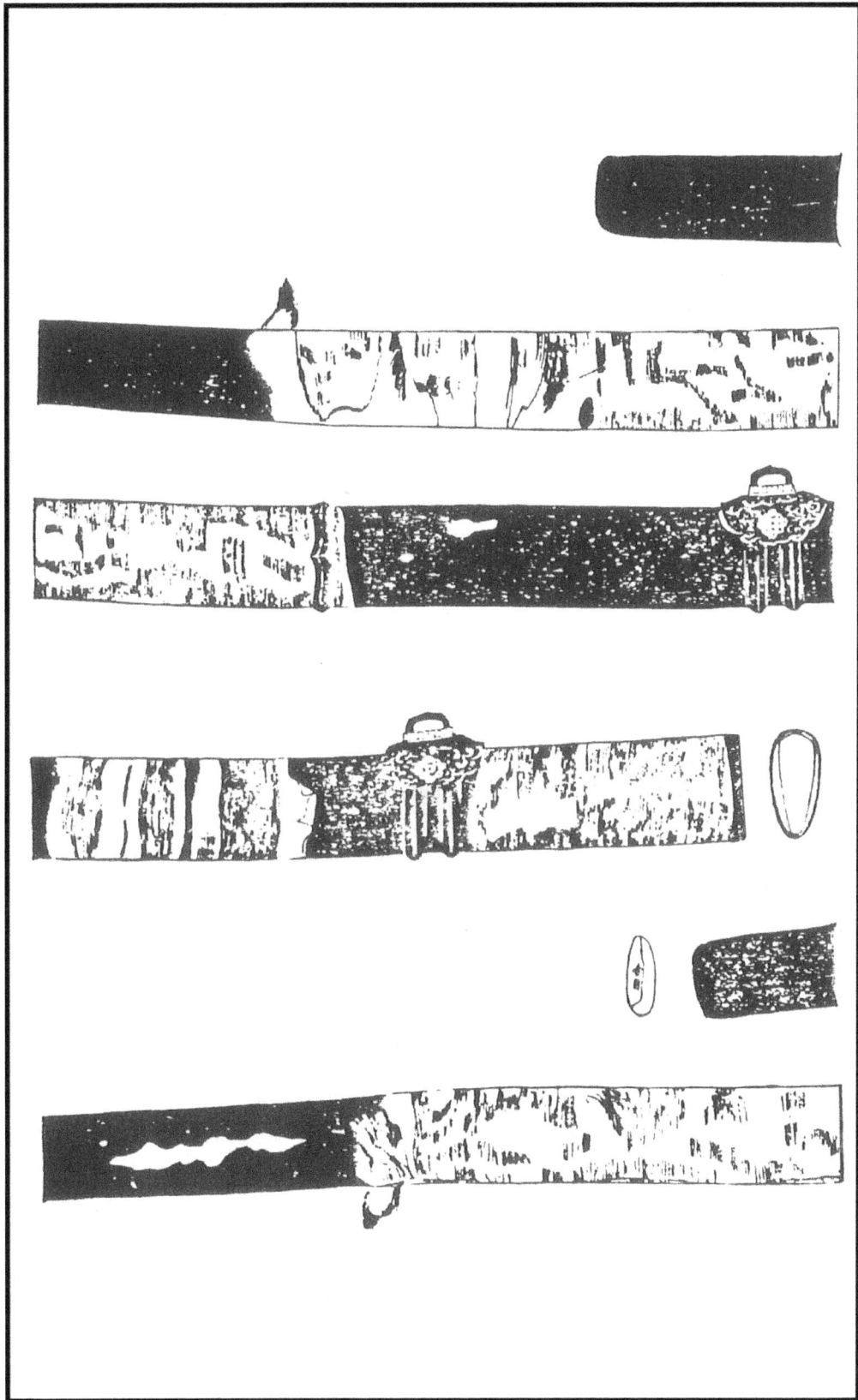

大阪商家藏櫛正成卿短刀圖　　大阪商家藏鳩丸短刀圖

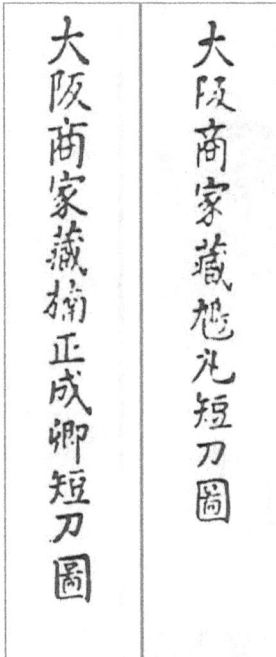

Figure 2.81 Tanto - Hatomaru.

Descriptions read, "Drawing of short sword (tanto) 'Hatomaru', Collection of an Osaka merchant;" and, "Drawing of short sword belonging to Lord Masashige Kusunoki, Collection of an Osaka merchant."

As mentioned earlier, Kusunoki Masashige (楠木 正成, 1294 – July 4, 1336) was a 14th-century samurai who fought for Emperor Go-Daigo in his attempt to wrest rulership of Japan away from the Kamakura shogunate and is remembered as the ideal of samurai loyalty. His origin has not been validated and it was merely six years between the start of his military campaign in 1331 and his demise in 1336.

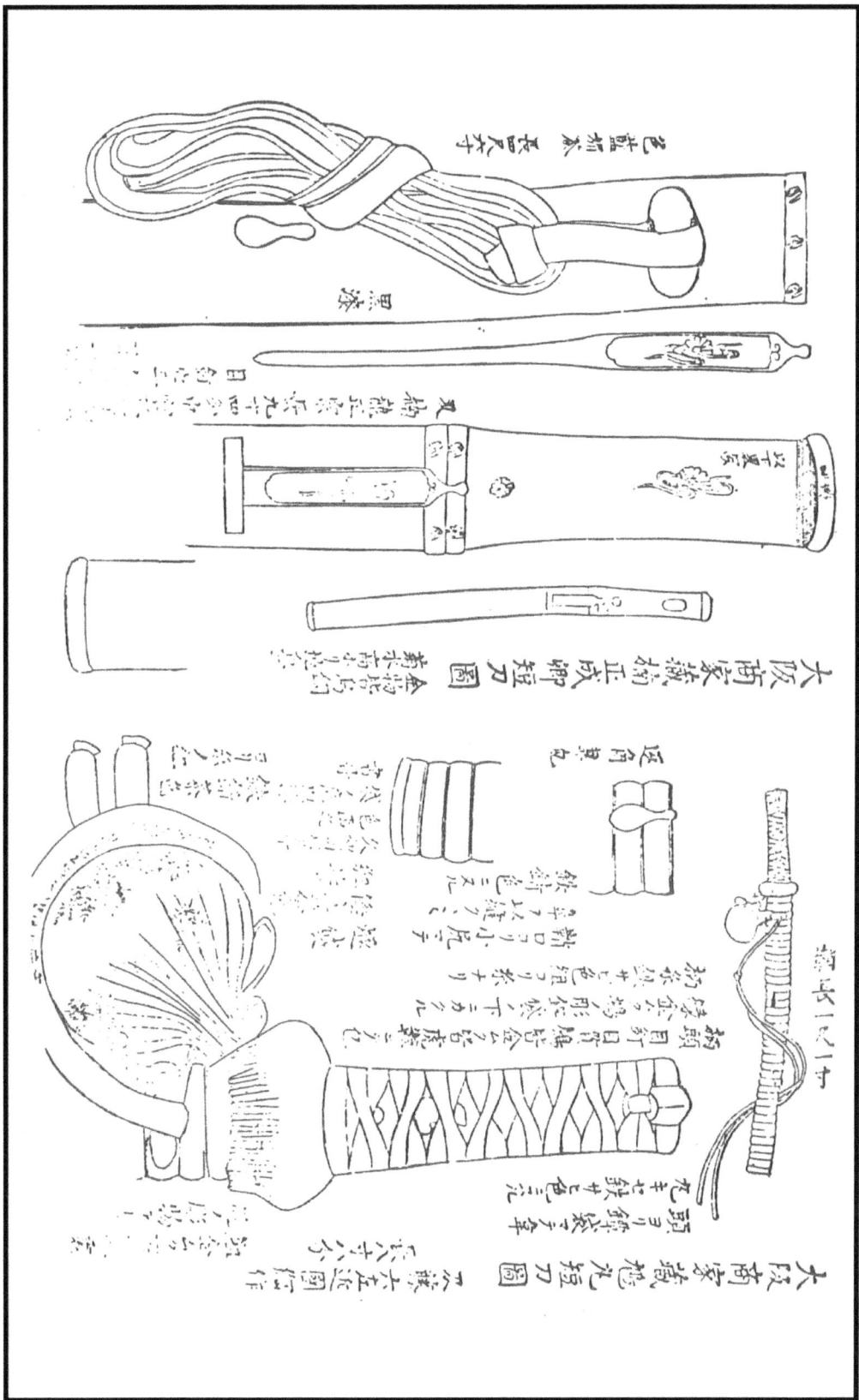

3 SWORD GLOSSARY

INTRODUCTION

The goal of this section is to give an overview of sword concepts and vocabulary through easy-to-understand definitions for quick reference, and guides to further research.

SWORD TERMS AND DEFINITIONS

A

Aikuchi – tanto up to 30 cm long (1 foot) mounted without tsuba.

Ara-nie – coarse or large nie (large nie crystals)

Arashiage – the rough finishing on a sword.

Asai-notare – a shallow undulating hamon.

Ashi – leg or foot. Short lines extending from patterns of nie or nioi.

Ashi sadamaru – a steady hamon pattern either straight or wavy.

Ashi-naga – long ashi.

Azuki midare – temper line like a row of small beans.

B

Bakufu – military government of the shogun

Bizen – archaic province of Japan, modern day Okayama prefecture

Bizen-to – swords produced in Bizen

Bizen-zori – deep curvature close to the tang area of the sword; also known as koshi-zori

Bohi – wide groove almost fitting shinogi surface.

Bohi soyebi – wide groove beside a narrow groove.

Boshi – shape of temper line at the kissaki (point).

Boshisaki – the very tip of the boshi temper line.

Bugei – military arts – use of sword, etc.

C

Chigau midare – oblique hamon of Bitchu blades.

Chiisa katana – a general term for all swords shorter than the katana but also used to indicate a length between wakizashi and standard katana, but also used to indicate a length between wakizashi and standard katana.

Chiji komasame – undulating fine straight grain of suwo nio smiths.

Chiji midare – wrinkled irregular hamon by miike & kongobyoe groups.

Choji – clove seed shape folds in hamon. Many varieties.

Choji-midare – clove shapes mixed with irregular patterns in hamon.

Chu-kissaki – medium sized point (kissaki).

Chu-suguba – medium width straight hamon (follows curve of sword).

D

Daimyo – feudal lord.

Daisho – (large-small) a matched pair of swords or fittings for same.

Daito – long sword (over 24 inches)

Dambira – very wide blade.

Dogane – a metal band around a sword handle.

Doran or *toran* – high wave patterns of hamon.

F

Fuchi – collar on hilt.

Fuchikanamono – the ornamental ring around the end of a tachi tsuka next to the tsuba.

Fuchi-kashira – set of hilt collar (fuchi) and butt cap (kashira)

Funagata – ship bottom shaped nakago (tang).

Furisode – a tang shape with the end deeply curved toward the back side which resembles a kimono sleeve.

G

Gassan hada – grain made by gouging with round chisel then flatten.

Gendaito – traditionally forged sword blades by modern smiths before WWII.

Gimei – a false signature on a blade. Usually a copy of a famous smith to increase the sword's value.

Gunome – undulating hamon.

Gunto – army or military sword mountings.

H

Ha – cutting edge of a sword.

Hada – grain in steel, pattern of folding the steel.

Hamachi – the notch at the end of the edge that the habaki rests against.

Hamidashi – tanto with small guard.

Hamon – temper pattern along blade edge

Handachi – tachi mountings used on a katana or wakizashi

Hi – grooves cut in a sword.

Hiki hada – leather scabbard cover.

Horimono – carving on blades.

Hyogo-gusari – the chain link or leather attachment that the tachi is suspended by.

I

Ichi – one or first.

Ito – silk or cotton hilt wrapping.

J

Ji – sword surface between the shinogi and the hamon.

Ji-hada – surface texture – course or fine of various patterns of hada.

Jin wakizashi – medium length sword worn with a tachi.

K

Kabuto-gane – tachi style pommel cap.

Kaeshizuno – a hook on the side of the saya ment to catch on the obi, or sash, of the wearer.

Kai gunto – naval sword produced during WWII.

Kanji – Japanese characters.

Kantei – study and appraisal of swords.

Kashira – cap on the end of handle – pommel.

Kasumi no oshie – a misty nioi in blades of hizen yoshikage.

Katana – long sword worn edge up in sash by samurai.

Katana mei – signature side that faces out when worn edge up.

Katana kake – sword stand for horizontal display.

Katana shin – blade or body of a sword.

Katana hira – flat of the blade.

Ken – straight double edged sword.

Kinko – soft metal sword fittings (not iron).

Kiri-ha – flat sword with both sides beveled to the edge.

Kiri nakago – tang cut off square, usually in shortened blades.

Kiri suji-chigai – file marks.

Kissaki – the point of a blade. Many shapes.

Kodomo daisho – a child's pair of swords.

Kogai – hair arranger fitted in pocket opposite kozuka, on some swords.

Kogatana – short knife with a hole or ring at the end of the handle so it can be used as a needle to draw a cord through the severed neck to mouth of an enemy head for carrying.

Koiguchi – the mouth of the scabbard or its fitting.

Kojiri or sayajiri – bottom end fitting on scabbard.

Kore – kanji on tang meaning "this" for example saku kore "made this".

Koshirae – sword mountings including scabbard, handle and fittings.

Koto – old sword period (prior to 1596).

Ko-uchi katana – short fighting sword before wakizashi came in style.

Ko-wakizashi – short wakizashi of 1 foot to 1 foot 4 inches long.

Kozuka – the small knife carried in a pocket on the side of a scabbard.

Kozuka – spike for hair arranging carried sometimes as part of katana-koshirae in another 'pocket'.

Kuchikanamono – the ornamental ring around the mouth of a tachi scabbard.

Kuni – province, town or city.

Kuri-jiri – chestnut shape tang end.

Kurikata – scabbard (saya) fitting for attaching the sageo

M

Maki ito – braid for handle wrapping.

Mei – signature chiseled on a blade, mostly on the tang. Signature is away from body when worn - katana - edge up, tachi - edge down. A few exceptions.

Mekugi – bamboo peg or metal rivet holding the handle on a sword.

Mekugiana – hole for mekugi. Katana 6.1cm down; wakizashi 4.6cm down.

Menuki – ornaments under handle wrapping to improve grip.

Menukio – handle wrapping. Same as udenukio.

Mi – body of a sword. Not including tang. The blade.

Midare choji – irregular clove seed shapes in hamon.

Mon – family crest.

Mumei – no signature (unsigned blade).

Mune – back ridge of sword blade.

Munemachi – the notch at the end of the mune that the habaki rests against.

Muso to – sword without mountings; a naked blade.

N

Nagasa – blade length (from tip of kissaki to munemachi).

Naginata – short sword blade on a long shaft. A halberd.

Nakago – tang of a blade.

Nakago jiri – the end of the tang.

Nakago mune – back of a tang. Several shapes; flat or rounded.

Nakago mune-maki – tip end of a tang. Many shapes.

Nakago saki – tip of the tang.

Nanako – raised dimpling (fish roe).

Naoshi – corrected or repaired.

Nie – fine white crystals formed in the hamon or ji.

Nioi – crystals like nie but much finer and darker. Hamon patterns may be made of nioi or a thread-like line of nioi may parallel or be mixed in with nie hamon (cloud like hamon). Presence of both is considered good.

Nioi-nie fukashi – wide area of nioi and nie.

Nomi ire – upper part of habaki.

O

O – large.

Obi – belt sash.

O-choji – hamon of large choji (clove seed) patterns.

O-dachi – very long sword (over 30 inches).

O-kissaki – large kissaki.

O-midare – large irregular hamon pattern.

Omote – side of sword away from body as it is worn. Signature side. The opposite side is called ura. Usually has the date, if any. Katana omote is opposite to tachi omote.

Origami – certificate of appraisal.

O-seppa – large seppa (usually on tachi).

Oshigata – rubbing of tang with inscription.

O-suriage – a shortened tang with the signature removed.

O-tachi – very long tachi, some are 5 or 6 feet long.

O-wakizashi – longer wakizashi – almost 2 feet long.

Rakka no suye – hamon starting large irregular at the base and becoming small to straight as it goes up the blade to the point.

S

Sageo – cord or braid attached to kurikata on side of scabbard.

Saguri – catch-hook on saya

Saka-choji – choji shapes slanting down toward base of blade.

Saka-gonome – slanted gonome.

Sakazuno – hook-like fitting on wakizashi or tanto scabbard.

Saki – tang end of a sword blade.

Saku – kanji on tang meaning "made".

Saku kore – made this.

Samurai – warriors hired by feudal lords before 1870.

Sanbonsugi – three cedar trees pattern hamon. Kanemoto.

Saya – scabbard. Many kinds, see books on koshirae.

Sayajiri – the end of the tachi scabbard.

Sayashi – scabbard maker.

Semegane – the bands on the scabbard of a tachi.

Seppa – washers to fill out space provided for tsuba on blade.

Shakudo – copper and gold alloy used for sword fittings

Shinogi – ridges on each side of a blade.

Shinogi ji – sword flat between the mune and shinogi.

Shinogi zukuri – sword with shinogi.

Shin no kurikara – horimono of dragon twined around sword.

Shinto – new sword period (1596 to 1781).

Shin-shinto – new-new sword period (1781 to 1868).

Shira-saya – plain wood storage scabbard.

Shitodome – small collars in the kurikata and/or kashira.

Shosei ken – mountings made according to old chinese rules.

Shoto – short sword (between 12 and 24 inches).

Showa-to – swords made by hand in Showa Period – 1926 on. Not gunto.

Shumei – red lacquer signature.

So mune – round back.

Sori – curve (general).

Sori – the curve of the blade (specific).

Sugata – shape of sword blade.

Suguha – straight temper line.

Suguba hotsure – straight hamon somewhat frayed in places.

Sun-nobi – longer than average tanto or wakizashi.

Suriage – shortened blade. All or part of tang cut off.

Suriage nakago – tang of a shortened blade.

T

Tachi – long sword worn with cutting-edge down.

Tachi kake – sword rack or stand for a tachi.

Tachi mei – signature facing away from body when worn edge down

Taka yamagata – small u-shape tang end.

Tameshigiri – cutting test of a sword. Same as kiritameshi.

Tameshi mei – gold inscription on tang describing test and by whom.

Tanto – dagger or knife less than one foot long.

Togari – pointed hamon patterns; saw teeth.

Togi mei – polisher's signature inscribed with needle at base of blade.

Tosu – an ancient short dagger worn on court dress.

Tsuba – sword guard.

Tsuba katana – sword with a guard for fighting.

Tsuchi – hammer for removing or replacing mekugi pin in handle.

Tsuka – sword handle.

Tsuka bukuro – sword handle cover.

Tsuka-gashira – pommel at the end of a sword handle.

Tsuka guchi – hole in handle to insert tang of sword.

Tsuka ito – braid for wrapping handle.

Tsukamaki – art/act of wrapping the handle of a sword.

Tsukamaki – the wrapping on the handle of the sword.

Tsukuri-zori – strongly curved blade.

Tsukuri-sugu – slightly curved blade.

Tsurugi – ancient name for ken type sword.

Tsukuri – shapes of blades.

U

Uchigatana – long fighting sword with tsuba, worn edge up.

Uchiko – powder for cleaning swords.

Uki menuki – menuki outside the wrappings. Same as hari menuki.

Ukyo tsuka – handle made of hard wood copying ancient fashion.

Ura-mei – signed on the ura (usually the date).

W

Wakizashi – medium length sword from 1 shaku to 2 shaku (12 and 24 inches)

Wakizashi no tachi – old term for wakizashi.

Ware – opening in the steel.

Y

Yaguragane – the suspension band attached to a tachi('s) scabbard by which it is suspended.

Yakigashira – head or ji side of a hamon.

Yakizume – temperline in boshi with no turn-back.

Yamazakura – small clove pattern resembling wild cherry blossoms.

Yamazakura no midare – choji pattern like cherry blossoms.

Yame – scar caused by arrow point on blade surface.

Yari – spear. Futamoto yari – 2 pronged; mitsumoto yari – 3 pronged.

Yasuri or yasuri mei – file marks on tang. Many styles.

Yasuri kiri – tangs having file marks rather than hammer or shave marks.

Yokote – line between ji and kissaki.

BIBLIOGRAPHY

Fuller, Richard, & Gregory, Ron (1987). *Military Swords of Japnan: 1868-1945*. New York, NY: Arms and Armour Press.

Hawley, W. M. (1981). *Japanese Swordsmiths Revised*. Hollywood, CA: Hawley Publications.

Irvine, Gregory (2000). *The Japanese Sword – The Soul of the Samurai*. London, England: Victoria and Albert Museum.

Kapp, L., Kapp, H. & Yoshihara, Y. (1987). *The Craft of the Japanese Sword*. New York, NY: Kodansha International.

Kapp, L., Kapp, H. & Yoshihara, Y. (2002). *Modern Japanese Swords and Swordsmith: From 1868 to the Present*. New York, NY: Kodansha International.

Kokubo, Kenichi. (1993). The complete illustrated book of the Japanese sword furnishings. Tokyo, Japan: Kogei Shuppan.

Nagayama, Kokan (1998). *The Connoisseur's Guide to Japanese Swords*. New York, NY: Kodansha International.

Nakao, Seigo (1997). The Random House Japanese-English English-Japanese Dictionary. New York, NY: Random House, Inc.

Ogasawara, Nobuo. (1994). The art of Japan 1, No. 332: The mountings of Japanese swords. Tokyo, Japan: Shibun Do.

Ogawa, Morihiro (2009). Art of the Samurai: Japanese Arms and Armor, 1156-1868 (Metropolitan Museum of Art). New York, NY: Metropolitan Museum of Art.

Roach, Colin (2010). *Japanese Swords: Cultural Icons of a Nation*. North Claendon, VT: Tuttle Publishing.

Robinson, B. W. (1961). *The Arts of the Japanese Sword*. London, England: Faber & Faber, Ltd.

Sato, Kanzan, & Earl, Joe (1983). *The Japanese Sword.* New York, NY: Kodansha International.

Sinclaire, Clive (2001). *Samurai: The Weapons and Spirit of the Japanese Warrior.* Guilford, CT: Salamander Books Ltd.

Smith, R. G. (2012). *Ancient Tales and Folk-Lore of Japan.* New York, NY: CreateSpace Independent Publishing.

Stone, G. C. (1961). A Glossary of the Construction, Decoration and Use of Arms and Armor, in all countries and in all times. New York , NY: Jack Brussel.

Takeuchi, S. Alexander. (2003). "Typology of *katate-maki* (i.e., battle wrap) and its relevance to historically accurate menuki placement." In *Dr. T's Nihon-to Random Thoughts Page.* Florence, Ala: University of North Alabama, , USA.

Tsuji, Kyojiro. (1973). Tsuka maki. In Tadashi Oono (Ed.), *Nihon-to shokunin shokudan.* (1st Ed.). Pp. 169-179. Tokyo, Japan: Kogei Shuppan.

Turnbull, Stephen (2004). *Samurai: The Story of Japan's Great Warriors.* London: PRC Publishing, Ltd.

Yumoto, J. M. (1958). *The Samurai Sword – A Handbook.* North Claendon, VT: Tuttle Publishing.

Zusho, Ichiro. (2003). *Satsuma Koshirae.* Tokyo, Japan: Ribun Shuppan.

PHOTO CREDITS

**Tsuka and Saya by
Kazuki Takayama & Yasuo Toyama
Courtesy of Kenji Mishina**
p. 12.

Christie's
p. 5.

**Japanese Imperial Collection
Courtesy of Nobuo Ogasawara**
p. 3, p. 4, p. 8, p. 9, p. 10.

Denver Art Museum
p. 11, p. 12, p. 13.

**All other Pictures and Diagrams
Created and/or Sourced by Author**

LIST OF FIGURES

ABOUT THE AUTHOR

Dr. Thomas Buck has been collecting and studying the Japanese Art Sword for over thirty years, acquiring his first Samurai Sword in October, 1975. In 1987, with the guidance of Dr. W. Y. Takahashi, Sensei, he began a three year intensive study/apprenticeship of the restoration and preservation techniques of John Grimmitt and Takahiro Ichinose, concentrating his research on Tsukamaki and Japanese Lacquer-ware. Since 1988, he has been performing restoration and research work on tsuka for various institutions, private collectors, and dealers.

ALSO BY THOMAS BUCK

Across the Spectrum: Historical Trends in Japanese Lacquer-ware

Ancient Japanese Swords and Fittings: A Collection of Restored Nineteenth Century Woodblock Prints

The Art of Tsukamaki

www.ingramcontent.com/pod-product-compliance
Lightning Source LLC
Chambersburg PA
CBHW081228090426
42738CB00016B/3224